A SCANDALOUS WOMAN
THE STORY OF
CAROLINE NORTON

A
SCANDALOUS
WOMAN

THE STORY OF
CAROLINE NORTON

Alan Chedzoy

a&b

*In memory of George Eric Winchcombe
and for Anna,
sometime tenants of Hardy's Cottage, Dorset*

First published in Great Britain in 1992 by
Allison & Busby
an imprint of Wilson & Day Ltd
5 The Lodge
Richmond Way
London W12 8LW

A catalogue record for this book is available from the British Library

ISBN 0 74900 166 6

Printed and bound in Great Britain by
Mackays of Chatham PLC, Chatham, Kent

CONTENTS

ILLUSTRATIONS

Except when stated otherwise, pictures are reproduced by courtesy of the National Portrait Gallery, London.

ACKNOWLEDGEMENTS

My thanks are due especially to two people: Mr Trevor Hearl for the loan of rare books, and Mrs Teresa Williams who discovered a great deal of interesting material and provided me with copies. May I also thank: Angus and Jean Newton of Send, Surrey, for information about Wonersh Park; the Reverend Canon Dr G. Tellini of Dunblane for information about Lecropt Church; the Reverend James R. Wilkie and his wife, who searched a Scottish churchyard for me over two days; and Mr A. Stirling of Keir, who made a remarkable discovery for me concerning his ancestor, Sir William Stirling-Maxwell. Patricia Brown of Weightman & Brown, Architects, of Acomb, York, provided me with valuable information concerning Kettlethorpe Hall and the funeral of Fletcher Norton. I am grateful to Fred Langford and Jill Bryant of the William Barnes Society for much helpful comment. Inevitably I have drawn much upon the two previous biographies of Caroline Norton by Miss Jane Gray Perkins and Alice Acland. Other information has been provided by Surrey County Library, Dorset County Library, Dorset County Record Office, and the London Library. It was most fortuitous that, when this book was in preparation, the British Library issued its Microfiche Publication on 'The Emancipation of Women', with the largest item devoted to the works of Caroline Norton.

I am very grateful to Natasha Fairweather and Peter Robinson of Curtis Brown & John Farquharson for their help and support, and to Peter Day of Allison & Busby.

A.C.

PART ONE

SHERIDAN'S GIRL

I

WAITING WOMAN

ONE MORNING IN SPRING 1877, a woman sat waiting in a Mayfair sitting room with a letter in her hand. Though she was sixty-nine years old, her raven hair was only a little streaked with grey, and her dark eyes and elegant neck were still remarkably handsome. Yet her movements were stiff with rheumatism, and she had no power in her legs to rise from her chair. Her name was Caroline Norton.

The letter was from her old friend in Scotland. He said that he would be coming down from Perthshire for the new session of the House of Commons and would hope to call upon her that day. He had some exciting news to tell her. So much she had expected, but it was his final comment that set her musing, for he added that he wished to consult her on a personal matter. She did not know what to make of this. If it was what she thought, there could be little purpose in such a thing now.

Chesterfield Street was quiet that day, so that only the occasional sound of footsteps or a clopping hansom reached her ears through the heavy curtains. The house was quiet too, but for an occasional clatter of plates from the kitchen, or a brief flutter of wings from the rear room. She could remember the times when her grandchildren used to visit the aviary. The little girl and boy would arrive from Italy, dazed by travel and the sheer size of London, and would wait solemn-eyed to hear the birds sing. Sometimes she would let the birds out to stand on the heads or hands of their delighted little visitors. How the children complained when the canaries and parakeets were put back in their cages! Caroline remembered that she herself could sing once, and had fluttered her own wings against the bars. But there were no little grandchildren now, and the birds were old.

Still she waited. She had spent most of her life waiting on men. Their portraits ranged on the mantelshelf and the book-cases beyond. Here were her two lost sons, the gentle Fletcher, and little William, so tragically killed. Here was her surviving son, Brinny, with her two grandchildren in Capri. Here also was Sidney Herbert, once Secretary at War and the hope of his generation, who had never recovered from overworking himself to send Miss Nightingale's expedition to the Crimea. Here were her literary friends, Tom Moore, the Minstrel Boy, and Samuel Rogers, the kindest and ugliest of poets. Here was her very own Prime Minister, Lord Melbourne, who had cheerfully deserted her for the company of the young Queen, and for whose sake she had first become a scandalous woman. And here was one who had preceded her but who even now seemed to watch her every move. She glanced up at Russell's portrait of her grandfather, the 'divine' Richard Brinsley Sheridan, author of *The School for Scandal*, with his intelligent eyes and decadent mouth. He had known what scandal was. Sometimes, obscurely, she felt that he was the author of her own story too, had foretold it all, and watched her waiting alone, on another morning, forty-one years before, on the eve of that dreadful day.

CHAPTER II

AT SPRING GARDENS

IN A PRIVATE ROOM AT HILL'S HOTEL, Spring Gardens, Westminster, Caroline Norton sat down alone to write a last note to the Prime Minister. It was 21 June 1836, and a beautiful sunny day. She found it difficult to control the pen because her hand was trembling. Normally she was an assured young woman, but now she was thoroughly frightened.

She did not know how this catastrophe might be avoided. She could only sit staring stupidly at the paper. Through the open window came the rumble of horse traffic in Trafalgar Square. She would have liked to go out for a morning drive in the park, but she knew that it was impossible; she would only be stared at, or cut, or made the subject of guffawed indecencies.

She dipped her pen and tried to explain to Lord Melbourne:

> I saw Uncle Graham on my arrival here, (where by my lawyer's advice I shall remain till after the trial.) He said he had expected daily to hear from you, in compliance with your promise that 'you would consider, and consult, & communicate ultimately on the subject with him, which you thought was the object of your interview with him – ' that he had not heard a syllable and therefore could tell me nothing.[1]

She could guess why Melbourne had not written to her uncle. He wanted no more to do with her, now that she had brought him such disgrace. She pictured the look of disdain with which he would receive her letter – if he bothered to open it at all. She could not forget the horror in his eyes when she had called upon him without notice, at 10 Downing Street. He had seemed panic-stricken. He was also very pale. They said he had been ill with worry since the whole business had started. Impulsively she sought to comfort him:

> It is the universal opinion that you will succeed – even one of

their own attornies let out as much, to a clerk who repeated it
to my lawyer . . .

She did not trust Melbourne. She believed he would agree to anything
– even her return to her husband – in order to save his own position.
All he seemed to think about was being the first Prime Minister in the
reign of the new Queen. But she would not let him barter away her
own freedom to achieve that ambition:

> You once said to me that in the event of N[orton]'s failing in
> obtaining a verdict you could 'arrange with him' & 'come to
> terms' – I forget the exact expression – except that he should
> 'Take me back'. I therefore tell you that it is my intention, (on the
> best legal authority Edinburgh contains) to proceed for divorce
> against him in the Scotch Court, & that I have all the papers now
> ready for that purpose as soon as he shall have failed here. So if
> it ever was your intention to communicate by attorney with him
> afterwards, it will not bind me in any way to come to terms with
> him. I thought that I had better tell you this as you generally act
> first, and then let me know what has been done . . .

Mechanically, she sealed and directed the letter, and rang the bell for
the servant to take it. She had nothing to do now but wait. She tried
to read but it was no good; her thoughts were always on the next day.
She paced the room, muttering and talking to the absent Melbourne.
Several times she had to restrain herself from scribbling yet another
note to him. Still she waited. At last her friends came to take her a
few steps down the street to an early dinner but they were unable to
distract her. Their inquisitive sympathetic eyes were intolerable to her.
Then, at the table, she whispered a sudden request to her mother who
nodded agreement. Even though she had promised her lawyers that
she would remain at Hill's Hotel, Caroline now decided that after
dinner she would leave London with her mother and go to their old
home at Hampton Court. The decision gave her another excuse to
write to Lord Melbourne:

> I am going to Hampton Ct with my Mother at 3 o'clk & shall
> stay there till something is settled. I will not say anything more
> to reproach or give you pain. I will not worry you. Only be well
> assured that you need not have shrunk. I would not have been

any burden or trouble to you or any other person under any circumstances.

The fault is in me – I do not attach people. I have always thought so and said so. I did what I could for my husband. I was of great service, of great comfort to him. I nursed him devotedly at a time when many young married women would have shewn great displeasure & resentment. I thought I owed him to replace the love that is involuntary, by every cheerful effort which can so easily be made voluntarily. No man ever admired me more or loved me less. I have been eight years his legal mistress & nothing more – no kindness – no tenderness, no clinging to the companion of younger days, no sentiment for the Mother of his children. He thought me beautiful and full of talent but I did not attach him.[2]

Now she could not stop the frantic scratching of her pen as she poured out her thoughts to Melbourne. All she wanted was for him to understand the depth of her feelings:

Well! I might say of him [her husband] that he is incapable of such love, as I might have earned from another . . . But you! I was of no service or comfort to you because I have never been in a position to render either – but my life has been divided (in my eyes) into the days I saw you & the days I did not – nothing else seemed of importance but you; your opinions – even your fancies . . . have been laws to me. Yet you are not attached to me . . . I was not two & twenty when you first visited me & thought merrily & carelessly about you . . .

I trust & believe that as far as you are concerned, this inquisitorial proceeding will produce nothing. It will be a great relief to me to hear that they give up your name – so great, that I shd. feel comparatively happy! Farewell – in leaving town, I destroy at least one restless feeling – the knowing that I am so near you & may not see you.

Caroline

At dinner she told her brother Brinsley of her new plans and he at once offered her his carriage. So, in the late afternoon, Caroline and her mother were driven out through the grime and roar of the London streets and along the sunlit fields by the river. At first she hardly noticed their new surroundings, but the sight of trees and fields, and the occasional flash from the summer Thames, put her in mind of that first journey she had taken as a schoolgirl, when she had been sent from home down to Surrey to the school at Wonersh. It was there that Norton had first noticed her, spying on her, no doubt, like some satyr, long before she had ever seen him. That was when her trouble started.

In those days, she had been full of great hopes and an appetite for life. Now she was appalled by the prospect she faced. She had lost everything: society, home, husband, and the company of the man she loved. Worst of all was the loss of her three little boys, from whom she could not bear to be parted, but with whom she could not hope to be reunited without a victory at the trial the following day. Her future depended on a favourable result. As the wheels turned beneath her, so her mind endlessly revolved the facts of her situation.

The next day, 22 June 1836, in the Court of Common Pleas, Westminster, her husband, George Norton, was to bring an action against the Prime Minister, Lord Melbourne, for 'criminal conversation' with his wife. This phrase was, they told her, the lawyer's cant for adultery. George claimed to know that Melbourne had been her lover. It was said that if Lord Melbourne lost the case, the result would finish him. He would have to resign, and his government would probably fall too. Her political friends told her that all the courts of Europe were watching for the result. But none of the newspapers pointed out that she too was on trial. A verdict for her husband would not only end Lord Melbourne's career, but would damage her own reputation irretrievably. Yet they would not let her speak in court and there was nothing else she could do to defend her reputation. So she had to wait, with her mother, through the long night and the whole of the following day before she could hope to hear news of the result.

Soon the great palace of Cardinal Wolsey came into sight. It was here that Henry VIII had brought Anne Boleyn, and here where the imprisoned Charles I awaited his fate. Now, among the long shadows of evening, the horses slowed and the small carriage with its freight of two silent women waited at the gate. A bell jangled; a lock creaked; and Hampton Court shut its gates upon them.

III

CRIMINAL CONVERSATION

THAT NIGHT, SIR JOHN CAMPBELL, the Attorney General, and Melbourne's Counsel for the Defence, lay awake with 'exquisitely painful apprehensions' of the morrow'.[1] His insomnia arose from the awareness that the future of the Government and many of his friends lay solely in his hands. Ministers counted on him to get Melbourne off, for the administration was too weak to survive a verdict of guilty. The trial had already 'excited more interest than any other since the beginning of the century, with the exception of Queen Caroline's case'.[2] The gutter press had been running scandalous stories for weeks, and the manager of the Theatre Royal in the Haymarket, with a shrewd commercial awareness that the Sheridan name was once again in the news, had revived *The Rivals*. Although Sir John believed Lord Melbourne was innocent, the weight of responsibility became 'more and more disagreeable' to him. He was unable to doze off until the early hours.

He awoke with a start to find that he had overslept. He hurried through his breakfast and rushed down to the Court of Common Pleas in Westminster. As he approached the courtroom, he was held up, several times, both by the mob and by officious policemen who claimed that they had orders to admit no-one. There was a great crowd outside the entrance and the various officials, lawyers and witnesses who were admitted were greeted with ironic cheers. There were shouts of 'Good old Melbourne', and hisses and counter-cheers for Norton, though neither of them was present in person. Sir John was glad to obtain the help of two burly constables to get inside the building.

Caroline, too, had been unable to sleep. She lay for hours, listening to the quiet breathing in the next bed, not knowing whether her mother was asleep. It was years since they had shared a room, not since she had lived here as a little girl. When the outlines of the casement slowly edged themselves in light, she rose quietly, and went, and looked down into the sombre courtyard. Gently she calmed a whisper from her mother's bed, before turning again to the grey day.

She guessed that, at that hour, learned counsel would be stirring in their beds and rehearsing in their dreams the eloquence that would win the day in the Court of Common Pleas. Old servants, bribed by her husband, would be rising in rough inns, to go to Westminster to practise perjury. Sadly, she had no need to prepare herself for the court, for she was not allowed to attend. But, had she been called to give evidence, she knew she would have roused their hearts at her story. Fifty years ago her famous grandfather had done as much, before he had sunk to his seat to the tumultuous applause of the House of Commons, after a triumphant speech of five hours and forty minutes in defence of the Begums of Oude. She knew she had the fire in her blood to do the same, but as a mere woman, she was not permitted to speak. So there she stayed, throughout the day, a solitary figure, waiting.

Since seven o'clock that morning, a 'considerable number of persons' had arrived at the court to try to get in early. The authorities were aware that the trial might provoke unrest and were determined to prevent it. So the jury was specially selected from the ranks of professional men only, and the constables were told to keep the mob away from the entrance to the court. The doorkeepers had strict orders to admit only authorized persons, such as reporters well known to the court and then only with a permit. What angered the crowd was the discovery that a private door at the side had been specially opened to let in those who could afford to bribe the doormen.[3] So the court soon began to fill up with the fashionable and well-to-do.

What worried these spectators was not the threat to Melbourne but the possibility that, if the trial were put off, they would lose a good day's entertainment. For, even at this late hour, there were many present who doubted that the authorities would really allow a British Prime Minister to be prosecuted in an open court. They feared that some legal pretext would be introduced to stop the proceedings. Their mood soon turned to indignation when, at half past eight, an inner door opened, and a set of young barristers, shouting 'Make way for the bar', forced an entrance into the room. These intruders then pushed their way on to the back seats and started loud arguments about the likely course of the proceedings. At the last moment, the large public door was opened and a 'tremendous rush of persons' was followed by a 'violent struggle' for seats. Arguments broke out all over the court, and there was more than one exchange of cards as a prelude to future duels.[4] The hubbub across the courtroom grew louder and tempers more heated until Lord Chief Justice Tindall took his place at half past nine. Almost immediately afterwards, Sir John Campbell bustled in, bowing to the judge and muttering apologies. Lord Tindall began by threatening to adjourn the court, and this brought order at once, for the spectators still feared they might lose their day's sport. Even then, there were shouts of disgust when, at the last minute, Lords Grantley, Litchfield and Lucan entered and took places of privilege on the bench.[5]

The proceedings began with the calling of the jury, and there was a buzz of surprise when the leader of the Tories, Sir Robert Peel, and his colleague, Mr F. Baring MP, were named, though neither answered the call. Then counsels were presented to the court. Sir William Follett appeared for the plaintiff, assisted by Mr Crowder and Mr Bayley, while Lord Melbourne was defended by Sir John, with the help of Serjeant Talfourd and Mr Thesiger. To the disappointment of the public, none of the principals in the case appeared in court. Neither Melbourne nor Norton chose to be present, and Caroline could not be called by Sir John, because she was the wife of the plaintiff.

Sir William Follett began his speech for the prosecution by urging the jurors to dismiss from their minds all newspaper chatter concerning the case. He said that the high position of Lord Melbourne was of no significance in the matter under consideration. All the jurors had to do, was to consider whether, after having obtained access to Mr Norton's house as his patron and friend, he had taken advantage of his host by inflicting on him the deepest injury which one man could give another. That is what adultery was, because it poisoned the source of all earthly affections – the love of a father for his child.[6] Follett then told the court the history of the Nortons' marriage, and pointed out that some years before, when Lord Melbourne was Home Secretary, he had helped Mr Norton obtain a post as Police Magistrate in the Whitechapel district. This appointment, he said, obliged Norton to leave the house early in the morning on three days of the week, when he returned after seven p.m. in the evening. By these means, Melbourne had ensured Norton's regular absences from his house at Storey's Gate, so that he could be sure of finding Mrs Norton alone. Occasionally he took care to visit the house while Norton was at home, for he 'professed to be the intimate friend' of both the Nortons, but his regular visits took place on two or three afternoons a week when Norton was out. Here was the opportunity for adultery.

Of course, Sir William was obliged to admit that he had no eyewitnesses who could testify that they had actually seen adultery taking place but he pointed out that this was usual in such cases. He recommended the jury to follow the guidance on such matters offered by Lord Justice Stowell in the case of Lovedance *v.* Lovedance.[7] Pausing for a moment at the laughter produced by the name of that case, he then quoted the judge's opinion: 'In every case the facts are concluded from fair inference; and unless this were so held, no protection could be given to marital rights ... The only general rule must be such as would lead the guarded discretion of a reasonable and just man to this conclusion.' Follett's audience of reasonable and just men took the point. They were not going to be presented with an eyewitness account of the Prime Minister and Mrs Norton in bed together, but they could settle back comfortably to infer that a nod is as good as a wink.

Follett now began to present his own inferential material. His first piece of evidence – he confessed he did 'not know whether much importance in the result may be attached to it or no' – was to point out that the Storey's Gate house had two entrances, one from Birdcage Walk, which was the public entrance, and one at the back from a passage leading off Prince's Court. Lord Melbourne 'invariably went in ... by the passage behind'. Sir William was taken aback by the burst of laughter provoked by this remark but it was quickly suppressed by the usher. The reference to secret entrances, however, was not lost on the jury who would have been well aware that there were many houses of assignation in the West End. Only a day after this trial, *The Satirist* was complaining that such a house in Bolton Street, Piccadilly, was doing a flourishing trade from the patronage of 'MPs, magistrates and parsons'.[8]

Sir William stumbled on. He described how, whenever the Prime Minister visited Storey's Gate, the servants were given orders that no one else, not even a relative, was to be admitted to the house; the blinds of the windows which looked on to the park were kept drawn, and no servant was allowed into the room unless called for by Mrs Norton. Even when she was ill in her bedroom, Lord Melbourne often went up and stayed with her for an hour or two. Servants would testify that they had sometimes found the door to the sitting room bolted, and also that they had seen kisses pass between the two parties; 'they have seen his arm around her neck; they have seen her hand leaning upon his knee, and herself kneeling in the room before him. They have seen familiarities of that sort between the parties, and they have seen what will leave no doubt in your minds, in that room, Mrs Norton, lying on the floor, with her clothes in a position to expose her person, and Lord Melbourne with her'. He paused dramatically and lowered his voice. Were these visits the actions of a friend? Surely such evidence was not consistent with innocence.

The jury was impressed and things were already looking black for Melbourne. Follett had the ear of the court and was beginning to score with his points. But he was too repetitive and rhetorical in manner to command such a sceptical crowd for very long and he also tended to overstate his case until it became absurd, as in his presentation of three notes written by Melbourne to Caroline. There was, he confessed, nothing much in the notes, but there was 'something in the style' which led him to something very like suspicion. The first read:

I will call about half past four. Yours

Why was there no proper beginning here, no 'Dear Mrs Norton' or something of that sort? The second read:

How are you? I shall not be able to call today but probably will tomorrow.

By this time, the onlookers were amused at the attempt to make a mystery out of such pedestrian little notes and there was some tittering in court. But Follett persisted. The third note read:

No House today. I shall call after the levée – about four or half past. If you wish it later let me know. I shall then explain about going to Vauxhall.

His suggestion that these were not the kind of notes that a gentleman would write to a lady with whom he was on friendly terms, only produced more laughter in the courtroom. At that moment, the reporter for *The Morning Chronicle*, Charles Dickens, had an idea for a comic scene for his *Pickwick Papers* which were then appearing. It would involve a court case, a pompous attorney, and the reading out in court of ridiculous notes. He later wrote it up as 'The Memorable Trial of Bardell against Pickwick'.[9]

Follett now tried to damp down a rumour that might have reached the jury. Some people had suggested that Norton knew very well what was going on, and arranged his absences from home as payment for a job Melbourne had got for him. Follett argued that there was no evidence for this view, except for the fact that Norton, like the great mass of people in the country, was obliged to leave his home to go to work. The 'special' jury, of eight merchants and a banker, all of whom went daily to their work, found much with which to sympathize in Norton's situation.

Then Follett made the mistake of reading out to the court a series of letters written by Caroline to George Norton, and arguing that these harmless little messages were evidence of a long-standing adultery. The first letter was written from Maiden Bradley in 1831:

> Our chicken [child] came safe to hand this morning. Your letters are too short. I dreamt last night that you were dying; that two old maids told you stories of me, and then persuaded you not to see me; but I rushed into your room and you said you were dying for my sake. Afterwards . . . you . . . died . . . wherefore I woke in a flood of tears.

Raising his voice above the laughter, he read out a second letter written in Scotland in 1833:

> Come back, come back, darling! I am wishing for you. To drive with four small piebald ponies and swing and fling beechwood nuts, is all we do, and very good sport it is.

The loungers in the court were now intent on ridicule, not only of Follett's arguments but also of the content of the letters. They howled with laughter at another one in which Caroline told her husband that Lord Melbourne had given her a book which argued that Mary Magdalene was the most virtuous of her sex. By this time, even Sir William Follett was aware that he was not creating the effect he intended. The jury could not take seriously his argument that these little notes were cunning messages but seemed instead to regard them as amusingly innocent. Follett decided to wind up quickly. He pointed out that, in considering damages against his client, the jury would take into account that he had suffered the worst injury a man could receive, which was the planting of the suspicion that those he called his sons were not his own children at all.

Now came the examination of witnesses for the prosecution. Joseph Compton Pott merely proved the marriage of the two parties, and Mr Fletcher Norton, George Norton's cousin, testified that it had been an affectionate one. Under cross-examination, he admitted that he always used the Prince's Court entrance when he visited Storey's Gate. Unlike the front door, it was furnished with a knocker and a brass plate. The park entrance was really a glass door leading privately to the dining room. This evidence was important because, by obtaining it, Campbell had shown that there was no entrance to the house kept private for Lord Melbourne.

Then followed the examination of some twelve servants employed by the Nortons at one time or another. In the early nineteenth century, servants were a tribe of people almost invisible to their employers but comprising a legitimized school of spies in every upper-middle-class household. Only very rarely, as in this case, were they allowed the luxury of public comment upon employers who had great power over their lives, and whose displeasure might mean destitution. Dismissed servants had old scores to settle. The names of Follett's witnesses suggest a villainous chorus from *The School for Scandal*: Benbow, Bulliman, Figgis, Fluke, Cummins, Lawly and Monk; their evidence conjured up a low-life world of servants, inn-keepers, ostlers and dealers, with such names as Fitness, Crook, Cumber, and Sly.[10] After the trial, Caroline Norton confided to others that she had been very much hurt by the willingness of so many of her ex-servants to give evidence against her. But Follett knew that it was from among her aggrieved or dismissed servants that he would find his evidence, while Campbell's strategy was to discredit them, or show that they had been bribed.

Georgia Veitch testified that, when she had been a housemaid in the service of Mrs Norton for three months in 1832, Lord Melbourne sometimes remained three hours at a time with her mistress, and left when Mr Norton returned at six p.m. Lord Melbourne visited the house two or three times a week, and it was 'generally understood' that, when he was there, other visitors were not to be admitted. Under cross-examination she agreed that 'a great many gentlemen' called, as well as Melbourne.

The next witness, Trinette Elliott, declared that, when Lord Melbourne was there, Mrs Norton frequently went upstairs to tidy herself, wash her hands and rouge. The prosecution used the buzz-word 'rouge' to smear Caroline. A lady who used make-up was trying to pretend that she was younger than her actual age; therefore she was telling a lie; therefore she was quite capable of lying on other matters. Furthermore, make-up suggested vanity and, implicitly, low sexual morality. Trinette was good at hinting improprieties. She swore that once, when she entered the drawing room, she had seen Lord Melbourne kiss Mrs Norton. On another occasion, she had found Mrs Norton and Lord Melbourne seated on the sofa, with her hand held in his. Furthermore, after the birth of Mrs Norton's second child, Lord Melbourne sat the whole afternoon in the bedroom with her, the window-blinds wholly down. By now, Trinette had the court spellbound, and was enjoying herself casting doubts about her ex-mistress. Why had Mrs Norton made use of so many pocket-handkerchiefs in putting herself to rights after Lord Melbourne's visits? The jury was expected to conclude that she was regularly rumpled by her visitor. It was Serjeant Talfourd, cross-examining for the defence, who dealt with Trinette. He made her admit that, when her mistress had kissed Melbourne, it was merely to greet him at the door, and neither of them had tried to hide the kiss from the gaze of the servants. Trinette also conceded that she herself had been obliged to leave Mrs Norton's service because she was 'in the family way'. When the defence had finished with her, the jury was left in no doubt that she was immoral and a liar.

Ellen Monk, maid to Mrs Norton for six months in 1834, confirmed that Lord Melbourne had, at times, sat alone with Mrs Norton in her bedroom, but admitted that this was only when she was ill. An ex-housemaid, Eliza Gibson, stated that, after one such visit, she had seen her mistress 'put her collar to rights', rouge, and adjust her tumbled hair. Eliza was asked whether Lord Melbourne had ever offered her a kiss, but she denied it. Later, she raised an easy laugh when she guessed his age to be about forty-five. More significantly, she let slip, under cross-examination, the fact that, on the previous Wednesday, Norton had coached her as a witness. With this admission, the defence succeeded in casting doubt on the motives of all Follett's witnesses.

Thomas Bulliman had been a general servant in the Norton household and then a coachman in the service of their friend Colonel Armstrong. He said he sometimes drove Miss Armstrong and Mrs Norton to Lord Melbourne's house but only Mrs Norton ever went in. When she did so, he would drive Miss Armstrong to make calls for about twenty minutes before coming back to pick up Mrs Norton. Once he had entered the drawing room at Storey's Gate with a message, to find Lord Melbourne and Mrs Norton close together on the sofa, he with his hand on her shoulder. They seemed confused when he went in, but he agreed that he had never been given any orders to keep out. A footman, Thomas Tucker, described how his mistress frequently needed to wash her hands and adjust her dress after Lord Melbourne's visits, but also agreed that this may have been because she was always drawing with her pastels or tending potted plants on the balcony. He denied having been down to Lord Grantley's place at Wonersh, previous to the trial, and could not remember who it was that summoned him to the court that day. William Lawly, coachman to Colonel Armstrong, admitted that he sometimes grumbled that he had to drive Mrs Norton round to see Lord Melbourne because she had no coach of her own. Still, he said, it was no use grumbling.

The evidence presented so far may have provoked suspicion but was not conclusive. The case for the prosecution largely rested on the next witness, John Fluke, who was the Norton coachman for the years 1830–34. He spoke for the servant class; for the shabby, the menial and the destitute; his weapons were intelligence, untruthfulness, ready wit and complete disregard for convention. He was cunning, philosophical, cheerful and very funny, and, like Doolittle, he could not afford a middle-class morality. The court loved him.

He began by describing how, on one occasion, having to go into the drawing room he knocked twice and entered. He opened the door and saw Lord Melbourne 'sitting on the left hand on a chair, with his elbows resting on his thighs, and his face resting on his hand; Mrs Norton was laid down with her feet towards the door and her head on the hearth rug'.[11] When he advanced to the middle of the room, Mrs Norton shifted her place a little, raising her body with her right hand. As she did so, Fluke saw that her clothes had been disturbed, and caught a glimpse of 'the thick at the knee part of Mrs Norton's thigh'. He said that he went downstairs and may have mentioned the matter to Mrs Figgis, the cook, and to his wife. On another occasion, Lord Melbourne entered the room, called out 'Well, dear Carry, how do you do?', and she kissed him.

The first part of Fluke's evidence was potentially very damaging. From the defence point of view, it was essential to discredit his evidence. Fortunately for Melbourne, Fluke, under examination, proved garrulous to the point of foolhardiness. As he teased the Attorney General, the atmosphere in the court turned from high drama to farce. Yet his answers fascinated the court because they took his listeners to a world far removed from the Society life of Mrs Norton, one of drudgery, drunkenness, and early death, the world of Sam Weller and Fagin.

Are you a married man? – I am.
Have you any children? – Three living out of ten.
They lived then over the stables in Fleece Yard and Bell Yard?
– Yes . . .

What did you do there? – I sold second-hand shirts and gowns.
Then you kept an old clothes shop? – Yes . . .
You lived in the cellar? – Yes . . .

Have you given up your business? – I can return to it again. I
have been to the country . . . I went to Wonersh.
What took you there? – I went down by the coach.
Is that your answer? – I went down with my wife and
children.
Bag and baggage? – Yes.

By now, Fluke felt that he was master of the courtroom, and began
to play his remarks for laughs.

Who gave you the money? – The solicitor gave me money to
pay my fare.
How much money? – About ten shillings . . .
How long did you live at the public house? – About a week.
What public house? – The Grantley Arms.

After demonstrating that he could swap sharp-talk with the learned
barrister, Fluke was quite happy to tell all. He had little to lose. Then
followed a rigmarole about how he and his family had gone down to
Wonersh where they had been entertained at the Grantley Arms at the
expense of the prosecution. From this it was clear that he had been
suborned. He told of a talk with a certain John Compass, the landlord
of the Robin Hood tavern, but would not admit that he had told him
that he had spent nine days preparing his evidence with Mr Norton's
lawyers. He also denied ever meeting Lord Wynford, the Tory MP
who was commonly thought to have persuaded Norton to bring the
action against Melbourne. His evidence on his own little failings was
punctuated by gales of laughter:

How was it that you left Mr Norton's? – To tell the truth I
got a drop too much. It was a court day and we generally
have a drop at such a time. Mr and Mrs Norton fell out in the
carriage, and, of course, they put the spite on me, and so I was
discharged . . .
And they put the spite on you? – Oh it's not the first time I
have had it like that.
You like to speak the truth sometimes, you took a drop too

much, eh? – I don't know who does not at times. We are all alike for that, masters and servants.[12]

Sir John then pushed Fluke hard for admissions. Did he not think that it was Mrs Norton, rather than her husband, who had insisted he be dismissed? Had he ever boasted that he was the 'premier witness against the Prime Minister of England'? Had he not said that, after the trial, he would get £500 to £600, and would retire to the country? Had he not said that he would prove Lord Melbourne's guilt? Did he not owe money in payment for horses to various people named Crook, Sly and Saunders? Had he not boasted that he was going down to Wonersh to 'fish' for witnesses against Melbourne? To all these and many similar questions, Fluke answered imperturbably that he may have said or done such things but that he could not remember. When re-examined by Sir William Follett, he partially regained the sympathy of the court by artfully revealing that he was a Waterloo veteran. He added that he had served in the West Indies and been discharged with 6d a day and a certificate of good conduct. He said that he wished he was still working for Mr Charles who, in his opinion, was a truly *Honourable* Mr Norton.

The nurse, Ann Cummins, had little to add, save that she had seen her mistress 'rouging and pencilling' and, at times, there had been mysterious marks on her linen. For the defence, Thesiger got her to admit that she was not really married, and, also, that she had gone down to Wonersh to be coached in her evidence, for which she had been paid by the prosecution. More importantly, the nurse, Martha Morris, declared that, before the Nortons' separation, they had quarrelled dreadfully, because Mrs Norton had insisted that she would go down with her boys to stay with her brother at Frampton Court in Dorset, even though she knew that Mr Norton was not welcome there. This was an important admission because, by obtaining it, Sir John was able to suggest that Norton had an ulterior motive for bringing this action which attempted to blacken his wife's name.

It was ten minutes past six when the case for the prosecution closed. Sir John Campbell then asked for an adjournment because, as he pointed out, the trial had already lasted some eight and a half hours, and he thought that the jury was too exhausted to give proper attention to his case. Sir William Follett objected to an adjournment unless the defence intended to call witnesses, in which case he conceded that there would need to be one. In the argument that followed, Sir John suddenly gave way. He had decided to switch his tactics. He had changed his mind, and decided not to call the witnesses he had assembled. He then rose to conclude the trial with his speech for the defence. Even when he later became Lord Chancellor, he still believed that there had been no moment in his professional life greater than this.

He began by pointing out that he did not need witnesses because no case had been made out against his client. Neither Lord Melbourne nor Mrs Norton was present in court and, therefore, there was no question of the prosecution extracting damaging confessions from them under cross-examination. Failing that, all the prosecution could have done was to present first-hand evidence of adultery being committed. It had failed to do so. Furthermore, the prosecution had failed to explain why, if Mr Norton had believed his wife had been unfaithful to him over all these years, he had done nothing about it before. If he had known, he must have connived at the adultery, but he, Sir John, acquitted Mr Norton of such a charge. Mr Norton had not forbidden Lord Melbourne's visits over the period of the marriage; on the contrary, there was ample evidence that he approved of them. Clearly, from 1831 to 1835, he had had no suspicions of adultery. In bringing forward this case against the Prime Minister now, he had been the tool of others who were acting for political purposes.

Sir John then turned to the evidence presented by the witnesses for the prosecution. Nothing was offered relevant to the years 1834, '35 or '36, 'a circumstance unexampled in the annals of such cases'. What evidence had been presented, derived from discarded servants, 'a race most dangerous in all cases, but particularly in cases of this sort'. He wondered why these servants had not told Mr Norton of their suspicions at the time of the alleged acts of misconduct, rather than coming forward with them only after they had been dismissed by Mrs Norton and after an interval of years. He pointed out that his cross-examination had made plain that many of these old servants had prepared their evidence with agents of Mr Norton who had also paid for their accommodation. No servants who were currently employed by Mrs Norton had been called. Why were not Mrs Gulliver or Mr Fitness asked to give evidence? The reason was because Fitness was present at the time of the quarrel between the Nortons, and could have explained the real cause of their separation. Fortunately, the fact of the quarrel about going to Frampton had been revealed by the witness, Mrs Morris.

Sir John dismissed, with some contempt, Follett's insinuations concerning the two doors to Storey's Gate. He reminded the jury that one of the first witnesses had confirmed that the park door to the house had neither knocker nor bell, whereas the Prince's Gate door, used by Lord Melbourne, was equipped with both and was, in effect, the street door. Suggestions that Lord Melbourne was in the habit of sneaking into the house were absurd. It was plain that the real reason for the separation of the Nortons had been their quarrel about going to Frampton. Adultery with Lord Melbourne was an afterthought, an excuse 'put into the plaintiff's mind by some insinuating rogue, by whom he had been played upon' for purposes of which he had never dreamed before.

Sir John maintained that there was evidence that the Nortons were happy together, though it suited his purposes not to examine this point too closely. He said they were a loving couple, and slept together from their marriage in 1827 until that same year of 1836. Was it likely that, for most of that time, Mrs Norton was carrying on an adulterous relationship with Lord Melbourne, without provoking suspicion and hostility in her husband? She was not only a loving wife but also an affectionate mother, and it was an evil hour when Mr Norton had been induced to part with her. At this moment Sir John contrived his most dramatic effect. Looking up at the bench on which Lord Grantley, Norton's brother, still sat, he demanded to know why that gentleman had not been called as a witness by the prosecution. 'He was sitting on the bench during the whole of the trial. He [Campbell] would say nothing of the taste which had led him to do so . . . but here he was – the brother of the plaintiff, the master of Wonersh, to which had gone down the Flukes and Cumminses; he could have explained the communications he had had with them' and might have given the court a clearer account of why the unhappy George Norton had taken this stand against his wife. Lord Grantley was not provoked, however; he glowered at Sir John, but did not speak. The jury enjoyed this dumb show as one of the most dramatic moments of the trial.

Sir John then contrasted the witnesses for the prosecution with others Sir William might have called. Mrs Norton still enjoyed the company of many respectable ladies, such as Lady Seymour and Miss Armstrong, who were her frequent companions and would never have connived at adultery had they reason to suspect it. Why had they not been called? Furthermore, Miss Armstrong often drove with Mrs Norton to visit the Duke of Devonshire – 'Was there any charge brought against His Grace'? Remorselessly, Sir John recalled the evidence and the character of the witnesses one by one. They were dismissed servants, of doubtful honesty, bearing grudges, with nothing more to swear to than a tissue of gossip. Almost all of them had been entertained by the prosecution at Wonersh, where they had been coached in their evidence and paid for their stories. Even then the respectable ones amongst them entertained no suspicions that Mrs Norton was committing adultery. The principal witness, Fluke, was a drunkard and cheat, who had sworn to make amends for his dismissal by Mrs Norton, and had boasted that he stood to earn £500 by giving evidence. What trust could be placed in such a witness? Sir John ended by reading out a statement from Lord Melbourne who had instructed him to say 'in the most clear, emphatic, and solemn manner, that he had never had any criminal intercourse with Mrs Norton, nor had ever done anything in the slightest degree to abuse the confidence of Mr Norton'. With this resounding declaration Sir John was done.

The Lord Chief Justice summed up briefly but dwelt especially on the evidence of Fluke: 'None of the other witnesses spoke to any act approaching to an act of adultery, but spoke to circumstances from which they were to infer it'. Fluke spoke to facts which would render it less difficult to come to a conclusion, but the jury 'had had the benefit of seeing him and would form their own judgement'. He then instructed the jury to retire to consider their verdict. It was fifteen minutes to midnight.

CHAPTER IV

From a Dark Wood

CAROLINE KNEW NOTHING of what was going on at the Westminster court that day, because Hampton Court was too far from London to receive hourly news. Nor did she expect a swift verdict, because she had heard that Sir William Follett would call a number of witnesses and guessed Sir John Campbell would do the same. So she had nothing to do but sit with her mother, or walk the gravelled paths, or stand alone at the window just thinking. Mrs Sheridan was especially tactful, and restricted her remarks to domestic matters. She knew her daughter's mind was elsewhere.

It was at this hour that Caroline missed her children most. She would wake to a sense of their absence, and then the recollection of her loss came as if her boys had been wrenched from her breast. She did not know for sure where they were. Perhaps they were at Miss Vaughan's house, with Fletcher ill, the baby crying, and little Brinny defiantly shouting that he wanted to see his mother. As the sun rose on another summer's day, her thoughts moved to Westminster and the trial. She knew that, at that very moment, the proceedings would be starting and everybody would be talking about her. Her name would be in the mouths of perjured witnesses, and reporters would be scribbling it down to supply gossip for the daily newspapers. These thoughts absorbed her. So her day wore on, while she and her mother clattered from room to room talking in hushed voices, till outside the shadows began to lengthen on the lawns. And still she meditated on the question which had occupied her all day. How was it that she, who had been raised among these grave gardens by this decent women, had become the most scandalous woman in England?

Caroline's first memory of her mother was of her arrival in Scotland in the autumn of 1817. It was at Ardkinglass, where Caroline and her brothers and sister had been left in the care of an aunt, while Mrs Sheridan took her ailing husband to the Cape of Good Hope. The six children had been playing in the garden when someone had come and said that their mother and sister, Helen, had arrived home from Africa, and the screaming children had bundled into the house to welcome them. But they had pulled up short at their mother's appearance. She was pale and weary, and dressed in black. She had come, she said, from a place far away, called the Cape. She and Helen had gone there, with Papa, so that the warm weather would make his cough better. But it had not made him better. Papa had died at the Cape. Now, she told the solemn-eyed children, they had brought him back to England in a big boat, called the *Albion*, so that he might be buried at home.

The prospect for Mrs Sheridan at that time was a bleak one. She was a thirty-seven-year-old widow with seven small children to bring up and launch into the world. Her husband and his famous father had left her very little money. Fortunately, though the Prince of Wales had withdrawn his friendship from Richard Brinsley Sheridan in his last years, the Prince, later George IV, remembered that he still owed 'Old Sherry' a debt of gratitude for his many services. Mrs Sheridan was given 'Grace and Favour' accommodation at Hampton Court and a small pension, and she began her struggle to bring up her family. It was, no doubt, difficult to restrain such a tribe of children among those austere courtyards. They *would* chase each other over the lawns, and shriek like wild birds across Sir Christopher Wren's dignified Fountain Court; and they *would* play games in front of the entrance of the Great Hall and Henry VIII's Chapel, without any awareness of the awesome history of these buildings.

Caroline was as wild as her brothers. She would charge through the Pond Garden and the Orangery, or run with them to admire the Great Vine which, they were told, had been planted in 1769. She would hop over the cobblestones, chanting her name to herself. She rather liked the sound of it: 'Caroline Elizabeth Sarah Sheridan, born on the 22nd of March, 1808'. When they heard it, people looked more closely at her, as if there were some significance in it. She was full of such thoughts. She loved to gaze up at the mysterious inscriptions on Nicholas Oursian's Astronomical Clock, which, a kind adult informed her, told the phases of the moon and high tide on the river, and also showed that the female earth was the centre of the universe and the male sun merely revolved about it. Sometimes she was taken into the Haunted Gallery, where people claimed to have heard the ghost of Catherine Howard, the fifth wife of Henry VIII, running towards the chapel door. They said that she had been 'unfaithful' to her husband, the King, and had made a last desperate attempt to see him, to plead for mercy, while he was hearing mass in the chapel. Catherine had been forced back, shrieking her innocence; three months later she was beheaded at the Tower. Caroline did not know what 'unfaithful' meant, but she liked to picture the young Queen in all her misery. She also liked the story of the fall and disgrace of Cardinal Wolsey, whose gloomy spirit seemed to her, to haunt the place still.

She pondered these tales as she trotted among the courts behind her brothers and sisters, a rather plain, elfin little girl, with dark eyes and raven hair. Even then she was drawn to the romance of suffering. She loved to hear of people in extreme and dramatic situations. She often begged her elder sister, Helen, to tell her how, when she was sailing sadly homeward from the Cape with Mamma, they had called in at St Helena, and glimpsed Napoleon himself, gloomily pacing the garden at Longwood.

Yet the Sheridans were a lively family, and she was the liveliest of them all. Their great hope was Richard Brinsley, the eldest, named after his grandfather. Then came the three girls, Helen, Caroline herself, and Georgiana who was a very beautiful child. Last came the three younger boys, Frank, Thomas and Charles. The children were noted for their good looks, high spirits, cleverness and mutual affection. They were artistic, played musical instruments, and put on little plays. Distinguished visitors such as the Duke of Clarence, afterwards King William IV, were sometimes invited to witness these performances:

> They were even in the nursery especially fond of private theatricals, and almost every Saturday and half-holiday was spent in preparing extemporary plays; tragedies were preferred, Turkish, so that they might wear a turband. [*sic*] Five minutes were allowed to an improvised speech to each actor, and ten minutes for Caroline to prepare her own essays at dramatic eloquence.[1]

The remembrance of that happy family life stayed with the Sheridan children throughout their lives. Many years later, Helen referred to it in a letter she wrote to Brinsley, then in India:

> One thing I remember that Mamma said to Caroline when she went to school: 'Ah, when once the branches of a family are divided, they seldom are all united again'. And it was quite true: we never did see a Christmas all together again. Caroline went to school, you to Harford; you never all of you had holidays at the same time, and then poor little Tommy went to sea, and so, though I sincerely hope to see you again my dear Brinny, yet I can never forget at Christmas or at any other time when we used

to be so merry together, that saying of Mamma's, and that we can never all meet together again, and I hate the look of the nursery where there used to be so many merry faces and cheerful voices.[2]

As the children grew older, Mrs Sheridan tried to explain to them how they came to be living at Hampton Court. She told them about their father, Tom Sheridan, who had died from consumption at the Cape. She told them how his father had been a famous playwright and the favourite of King George IV in his younger days. And she told them how, through the Duke of York, the King had looked after the family of his old friend by allowing them to live at Hampton Court. So the Sheridan children came slowly to understand why it was they lived among such grand surroundings and merited the kind attentions of the Duke and Duchess of Clarence.

What they could not understand was why they were poor. It had to do, Mrs Sheridan explained, with the early death of their father, who, she added significantly, had always suffered from being the son of a famous man. Tom Sheridan, she told them, was the only child of Richard Brinsley Sheridan's first marriage. He had inherited his father's exuberance and the good looks of his mother's family, the Linleys. But he was a wild young man and could settle to nothing. When he was a pupil at Harrow, Dr Parr had said that he had 'great acuteness, excellent wit and humour, but not a particle of understanding'. After his mother's death he merely lounged about in his father's house at Isleworth, and Mr William Smyth his tutor said that he despaired of teaching him anything.

The trouble was that Richard Brinsley Sheridan never gave his son any clear direction in life. Eventually, though, he was obliged to buy Tom a commission in a smart regiment, and the young man became the aide-de-camp to Lord Moyra in Edinburgh, where his high spirits soon made him a general favourite in the mess. The younger officers admired the cool cheek with which he disregarded regimental rules. He was often late and always in scrapes but this made them like him even more. He was a sociable, cheerful fellow. Entertaining in the mess made him an accomplished singer and dancer, and a writer of squibs and satirical verses. He was also a boxer, a gambler and a drinker. And even when his exploits were serious ones, he usually managed to extricate himself from them. Once, while hunting on a private estate without permission, he found himself obliged to run the gauntlet of the local squire and his dogs, but by the end of the day, he had so charmed the man that he was invited into the house for a drink. On another occasion, he lost almost all his money while gambling at Watier's Club in London, until he was rescued by 'Beau' Brummell, who joined forces with him, and helped him to combined winnings of £1000. He did not always get off lightly, however. At one time, he became entangled in a love affair which ended with his father having to pay £1000 damages on his behalf.

Tom learned nothing from this episode, and still his father was alternately driven to rages by his irresponsibility or beaming pride by his wit. But they fell out seriously one day when Sheridan visited the mess and publicly threatened to cut his son off with a shilling. Quick as a flash, Tom retorted: 'You will have to borrow it first'. The shout of laughter from the young subalterns embarrassed Sheridan, and he would not speak to Tom for weeks afterwards. Tom would not have minded this so much if his father had not been his sole source of income. But prudence was no part of his nature. He was a charming, romantic rebel, whose life was guided by his heart rather than his head. In 1805, he fell in love with Caroline Henrietta Callender, a beautiful and intelligent girl, the second daughter of Colonel, afterwards Sir James, Callender. When he found out about the attachment, Colonel Callender was furious and positively refused to allow his daughter to marry a penniless rapscallion like young Sheridan. So there was nothing for the lovers to do but elope. Luckily, Caroline's family came round after her marriage to Tom, and the lovers were even invited to spend part of their honeymoon at the Callender home in Scotland. But Caroline's back-biting relatives observed with grim delight that young Sheridan stayed up playing billiards till four or five in the morning even though he was on honeymoon.

Within a few years, Tom Sheridan found himself the father of four sons and three daughters, and, over that period, his financial situation grew progressively worse. In the end he was obliged to leave the army, to help his father manage the Drury Lane Theatre. Tom had a quarter share in the enterprise which was supposed to bring him about £225 a year. Unfortunately, his father rarely paid him his share. Sheridan's contribution to the management was merely to call at the box office in the morning, at an hour early enough to dodge his creditors, to pocket the takings and then to spend them on drink. Tom spent his days dealing with destitute actors pleading to be paid, reading play scripts, and trying to keep the affairs of the theatre in some sort of order. Even so, he was still thought of as 'Young Sheridan', the brilliant son of a brilliant father, and a coming man. When he attempted to follow Sheridan's second career in politics, however, the result was a disaster. In an election at Liskeard, he received a derisory number of votes. Worse was his reception at Stafford, his father's old seat. He had hoped that, in this constituency, the Sheridan name would count for something but the Stafford electors were not interested in his family or ability, and expected their votes to be bought with ready money. When it was plain that Tom expected them to give him their votes for nothing, they turned out in a crowd to meet him, pulling an open carriage to conduct him away from the town.

As his hopes declined so did his health. His mother's family, the Linleys, were noted for their beauty, but it was of the fragile, tubercular kind. In early middle-age, Tom Sheridan began to cough, and it became very plain that he had inherited the family disease. His depressing days at the theatre, the collapse of his father's career, and the burden of an ever-growing family became too much for his health. Soon he was coughing all the time and he realized that, if he did not travel to a warm climate, he would quickly die. He went on several trips to southern Europe in the following years but his coughing only started again when he came home to the smoking chimneys of London. Then, when he was in despair, his father's estranged friend, the Prince of Wales, stepped in to help him. Tom was appointed Paymaster General at the Cape, on a salary of £1000 a year. It was his last chance to save his life. So, leaving the six younger children with a relative at Ardkinglass, he, his wife and Helen their eldest daughter, set sail for the Cape. But it seems that even before he went, Tom Sheridan had given up hope, for, when he met his old dancing master, Angelo, in the street, he told him that he was a dying man. Yet his old liveliness returned for a while when he first arrived in the colony, and he soon became a popular figure. When news reached him of his father's death, however, his spirits sank and the tuberculosis strengthened its hold upon him. On 12 September 1817, just fourteen months after the death of his father, he died at the Cape, aged forty-two.

It was then that the Royal Family stepped in again to help, and offered Mrs Sheridan the Grace and Favour apartment at Hampton Court. Her income now consisted of her modest pension from the King, a small allowance from her own father, and her husband's doubtful share in the Drury Lane estate. Her task was to educate her children, get each boy into a profession, and marry off each of her girls into the nobility. She dedicated her life to this business and she succeeded remarkably well. In later life she also tried to make some money writing novels. She brought out *Carwell* in 1830, which attempted to expose the irrational sentencing procedure meted out on forgers, and followed it with *Aims & Ends* in 1833 and *Oonagh Lynch* in the same year.

It was the daughter named after her who gave her the most trouble. To start with, Caroline seemed to be the only one who had not inherited the Linley good looks. Helen and Georgiana were beautiful girls but Caroline was so plain that her mother was concerned that she might not attract a husband. Perhaps, because of this, Caroline was difficult and constantly demanded attention. She loved the theatricals which she organized for her brothers and sisters and announced that she would be a famous actress, and a writer like their grandfather. To this end, she persuaded Helen to join her in writing a book. Some months before, they had been given a copy of *The Dandy Book*, with its caricatures of Dandies of the day. Now they wrote a sequel entitled *The Dandies Rout*. A bookseller named Marshall was so impressed with their efforts that he gave them £50 for the copyright. After *The Dandies Rout*, Caroline announced to her awestruck brothers and sisters that she was about to compose a Romantic poem in Spenserian stanzas, entitled *Amouida and Sebastian*, set in America. She started it off in bold lettering, but never finished it.

In later life, Caroline became more sensitive to the plight of her own mother bringing up all those boisterous children, and she wrote a poem about her:

> In thy black weed, and coif of widow's woe;
> Thy dark expressive eyes all dim and clouded,
> By that deep wretchedness the lonely know;
> Stifling thy grief, to hear some weary task
> Conned by unwilling lips, with listless air;
> Hoarding thy means, lest future needs might task
> More than the widow's pittance then could spare.
> Hidden, forgotten by the great and gay,
> Enduring sorrow, not by fits and starts,
> But the long self-denial, day by day,
> Alone amidst thy brood of careless hearts!
> Striving to guide, to teach, or to restrain
> The young rebellious spirits crowding round,
> Who saw not, knew not, felt not for thy pain,
> And could not comfort – yet had power to wound![3]

Of all the girls, only Caroline was sent away to school, and this was probably because she was so difficult. In recollection, she had to admit that there always had been something of the devil in her. Her grandfather had seen it. When, as an infant, she had been placed in the arms of Richard Brinsley Sheridan, he had inspected her closely and then pronounced his verdict. She was not a child he would care to meet in a dark wood. When she was a girl and people told this story in her presence, she would cover her face, and blush, because she found it embarrassing; but, while doing so, she would spy through her fingers at the expressions on the faces of the listeners. For, even then, there was something else in her which delighted in the dramatic nature of the story, and she was well aware that she would have braved any amount of embarrassment to be the centre of a sensation.

CHAPTER

V

A School for Scandal

IT WAS ONLY WHEN SHE WAS OLDER that Caroline understood what part her dead grandfather played in shaping her life. For example, she would never have gone to the finishing school at Wonersh if he had not been both so brilliant and so recklessly extravagant. His luminous career and lofty friendships had raised the Sheridans to an eminent place in Society, but his profligacy, coupled with the burning down of the Drury Lane Theatre in 1809, had ensured that they had very little money with which to keep up their pretensions. Because of this, Caroline's brothers were obliged to work their way up in gentlemenly professions, and she and her sisters were required to marry for money. Mrs Sheridan knew her daughters Helen and Georgiana would be very attractive to the right sort of young men, when the time came. Only Caroline was a problem. Besides being plain, she was unruly, subject to tantrums, and an unspeakable show-off. If she were to find a husband she had to be taught how to make herself amenable to people. She had to learn not to argue with men but to please them. So she must be sent to a finishing school.

Caroline wept and pleaded not to go but it was no use. Mrs Sheridan was gentle but firm. There had been too many occasions on which Caroline had quarrelled with her sisters, or had indulged in sulking fits and jealous rages. Words had had no effect on her. Caroline did not seem to be able to control herself and conduct herself at all times as a young lady should. Perhaps a brief course in a school would help her to moderate her passions. So it was decided. When Caroline was sixteen, her name was entered for a young ladies' academy at Wonersh in Surrey. She was heart-broken at leaving her comfortable home, her gentle, long-suffering mother, Helen, Georgiana, and the lively brothers whom she had led into all sorts of scrapes. When at last, the dreaded carriage came to haul her away from all her loved ones, she could not, at first, look out of the windows for sobbing, and, when she did so, the turnpike road from Guildford to Shalford was fringed with misery. It was 1824 and she remained at the school for nearly two years.

At first she had determined to be miserable but, to her surprise, she rather liked school. She became the centre of a group of companions who giggled their way through mornings of French and handwriting instruction, and afternoons of sketching, watercolour, practice at the pianoforte, dancing, and tuition in etiquette. There were occasions when she got into trouble for speaking her mind too plainly, and more than once she shocked the teachers by her language which, she was told, was far too coarse for a gentlewoman to use. But she had an open nature and quick affections, and was soon a favourite among both teachers and pupils. To her surprise, she now found that the other girls regarded her as a beauty, for, between the ages of fourteen and sixteen, her appearance had altered considerably. Her dark eyes and hair had always fascinated people but now her figure had filled out, and her white neck arched gracefully from her full bodice. And she was not unaware that, when she was reciting poetry to her classmates, the colour which came and went in her cheeks and the tears that came to her eyes in particularly passionate moments only increased the dramatic effect of what she was saying. She had become desirable.

On fine afternoons, the young ladies were taken out to walk two by two in the Surrey countryside, and a favourite route went through the grounds of Wonersh Park. Their teacher had a connection here, and one day she announced that she had succeeded in getting permission for them to tour the house itself. As she clumped through the rooms with her chattering companions, Caroline joined in their gossip about the Norton family, of which Lord Grantley was the head. Privately she liked to invent stories about them to entertain herself. One day, however, she found that she had attracted the attention of one of the real owners:

> . . . the governess to whose care I was confided happening to be the sister of Lord Grantley's agent, the female members of the Norton family, from courtesy to this lady, invited her and such of her pupils, as she chose to accompany her, to Lord Grantley's house. A sister of Mr Norton's, an eccentric person who affected masculine habits and played a little on the violin, amused herself with my early verses and my love of music, and took more notice of me than my companions.[1]

Miss Augusta Norton was the sister of Lord Grantley. She seemed a strange lady to Caroline, for she habitually wore breeches, and kept her hair severely cropped. The moment she spied Caroline passionately reciting verse to her group of schoolgirl companions, Miss Norton took a fancy to her. Soon Caroline was invited to the house alone. Miss Norton asked her to play the piano and to recite her own poems, which Caroline was happy to do. But she found her hostess's sudden swings of mood from pride to playful whimsy both puzzling and alarming.

Then came a new development. One day, Caroline was sent for by her teacher, whom she found in an agitated state. At first she seemed at a loss for words but then puzzled Caroline by announcing abruptly that she was not prepared to take her again on walks to Wonersh Park. She seemed unwilling to give a further explanation but Caroline begged to know in what way she had offended. She could only guess that she had, perhaps, unintentionally annoyed Miss Norton, which would not have been a difficult thing to do, and it was true that that lady's behaviour had seemed even more odd when last they had been alone. But her teacher's reply did not concern Miss Augusta. It was of young Mr George Norton that she spoke. Apparently, he had seen Caroline walking through the rooms of the house, and now wanted to marry her.

At first, Caroline had difficulty in taking the matter in. Who was Mr George Norton? Then she remembered a heavy young man, some six or seven years older than herself, who had silently stared at her among her schoolgirl friends, as they giggled along a corridor in Wonersh House. One of her friends had noticed his interest and made a remark. When she had asked about him, she learned that he was the younger brother of Lord Grantley and the heir to the estate. It seemed that this was the man who now wanted to marry her. He had never even spoken to her, and yet here he was, asking the address of her mother, so that he could write a formal proposal of marriage.

Caroline's flustered teacher did not quite know what to do about all this. Apparently she had doubted the propriety of passing George Norton's message to Mrs Sheridan, but had finally decided that she must. She kept repeating that she was responsible for Caroline, who was only sixteen, and that she owed it to her dear Mamma to take the greatest care of her. On one thing, however, she was clear from the start. Caroline was not to visit Wonersh Park again, unless her mother wrote to give her permission. Caroline's reputation must never be compromised. She also advised her pupil to write to Mrs Sheridan. Caroline realized that her teacher was not entirely convinced by her own assurances that she had never spoken to Mr Norton, and had never enticed him. Indeed, she could hardly blame the woman, for who would believe that a man might propose to a girl without even speaking to her? That evening, Caroline wrote to her own mother to explain that Norton's proposal was a complete surprise to her. She had never (she underlined the word) encouraged him. But, even while she scribbled away, she found herself strangely flattered. He must be very smitten with her.

While she waited for her mother's reply, Caroline found out as much as she could about the Nortons. Lord Grantley, the head of the family, was married but there were no children, and it was said that he and his wife rarely met. Wonersh Park was the family home, although the Nortons were a Yorkshire family and had large estates in that county. Lady Grantley lived at Wonersh, as well as several of her sisters-in-law, though her husband went there very little. His only brother was this George Norton, who was a barrister but never practised. He was said to be a typical Norton, heavy in face and features, indolent, undemonstrative and a Tory. His proposal seemed preposterous to Caroline. What would her brilliant, Radical grandfather have said about an alliance with such a family?

It is unlikely that Mrs Sheridan ever suspected her daughter's behaviour, for she knew that Caroline was not underhand. In her reply to Norton, she acknowledged the honour he had done her family in asking for her daughter's hand, but refused it because Caroline was only sixteen years old and, therefore, far too young to be married. In his answer, Norton said that he entirely understood the reason for Mrs Sheridan's refusal but added that, if her daughter's youthfulness was her only objection, he would be prepared to wait three years more, for a time when it would cease to be an obstacle.

Caroline must have been thrilled by all this drama. She was only sixteen and yet she had already provoked a passion and made a conquest. She dismissed the possibility of her ever marrying Norton even in three years' time. She was going to marry Lord Byron, or rather – as he had just died – a handsome young poet very like him. She had decided that her husband would have a noble brow and imperious looks, and would speak nothing but verse. Mr Norton, from what she had seen of him, was a very ordinary young man, who spoke nothing at all. He was certainly not the Byronic soul-mate she intended to be her husband. Yet she was flattered by the thought of this moody lover yearning for her. Perhaps, when she refused him again in three years' time, there would be scenes of duels and horse-whippings? She certainly hoped so. Meanwhile, she would soon leave school to 'come out' in Society, and her love-life would begin in earnest.

Caroline had never met anybody like Norton and had little idea of the sort of person she was dealing with. She might have guessed from his silent, arrogant stare that she had stirred something in him but she would never have understood at that time that his was a coldly egotistic nature which had been awakened to quick passion by her presence. Her family life among the warm, witty Sheridans had not prepared her for such a person. Besides, how could such a lively, innocent schoolgirl know anything of the unemotional, joyless sensuality which was Norton's? Even Mrs Sheridan did not see the danger, though she might have reflected that there was something profoundly wrong in a lover who did not even stoop to speak to her daughter. Later, when she got to know him better, Caroline understood Norton well enough. His chief characteristics were pride and lethargy. To propose to a young girl directly, and to risk a public refusal, would have been unendurably humiliating to him. He was also very conscious that he was doing the stooping. Caroline had practically nothing in the world, while he was a barrister, a prospective MP, and the heir to a peerage. But he was determined to have her, however long it took. His was a vegetable sensuality. He never condescended to be urgently enthusiastic about anything. He was always slow-moving; even at school they had called him 'the late George Norton'.

Some eighteen months after the drama of Norton's proposal, Caroline found herself getting into the coach to leave the school at Wonersh, to rejoin her family at Hampton Court. She had changed greatly, and the experiment of sending her away had been a success. She was now ready to enter the world. At home she found her mother and sisters delighted to have her company again, and full of compliments about her appearance. Helen was eighteen now, and was to 'come out' in that very year, 1825, with Caroline in the following season, and Georgiana after that. Caroline's sisters were in nervous high spirits. Their talk was all of balls and gowns, and the various young men that Brinsley brought home to introduce to the family. They speculated endlessly on marriage. Caroline's curious conquest had excited their imaginations. They discussed what it would be like to be married, and what sort of men they would choose as husbands. Caroline was surprised to find that, at times, she was rather bored, but, nevertheless, she was cheerfully prepared to join in her sisters' conversation.

But though the talk was all of pleasure, the girls understood that all these amusements had a deadly serious purpose. They *had* to find husbands, because they had no money of their own. If any of the girls failed to marry, then there was nothing for her to do but to act as a penniless companion to their impoverished mother. To refuse a good match was the most irresponsible of actions, and an old maid was the most ridiculous of creatures. After her marriage, Caroline wrote some verses about a girl who was foolish enough to turn down any number of suitors and was, consequently, left on the shelf:

RECOLLECTIONS OF A FADED BEAUTY

Then Mr Humley asked aunt's leave to wed,
And winked, and asked if love was in my head,
Or heart, and then proceeding things to settle,
(Helping my aunt the while to lift the kettle,) –
Said, 'you shall have a cozy home my dear,
And fifty pound (to buy you clothes) a year.
And we must get your aunt, or some kind fairy
To teach you how to churn and mind the dairy'.
'A cozy home!' why, did one ever hear
Of such a man? and, to call me 'my dear'.
Me – I was Frederick Mortimer's 'heart's Haidee';
Young Minton's star of hope and gladness – me!
But I refused him; though my aunt did say
'that it was an advantage thrown away';
(He an advantage!) that she'd make me rue it –
Make me a nun – I'd like to see her do it!
Down, down rebellious heart! I am a nun,
At least, the same as if I had been one.
I do repent I thought myself too comely;
I do repent I am not Mrs Humley![2]

But though they were positive they would soon be married, the three Sheridan girls were not entirely sure about how it was done, and Mrs Sheridan had little advice to give. When they pressed her about her own romantic courtship, she would only smile and observe that the Sheridans never did things like other people, not even love-making. In fact, the family tradition was elopement. Not only had Mrs Sheridan herself run away from home with her husband, but the Sheridan grandparents had also eloped. Indeed the tale of how Richard Brinsley Sheridan had courted his wife, and then turned the episode into a dramatic masterpiece, was hardly a suitable example of courtship for Mrs Sheridan to recommend to her daughters.

The Sheridan girls had been long familiar with Sir Joshua Reynolds's painting of their grandmother, the ethereal Elizabeth Linley. He had depicted a young woman in the role of St Cecilia; she was seated at the piano and was accompanied by two angelic little choirboys, her brothers. The Linleys were noted for their ravishing looks and their musical talents, and Caroline's family were often compared to them. Thomas Linley, Elizabeth's father, had flourished in the 1770s as a musician, and he frequently featured his own children in the concerts he gave in Bath. Elizabeth was the most celebrated of all the Linleys; with her clear soprano voice and delicate features she became a sensation in the city. When she was only sixteen, the famous artists Reynolds and Gainsborough were wild to paint her, and she was also pursued by many unsuitable men. At one time, her father insisted that she became engaged to an elderly miser named Walter Long, who later settled £3000 on her, before she adroitly broke off the match. Another man, named Captain Mathews, though married, pestered her from day to night. It was even whispered that King George III had ogled her from the pit, while excusing himself by declaring that he had never heard a finer voice.

Elizabeth was miserable, and wanted to get away from all these tedious lovers. The last straw came when she heard rumours of a new play at the Haymarket Theatre, called *The Maid of Bath*. The author, Samuel Foote, had presented her on the stage in the guise of a character named 'Miss Linnet'. In the play, she was pursued by an old miser remarkably like Long, while a certain 'Major Racket', modelled on Mathews, constantly attempted to seduce her. Her acquaintance in Bath seemed to think it was a huge joke. It now seemed to the poor girl that people were either sniggering at her or trying to make love to her. What she needed was a protector.

It was her friend, Alice Sheridan, who suggested a suitable person. She had a young brother, Richard Brinsley, who had absolutely nothing to do but drag after their father round the country while he gave his lectures about elocution. Young Brinsley was handsome and charming and, what was more important, the soul of gallantry to women. She was quite sure that he would be willing to accompany Elizabeth across the Channel to France, where she could take sanctuary in a convent. It was true that he had no money, was only twenty, and could not speak French, but he had always shown a 'delicacy and tender compassion for Elizabeth' and was sure to agree. So it proved, but, soon after the couple left Dunkirk, young Sheridan declared to her that he would not conduct her to the convent, unless she first consented to marry him. He confessed that all along he had been hoping to make her his wife, and, anyway, she must know that if she ever returned to England unmarried, she would cause a scandal. In return, Elizabeth admitted that Brinsley was the only man she had ever truly loved, and she was not averse to marrying him. So they found a French priest who frequently obliged English runaways, and were married at once.[3]

For a month, the young lovers sat in an hotel in Lille, while their money was running out. Then Elizabeth fell ill, and, when her father appeared, to take her back to England, neither lover was truly sorry to see him. Afterwards, Richard Brinsley returned to Bath alone, and found the town agog with the story of his elopement. Captain Mathews, who was beside himself with jealousy, denounced him in *The Bath Chronicle* as 'L[iar] and a treacherous S[coundrel]'. Brinsley swore he would have his revenge for this, and fought two duels with Mathews. In the first, he broke the captain's sword across, and held his own at Mathews's breast to make him take his words back. He also forced him to swear to print a retraction in *The Bath Chronicle*, which oath was honoured in the issue for 7 May 1772. But Mathews's pride was now so inflamed that he challenged Brinsley to a second duel. It took place on Kingsdown, and, this time, Brinsley was seriously wounded. He was almost given up for dead, but put to bed at the White Hart, where, in eight days, he was pronounced out of danger. Once again, all Bath rang with his doings.

Brinsley was now sent to Waltham Abbey, to study for the Bar, in order to keep him as far as possible from his Elizabeth. But it was no good. The two insisted on being together, and, on 13 April 1773, they were married for the second time. They had nothing to live on save Mr Long's £3000. Brinsley had no profession, and he would no longer allow Elizabeth to sing in public, for fear that she should be leered at from the pit. One day, however, his family were amazed when he informed them that a play of his was to be performed at Covent Garden. It was called *The Rivals*, and seemed to draw very heavily on his own recent adventures. It was set in Bath and featured an attempted elopement and a duel. Friends also noticed that the dictatorial Sir Anthony Absolute, in the play, tended to resemble Sheridan's own irascible father; while Bob Acres had something of Captain Mathews about him. The first performance on 17 January 1775 was not a success, partly because it was overlong, and partly because the chief actor, Shuter, had not mastered his lines. But the play was not damned outright, and, when these matters were put right, it was presented again on 28 January to such a rapturous reception that it was repeated for fifteen nights. Overnight, Sheridan became 'the divine Brinsley' with a national reputation for wit, and a good income from the box office.

Throughout her life, Caroline revered the memory of her grandfather and loved to hear stories of him. She too would have preferred a life of passions, jealousies, duels and drama. It would have been thrilling to be carried away to France, and to be married in a convent by a handsome young lover. That was romance! It was like a tale from *The Castle of Otranto*. And her handsome, witty grandfather seemed to her to be the model of what a man should be. In a way, she was a little in love with him, but she also envied his freedom to live such an exciting life. Like poor Elizabeth Linley, she could only wait for such a hero to come along.

Like her grandfather, she always had a weakness for dramatic gesture. Any misfortune could be endured provided it enabled one to show off. Sheridan had made use of such an occasion when his theatre burned down and he had lost his fortune. For, within a few years of the presentation of *The Rivals*, he had become a wealthy man. First he wrote a series of successful plays including *St Patrick's Day*, *The Duenna*, and *The School for Scandal*. Then, having borrowed the £35,000 to do so, he became the manager, and half-owner, of the Drury Lane Theatre. This property was the security for all his many borrowings over the next thirty-three years, and it seemed a good one, for he had perceived that it was quite safe to borrow at 5% on an investment that offered 10%. He also took £4000 a year as his own salary, which sum he spent almost as quickly as he could collect the cash from the box office.

But on 24 February 1809, when the House of Commons was debating the war with Spain, its windows were lit up by a vivid glow. News soon reached the members that the Drury Lane Theatre was on fire. Sheridan, who was an MP, was in the House at the time, and was accorded a unique privilege when Lord Temple and Mr Ponsonby both offered to move an adjournment motion: 'in consequence of the extent of the calamity which the event just communicated to the house would bring upon a respectable individual, a member of that house'. Sheridan politely refused the offer, and strolled down to watch his beloved theatre in conflagration. It was an occasion for panache. So he took a table at the nearby Piazza Coffee House, and sat drinking wine while watching the fire that spelled his utter ruin. When his friends expressed surprise at his calmness he smiled. 'Cannot', he asked, 'a man take a glass of wine by his own fireside?'

Caroline loved that story. She so admired her grandfather's command of himself, his cool disdain for mere money matters, and his contempt for conventional responses. To her it seemed a magnificent thing to scorn the fates with such an attitude. For her grandfather was ruined by the fire, and recognized his ruin at once. Within months he was arrested for debt.

But Mrs Sheridan did not share her enthusiasm for the story, and was annoyed that Caroline did not seem to understand its significance. The Drury Lane fire was not only a catastrophe for Sheridan, but for all of them. Because Richard Brinsley had lost most of his money following the fire, he was unable to offer customary bribes to his electors in Stafford and lost his parliamentary seat. Because he was no longer an MP, he was liable to arrest, and because of this, he was often in a debtors' gaol. Because of this, his last days were miserable, and spent in destitution, and because of this, Caroline's own father was worried into his grave by money troubles. Because of this, their family had no fortune to speak of, and the Sheridan girls had to find rich husbands. Because of this, Caroline had to accept the best offer she could get as soon as she 'came out'. Her grandfather had left her no choice.

VI

IN THE MARKET

IN THE SPRING OF 1825, Mrs Sheridan launched her girls upon the fashionable world. She took rooms for the Season in Great George Street, Westminster, hard-by the Houses of Parliament with their plentiful supplies of rich and relatively young men. Helen was to 'come out' that Season. Throughout the summer, Caroline and Georgiana, now seventeen and fifteen respectively, spent their days waiting for Helen to get up, listened to tales of the ball she had attended the night before, helped to dress her for the coming evening, and often lay awake to welcome her home. And, through many early-morning hours, the girls' bedroom was enlivened by whispered accounts of presentations at court, splendid receptions, the latest fashions in gowns, and what the young men said.

From the first, they teased her about her admirers, and were disappointed when she said that she had not fallen in love with anyone, nor had she found any man especially attractive. But, as May gave way to June, they began to hear more about a certain Captain Price Blackwood, the young heir to the Irish peer, Lord Dufferin. It seemed that he was being very attentive to Helen. When pressed by her sisters, she was impatient and curiously anxious. She said that she was not in love with him, he was merely being kind. In this she was speaking the truth. She had not fallen in love with Blackwood and probably feared to commit herself to a match that was certain to provoke the hostility of his family. However charming, the Sheridan girls had no money, and their family lived only on the fringes of aristocratic society. Besides, the name of Richard Brinsley Sheridan was not always an asset in such circles. Whatever the reason, there was no proposal for Helen that year, and when the Season ended in early July, the three girls and their mother took the carriage back to Hampton Court.

In the spring of 1826, Mrs Sheridan again took the rooms in Great George Street, and this year it was Caroline's turn to be presented at court. She was well aware that her business was to find a husband, and she was supremely confident of doing so. It was for this that she had spent hours learning the waltz and mazurka in the arms of great gawky schoolgirls at Wonersh. It was for this that she had committed to memory tables of irregular French verbs, and had spent long, tedious afternoons with her needlework, sketch-pad and water-colours. She also had an uncommonly witty tongue which, as she already knew, some men found attractive.

By the time she was seventeen, Caroline knew better than most girls how to capture male attention. She was very aware of her charms and how to use them. For example, she learned to employ a certain slow movement of the neck the better to show off her bust. She also perfected a characteristic eye-movement by practising in front of a mirror. Having lowered her lids for a few moments, she would approach the glass, and then, when no more than three inches from its surface, would slowly raise them and gaze deeply into the image of her own eyes. Few men were impervious to this display. She also liked to exchange banter with her admirers, and ignored the disapproval of older ladies. She was a good mimic, and told stories in an affected Irish brogue, for she liked to be thought of as Irish though she had never been to that country.

In the 1826 Season, the Sheridans' small apartments were regularly crowded with guests. Mrs Sheridan was still regarded as one of the most charming hostesses in London, and the good looks of her daughters were now famous. Helen was handsome and Caroline attractive, but Georgiana, now sixteen, had been seen at afternoon receptions, and promised to be even more ravishing than her sisters. And, though the Sheridan girls were much admired individually, together they were a sensation. People began to call them: 'The Three Graces'. Years later, Helen explained their relative merits to Disraeli; 'You see', she said, 'Georgy's the beauty and Carry's the wit, and I ought to be the good one, but I am not.'[1]

Looking back, Caroline pitied the simplicity of her younger self. At the time, it had all seemed so innocent to her. Of course she had understood that her embroidery and dancing lessons were preparations for the business of husband-hunting, but she still believed in romance, and the impulse of a free heart. How could she have understood then that many of the young bloods who crowded round to be introduced to her, and pressed her hand rather too firmly, might well have left her mother's apartments and sauntered over St James's Park, to White's Club, where they would gamble, and guzzle strong liquors till the early hours? And how could she have guessed that some of her more fulsome admirers would walk straight from her company, to houses of assignation especially reserved for Members of Parliament,[2] or might stroll out on to the cool pavements to buy themselves the favours of working girls, who came rather more cheaply than the hot-house beauties exhibited for sale in the salon?

Of course, ladies knew of White's Club only by report, for they were not allowed in but there was another institution close by, in King Street, Westminster, which in the 1820s was the centre of Caroline's social world. It was Almack's assembly rooms, later known as Willis's. Here, subscription balls were given on Wednesday nights throughout the Season. Admission was strictly limited to the upper classes, and there in the Season, between ten and half past eleven in the evening, girls danced their quadrilles, mazurkas and waltzes, and were permitted to talk to the young men who came to look them over.

Even to be admitted to one of Almack's subscription balls was a significant social achievement. To get an entrance ticket, a young lady needed a good measure of 'ton' (or fashion), and an impeccable reputation. Each Monday the patronesses of the Ball decided upon the list of girls fortunate enough to receive them. These six arbiters of Almack's list were ladies of the highest fashion, and included Princess Lieven who was the wife of the Russian ambassador, Lady Cowper, and Lady Jersey. Each patroness used three baskets in order to select her list and all eighteen baskets were spread upon a red baize table. The first basket of each contained the names of those young ladies who had applied to her for tickets; the names of those chosen went into the second basket; and of those rejected into the third. Unlucky candidates were divided between ladies who might re-apply, and those who would never be granted admission. As each patroness brought out a name from her first basket, the others would raise objections on the ground of social status, suitability, the wealth of the young lady's parents and the propriety with which she conducted herself. Almack's must never become a centre for scandal. Fortunately, there were no such fears on account of Caroline and she was granted a ticket.

She was soon noticed. In April 1826 at the Spitalfields Ball, she was chosen, with eleven other of the prettiest young ladies, to perform an exhibition quadrille representing the twelve months. She was August, and had to dance with great care, so as not to upset her headdress decked out with the fruits and flowers of the month. To her delight, she heard that the dance was to be repeated at Almack's a week later, but was desperately disappointed when she was told that it had been cancelled because the sister of one of the months had died. The patronesses were obliged to make hurried arrangements, because of the cancellation, and, once again, Caroline found herself in demand.

On 7 May she danced a quadrille of 'Paysannes Provençales' with some of the most specially favoured of all Almack's young ladies, including the daughter of Lord Talbot, and the Miss Duncombes.[3] The applause at the end was rapturous, and she specially noticed a middle-aged little man who clapped her enthusiastically.

Shortly afterwards, to her surprise, he called at Great George Street, and introduced himself. It was in no way improper that he should, for he turned out to be an old friend of her grandfather's. It was Tom Moore, the Irish poet, the author of the famous *Irish Melodies*, many of which she already knew by heart. He told her that he had thought her the prettiest dancer at Almack's and that she was 'strikingly like old Brinsley'. And he made it plain that he considered her just as pretty without her nutritious millinery.

They laughed together, but afterwards he told her sad stories of her grandfather's last days of poverty. Sheridan's end resembled the final scene from Hogarth's *The Rake's Progress*. The house in Savile Row was almost empty. The books, pictures and most of the furniture had all been sold. The second Mrs Sheridan lay in a first-floor bedroom dying of cancer of the womb, and the one maidservant left to attend her only stayed on because she was waiting to be paid. Sheridan lay in the garrett above, on a sodden mattress, covered by an old red and blue blanket. He was unable to get up even to answer calls of nature, and there was no-one to help him. None of the grand friends of his youth were interested in him now.

That is how Moore found him. He had been alerted to the situation by Samuel Rogers, the poet, who had received a begging letter from Sheridan: 'They are going to put the carpets out of the window, and break into Mrs Sheridan's room and take me – for God's sake let me see you'. Moore and Rogers went there at once to give what help they could. They called in the Dorset physician, Dr Bain, to examine Sheridan, but he pronounced the case hopeless. The two friends then wrote to the newspapers to make it known to the public that Richard Brinsley Sheridan, the author of *The School for Scandal*, was lying ill and destitute. That brought in offers of help. Even the Prince of Wales sent money through an intermediary, but on his deathbed, Sheridan insisted in sending it back to the Prince he believed had forsaken him. Help had come too late. Sheridan died in Savile Row on 7 July 1816, looking much older than his sixty-five years.

Moore paused, and there were tears in his eyes as he spoke of it, for, as Caroline was to discover, he was a tender-hearted little fellow. They agreed that Caroline must have been about eight years old when her grandfather died, a little girl running about the grounds of Hampton Court. Moore wanted to know if she had heard about the funeral. For Sheridan's funeral was a great contrast to his dying. All those who had neglected him in his last days turned out to share some of the glory of his great name. It was at Westminster Abbey. The pall-bearers were the Duke of Bedford, the Earl of Lauderdale, Earl Mulgrave, the Bishop of London, Lord Holland and Lord Spencer. The mourners included three dukes (two royal); fifteen other members of the nobility; the Lord Mayor; many knights, baronets and MPs; and the whole of the Drury Lane company. But none of them would subscribe to a memorial for Sheridan. In the end, an unknown man, Peter Moore, put up a stone at his own expense. It read

RICHARD BRINSLEY SHERIDAN:
born 1751; died 7th July 1816:
THIS MARBLE IS THE TRIBUTE OF AN ATTACHED FRIEND.

But Sherry's most powerful valediction had come in a letter Moore had received from Lord Byron, who had just been hounded out of the country. Byron wrote of his old friend: 'Sheridan was too good for that gang, and 'though he had nothing to help him in the way of family or influence or fortune, he beat them out and out in every thing he tried.'[4]

Caroline found a true a friend in Tom Moore, and one who seemed somehow to come as a bequest from her grandfather. Moore remained loyal and affectionate through all her later troubles until he died in 1852. They shared many things: a veneration for the memory of her grandfather, a sentimental love of everything Irish, and a joy in poetry and song. His *Irish Melodies* included such ballads as 'Love's Young Dream', 'The Minstrel Boy', and 'Believe Me if all those Endearing Young Charms'. He would perform these in aristocratic drawing rooms where, in later years, Caroline's own splendid contralto sometimes entwined with his pure Irish tenor. But though his friendship brought her much pleasure, Moore also painted for her an awful image of worldly failure; it was of a penniless old man who lay dying beneath a red and blue blanket.

As the Season of 1826 progressed, there grew a tension among the Sheridan girls. Helen and Caroline enjoyed their trips on the Thames, their drives in Rotten Row, and their mother's receptions, but they were both aware that the precious days of the Season were coming to an end with nothing gained. It was the tradition that the eldest girl in a family must find her husband first, and Helen's matrimonial fortunes inevitably affected her two younger sisters. Georgiana was due to 'come out' in the following Season and her beauty was already such that there was no doubt she would have many suitors. Helen was still indifferent to Captain Blackwood, though he was as attentive as ever. His interest, however, seemed to annoy her rather than to gratify. Then came days when Helen and her mother remained closeted together for hours at a time. Helen would emerge from these meetings red-eyed, and her mother with uncustomary tight lips. At last the crisis was over, and Mrs Sheridan joyfully summoned her family to tell them that Helen was to marry Captain Blackwood. It was the end of the Season. The wedding took place on 4 July 1826, at St George's, Hanover Square, with Caroline and Georgiana as bridesmaids. Mrs Sheridan led the contingent of adoring Sheridans. She explained the absence of Lord Dufferin as a matter of petty family hostility. After the wedding, Blackwood took Helen to Italy for their honeymoon. Mrs Sheridan said that he did so to protect her from his disapproving relatives.

Now it was Caroline's turn to land a husband and she felt that such a thing was surely not difficult. She was handsome, quite willing to fall in love, and very susceptible to the beauty of young men. She was the subject of universal admiration, and her performance as 'August' had brought her many admiring glances. Yet, for some reason, 1826 was not her year. It has been suggested that she had an unhappy love affair during the Season, and that this may have been the cause of her subsequent cynicism and restlessness. Or perhaps it was grief that unsettled her, for hard on the heels of Helen's wedding, came the news of Tommy Sheridan's death at sea. August brought no flowers and fruits for her, only the memory of a little brother lost.

After the Season, the Sheridans stayed on for a time at Great George Street, until the new parliamentary term brought its crop of MPs. Their Westminster tea-parties were crammed with members talking of Canning and Wellington. Most of their guests were Whigs, for the family was still passionately partisan in politics. Caroline's older brother, Richard Brinsley (to whom they all referred as 'Brinny') was beginning to show an interest in public affairs, and it was hoped that, one day, he would become an MP like his grandfather. Caroline loved to hear political talk, for she was an ardent Whig and all for reform. She delighted to exchange gossip about the great Whig grandees, and to discuss such matters as the prospects for a reform bill and the future for 'auld Ireland'. She learned that Lord Grey might form a Whig government, or perhaps Lord Althorp, but she held stoutly to the view that the true prospective leader for their party was Mr William Lamb, even though he had resigned his seat at Hertford. For she had discovered that he was that same William Lamb who had been a friend of her grandfather, and had written an Epilogue to his play *Pizarro*:

> Mine is the task, to rigid custom due
> To me ungrateful, as 'tis harsh to you,
> To mar the work the tragic scene has wrought,
> To rouse the mind that broods in pensive thought,
> To scare Reflection, which, in absent dreams,
> Still lingers musing on the recent themes.[5]

There was, of course, little chance that she would ever meet Mr Lamb, because, having resigned his seat, he seemed to have retired from public life altogether. All the world knew of his troubles; his wife, Caroline, had conducted a tempestuous affair with Lord Byron, which had ended with her slashing her wrists at Lady Heathcote's Ball in 1813. In 1826 Caroline Lamb was ill and living in seclusion. Their only son, Augustus, who lived with his father, was an epileptic and mentally enfeebled. It seemed that the world might have heard the last of William Lamb.

Christmas was spent by the Sheridans at Hampton Court, as usual, with only letters from Helen to give the days interest. She wrote to say that she was blissfully happy. Her husband was very kind, and she was learning to love him very much. True love, she concluded, was not always an instantaneous thing, but might grow in marriage between a man and his wife. A later letter informed them that she was going to have a baby.

In the spring of 1827, the trees in St James's Park put forth their new leaves and the Season began with its familiar round of parties, balls, fêtes and expeditions. Georgiana 'came out', and was at once surrounded by elegant admirers. Fond as she was of her sister, Caroline watched the young girl's instant success with alarm. She did not wish to stand in the way of Georgiana's brilliant opportunities, but it would have been a humiliating thing if convention were to be broken, and Georgiana got married before she herself had been asked. She would have been stranded at twenty, a Society spinster overtaken by her sisters, ready to decline into a useful companion to her mother, and a loving aunt to her sisters' children. She had too much spirit for that, and was determined to find a husband. Yet somehow no suitable man came forward.

That year there was a new government. Lord Liverpool's long administration ended with his stroke, and Canning succeeded him. In May, when Caroline was preparing for the new Season, William Lamb was on the high seas, for he had been appointed Chief Secretary for Ireland. But the world of Society was much the same, and the warmer weather brought out yet another generation of fashionable young women like the butterflies in the park. Their coyness and delicate airs, their fancy quadrilles and mazurkas, their sentimental songs and delicate pastels were all traps for suitably rich young men. Of course the business was dressed out in the language of romantic love, and, indeed, Caroline knew of many a true affair of the heart among her set. But such passions might not interfere with the real business of life, which was money. A woman who foolishly placed her affections with an impecunious younger son, or, worse still, with a married man, was heading for disaster. And these young girls in the marriage market were at the centre of the gossiping attention of older women seated round the room at Almack's. An indiscreet glance between a couple, a scrap of servant's rumour, a young lady's fainting in the heat of the hall, could set them all whispering among themselves. There were, among the lookers-on at Almack's, many a Lady Sneerwell and Mrs Candour, who would pull to pieces a young lady's reputation out of malicious pleasure, and there were also many indiscreet young Lady Teazles there, to give them sport for the evening.

Why was it that no suitable young man proposed to Caroline? Perhaps it was her air of indifference that just hinted at contempt which alarmed them. They admired her beauty, no doubt, but her talk frightened them off. She had a way of taking a man up on his words, and making him feel foolish. Older men rather liked it, but the younger ones were afraid. Few of them wanted clever wives. So they held back. And Caroline remembered with regret the many times when a sharp aside from her had raised a laugh among the seasoned bystanders but had reduced a stammering, red-faced boy to silence. Her tongue was her temptation. She could not resist the delights of wit.

Then her mother received another letter from George Norton. Incredibly, he announced that he still wished to marry Caroline, and reminded Mrs Sheridan of his offer three years before. It was now nearly the end of the Season and Caroline sensed failure again. For the first time she considered his offer seriously. He was, after all, quite good-looking in a heavy, thick-set sort of way, and he would probably be Lord Grantley one day. He was surely rich and certainly constant. He would make a usefully tame husband for a woman of strong personality like herself. He was the sort of dull man who might easily be managed. Besides, if Helen's experience was anything to go by, she might grow in affection, if not love, for Norton. So she made up her mind and told her mother that she would marry him. The wedding was on 30 June 1827, at St George's, Hanover Square, and exactly a year after Helen's. Caroline was nineteen and Norton twenty-six.

VII

BRAVING MR NORTON

GEORGE NORTON HATED MOST what he called 'cleverness'. He told her so soon after they were married. He disliked her to be 'clever'. Indeed, he did not like her to talk very much at all. Caroline had expected him to discuss everything with her: their plans to take a house in London; his prospects as Lord Grantley's heir; his career as a barrister; their current financial situation; and, more immediately, their honeymoon. But he would not say a word about these matters, and, when she kept on at him, he would flush up and glower at her. She told him that her father had always taken his wife into his confidence but Norton intimated that he was not that sort of husband and she had better know her place. And when she persisted, by pointing out that it was not unreasonable for her to want to know something of their circumstances and prospects, Norton would take another sip from his glass, and tell her not to argue. If she remarked that she was not arguing but merely asking him to be reasonable, he would repeat that she was being clever again, and he did not like it.

Of course, Caroline was clever. It was only to be expected. Her great-great-grandfather had conversed with Swift; her great-grandfather had been the friend of Dr Johnson; her grandfather had been the greatest comic dramatist of his time. The Sheridans were a clever lot, whereas the Nortons ... were not. Some such remarks passed between Caroline and her husband from the first days of their marriage. And she was so incensed at his refusal to consult her about family matters, that she began to goad him. He was slow-witted and did not always understand her ironies but he was conscious enough of the contempt in her tone to resent it. Whole evenings would be spent in desultory bickerings until a point was reached when Norton would put down his head and stare at her with that look of baffled fury she came to know so well. So the clock would tick, and he would go on tippling brandy and puffing at the hookah that she grew to detest, and there was nothing for her to do but pace the room. Often, the old woman who looked after Norton went to bed early, so it fell to Caroline to draw the curtains herself, but not before taking one last look outside. Even on a summer's evening, the Temple was a dreary place.

Norton had brought her to his chambers soon after the wedding, and Caroline was puzzled to find herself there. She did not know if Norton intended that they should live there permanently. She had not taken part in the marriage settlement herself but her mother had supposed that the Nortons would take a splendid town house, and, perhaps, be granted a lodge on Lord Grantley's estate at Wonersh. Of course, Caroline knew by now that she could get Norton to tell her his plans if she sat on his lap and called him her 'Geordy boy'. But though she was not averse to these demonstrations of affection, she considered them no substitute for rational conversation. She would not be the pretty pet that Norton seemed to want in a wife.

She spent much of her time now writing to her mother, and their daily exchange of notes was sometimes the only intelligent diversion she got. But Norton did not like her doing so, for he said she was only complaining to her relatives. One day, his reaction took Caroline by surprise:

> After our honeymoon, we lived for a short time in chambers Mr Norton had occupied as a bachelor, in Garden Court, Temple; and, on the first occasion of dispute, after some high and violent words, he flung the ink-stand, and most of the law-books, which might have served a better purpose, at the head of his bride. We had no servants there, but an old woman, who had taken care of these chambers for some years, and who offered me the acceptable consolation, that her master was not 'sober' – and would regret it 'by-and-by'.[1]

It was a terrible shock. She had never experienced physical violence before. The Sheridans were far too civilized even to suspect private brutality among their own acquaintance, and her brothers and sisters would have been horrified had they learned of this incident. She knew that Brinny would never have stood for such violence towards her. So she resolved to keep the matter a secret, and took refuge in the idea that Norton's brutal outburst had been provoked by drink. What she had to do was to help him lose his bachelor habit of brandy-drinking. When she had weaned him off spirits, he would become more amenable. She had no doubt that she could reform him.

Shortly afterwards, Norton informed her that they were to go on a honeymoon visit to the Menzies family, in Scotland, for his sister,

Grace, had married Sir Neil Menzies of Rannoch Lodge, Perthshire. So, in the late summer of 1827, they took the steam-ship up the east coast, for the first of many seasonal visits to the Menzies. Caroline was determined to be liked by her husband's relatives, and from the first, put on all her winning ways which had proved so effective in Westminster drawing rooms. It worked with Sir Neil, and she soon became a favourite with him. They would often take evening walks together along the shores of Loch Rannoch, chatting as they walked. It was the first time she had been in Scotland since she was a little girl, when her parents had been at the Cape. Now she found herself moved by the beauty of the Highland scenery: she admired: 'the blue lake and purple hills . . . the aromatic scent which loads the atmosphere in spots thickly planted with firs . . . the bloom of the heather, spread out for miles and miles, the rush of the tumbling, turbid streams, whose banks were blocks of stone, whose shining pools seemed fathomless'.[2] 'The lake', she told the delighted Sir Neil, 'lay like a sapphire dropped from the crown of some monarch mountain'. It seems that her brother-in-law was very taken by her poetic enthusiasm for his native heath. Indeed, when Caroline opened her eyes in ecstasy, there were few men who could resist her. And masculine admiration was becoming meat and drink to her.

Lady Menzies was less charmed with Caroline's whimsy. She was jealous of this young, beautiful woman who, as soon as she arrived, had captivated her husband and any male guest who turned up. But there was more than jealousy in her dislike of Caroline. Grace was a true Norton; she had no conversation, she was not interested in poetry and wit, she had few generous impulses herself and suspected them in others. Her passions were money and worldly influence. There can be little doubt that she resented her brother bringing this penniless, chattering flirt among them. When Caroline understood Grace's hostility, her response was to flirt even more outrageously with the innocent Sir Neil, and the upshot was that Grace Menzies soon became the first of her many enemies among the great tribe of plain women.

George Norton was infuriated by his wife's behaviour at the Lodge, not because of her friendship with Sir Neil, but because she exhibited a cool contempt for his opinions in front of his friends and relations. With her ready intelligence she could easily out-argue him, and frequently did so. What was worse, he fancied that these public contests made people laugh at him. Norton's attitude to life was nothing if not hierarchical. He expected his animals, tenants, servants and his wife to obey his orders and accept his views without question. The trouble with Caroline was that she just did not seem to understand that she was to be his creature in everything. He decided that he would have to teach her not to set herself up against him. Later, she wrote an account of the incident:

> After this happy beginning, I accompanied my husband to Scotland. We had been married about two months, when, one evening, after we had withdrawn to our apartments, we were discussing some opinion he had expressed; I said (very uncivilly), that 'I thought I had never heard so silly or ridiculous a conclusion'. This remark was punished by a sudden and violent kick; the blow reached my side; it caused great pain for many days, and being afraid to remain with him, I sat up the whole night in another apartment.[3]

There was no longer any doubt. Norton's earlier display of brutality was no drunken exception. She knew now that he might prove physically aggressive at any moment. So it proved, and she became a battered wife. During the next nine years, while they were living together, Norton not infrequently subjected her to a beating. This was not an entirely unknown story even in their class, but Caroline was one of the first women to write an account of such treatment.

She now lived in nightly dread of him. His forced caresses were even more repugnant to her than his brutality. Soon the two of them began to enact a routine which became familiar: there would be an argument; she would mock him; he would assault her; and then would come his weeping and pleadings for forgiveness. All he wanted at the end of their quarrels was to be taken back into her affections, so that he might become her 'Geordy boy' again. After such quarrels, there was little she could do but forgive him. But her spirit was bruised by such occasions. Her tongue became sharper, her mockery more acid. And she could not resist braving him when his black mood came upon him, and this brought more blows.

They often quarrelled about money, for Norton never seemed to have any. It was his meanness that first puzzled her. She could not understand why they were living in chambers rather than a town house. And she could not understand why her husband did not practise as a barrister if they needed more money. As usual, Norton was not very informative about his affairs, but he left her in no doubt that he objected to any profession as unbecoming to a gentleman. Besides, in

1826, he had been elected Tory MP for Guildford, and he protested that this took much of his time, although, of course, the post was unpaid.

Norton was of the opinion that, because he was a gentleman, life owed him a living. He even blamed Caroline for their lack of money. He said he had expected, when they married, that her grand Court friends would find him a sinecure appropriate to his rank. He frequently reminded her that she had brought him only £50 a year as a dowry and that, consequently, she was a charge on him. He said that his mother-in-law ought to persuade her connections among the Royal Family to grant him 'a small legal appointment'. In the end he got his way. Mrs Sheridan swallowed her pride and requested that he be given something. Shortly afterwards he was appointed a Commissioner for Bankruptcy.

Even this post did not satisfy his need for money, however, and Caroline sensed the lack of it in everything he did and said. It was puzzling. He had seemed a good match, being the heir to the childless Lord Grantley. When Mrs Sheridan had negotiated the marriage settlement, Norton had led her to believe that a sum of £30,000 had been set aside for Grantley's brothers and sisters and that, as the eldest brother, most would come to him. Now that Caroline had married him, it slowly became clear that Lord Grantley had little intention of settling anything on his siblings and that, consequently, George Norton had almost no income of his own. Mrs Sheridan was shocked. Norton had cheated her. The Sheridans never forgave him for his duplicity. In fairness to Norton, however, it must be acknowledged that both he and Caroline had married in the hope of financial gain, and both had been disappointed.

The post of Commissioner for Bankruptcy afforded them only a small income and a large London house was out of the question. When they returned from their honeymoon in the spring of 1828, they took a lease on the tiniest property commensurate with their social status. It was 2 Storey's Gate, Westminster, just round the corner from Mrs Sheridan's rooms in Great George Street. The little house was hard by St James's Park and Birdcage Walk. Norton had merely to saunter round the corner to call in at the House of Commons.

Despite the fact that her house was so small, Caroline sensed it had real possibilities and set to work to make the most of it. She had the tiny first-floor sitting room painted entirely white, and added to the effect with white muslin curtains. Then she chose an enormous blue couch for the room. It was so large that it took up almost all the available space. As there was little room for any other furniture, guests had little option but to sit next to her on the couch, and the sheer proximity to Caroline then obliged them to enter into the intimate conversations she loved. In this room she established her small salon. Sometimes her guests would find her surrounded by her books, drawings and pastels, or on the balcony overlooking St James's. That spring she had the balcony doors open all the time, for she liked to tend her geraniums while listening to the sounds of the horses and carriages, the talk and laughter, coming up from the park below.[4]

Then came an incident which made it no longer possible for Caroline to hide Norton's brutality from her relations. It started when he made unpleasant remarks about her sister, Helen. Caroline was never prepared to accept criticism of her family:

> Four or five months afterwards, when we were settled in London, we had returned home from a ball; I had then no personal dispute with Mr Norton, but he indulged in bitter and coarse remarks respecting a young relative of mine, who, though married, continued to dance, – a practice, Mr Norton said, no husband ought to permit. I defended the lady spoken of, and then stood silently looking out of the window at the quiet light of dawn, by way of contrast. Mr Norton desired I would 'cease my contemplations,' and retire to rest, as he had already done; and this mandate producing no result, he suddenly sprang from the bed, seized me by the nape of my neck, and dashed me down on the floor. The sound of my fall awakened my sister and brother-in-law, who slept in a room below, and they ran up to my door. Mr Norton locked it and stood over me, declaring no one should enter. I could not speak, – I only moaned. My brother-in-law burst the door open, and carried me downstairs. I had a swelling on my head for days afterwards, and the shock made my sister exceedingly ill.[5]

Her marriage was fast becoming a nightmare. Just recently, she had been a carefree young woman, full of the appetite for life. Now, a few months later, she found herself yoked to a man who had little money, large pretensions, and no scruples at all about assaulting her.

Many and many a day after that one which sealed her fate it seemed to be a dream that she was indeed a wife, and she would start from her uneasy sleep with a vague feeling of remorse and regret, or that still vaguer sensation which comes upon us after great sorrow – the consciousness that we have some cause for grief without the perfect memory of what it is. Then, as gradually the whole truth became present to her mind, she would close her eyes and strive to sleep again, to dream that she was free – sometimes the effort would succeed, wild, wandering visions would give her back all the bartered liberty of her youth; the days would return when she had still the power to choose, and to refuse; and she started and shrank to find how bitter was the waking which brought back the truth to her heart.[6]

But though Norton's brutality hurt her feelings as much as her body, in the early years of her marriage she still had plenty of the recuperative powers of youth. She took consolation in her social life. In the 1828 Season, few of those who met her in the brilliantly lit drawing rooms of London would have guessed from her demeanour that she was subject to fairly frequent acts of brutality. Perhaps only a certain feverishness in her gaiety might have betrayed to the observer that all was not well with her. But only her family really knew what was going on, and her mother was her special confidante:

> On another occasion, when I was writing to my mother, Mr Norton (who was sipping spirits and water, while he smoked his cigar) said he was sure 'from the expression of my Countenance' that I was 'complaining'. I answered that 'I seldom could do anything else'. Irritated by the reply, Mr Norton said I should not write at all, and tore the letter up. I took another sheet of paper, and recommenced. After watching and smoking for a few minutes, he rose, took one of the allumettes I had placed for his cigar, lit it, poured some of the spirits that stood by him over my writing book, and, in a moment, set the whole in a blaze. But Mr Norton vouchsafed no other notice of my alarm than that it would 'teach me to brave him'.[7]

The struggle between them had begun in earnest. Caroline did not know it then, but she would go on braving Mr Norton for years to come, and the record of it would enter the annals of English history and law. But even at this early time in her marriage, she understood Norton well enough to realize that he would expect her to do exactly as he told her, and herself well enough to realize that she could never endure such domestic tyranny. He may have been an English High Tory, who demanded obedience from all his subordinates, but she was from Radical stock and Irish at that. She would never give in.

VIII

TEMPTATIONS

CAROLINE'S FAMILY was a great support to her. In the spring of 1828, the first Season after her daughter's marriage, Mrs Sheridan again engaged the rooms in Great George Street and lived there with Georgiana, who was still unmarried, and her two younger sons, Frank and Charles. Richard Brinsley was away in the Indian Service, but Sheridan visitors to Great George Street and Storey's Gate included Helen and her husband, Captain Price Blackwood, back from their Italian honeymoon, and Caroline's Uncle Charles, her father's half-brother, now a bachelor of thirty-two.

In that Season, Mrs Sheridan's small rooms were often crowded with guests come to admire the beauty of the 'Three Graces'. One of them, Fanny Kemble, remembered, years after, the drawing room 'literally resplendent with the light of Sheridan beauty male and female'. Mrs Sheridan, she thought, was 'more beautiful than anybody but her daughters', and her sister, Lady Graham, was decidedly 'handsome'. As for Charles Sheridan junior (Caroline's brother), he was good-looking enough to be 'the younger brother of the Apollo Belvedere'. 'I never saw', wrote Fanny, 'such a bunch of beautiful creatures all growing on one stem.'[1] Caroline agreed. 'Yes,' she added, looking round with an amiable complacency, 'we *are* rather good-looking people.'

Even among the Sheridans, however, it was generally agreed that Georgiana was the outstanding beauty, but there is nothing to suggest her sisters were ever jealous of her. It was Caroline who was more frequently the centre of attention because she had more wit and vivacity than her sisters. As a married woman, it was now much safer for her to tease and flirt with her admirers, though even now she was sometimes misunderstood. For example, not long after her marriage, at a house party in Scotland, where she was staying without her husband, the eldest son of the Earl of Tankerville entered her bedroom at two o'clock in the morning, quite sure that she wanted to sleep with him. It took her half an hour to talk him into leaving. Clearly, her signals were sometimes misread.

She soon became a consummate drawing-room actress, however, who could calculate to a nicety the impression she was making on an admirer. Norton gave her no affection so she was forever trying to persuade other men to fall in love with her. Of course such passions were of the hopeless kind, but, as a Romantic, she rather liked that. In one evening she might act many parts. By turns, she might be roguish, worldly-wise, vulnerable and tragic. And, though she was not a conventional beauty, her looks were impressive. Fanny Kemble wrote of her that: 'She was splendidly-handsome, of an un-English character of beauty, her rather large and heavy features recalling the grandest Grecian and Italian Models, to the latter of whom her rich colouring and blue-black braids of hair gave her an additional resemblance.' People said that her beauty was 'classical'. Young Percy Fitzgerald was always remarking upon her 'antique stateliness and classical air' and the fine outline of her 'massive tresses'. Caroline thrilled to this sort of flattery. Singing was another way in which she could command admiration. She had a 'peculiar deep, rich contralto', and was often asked to sing in Society drawing rooms, either the Irish ballads of her friend, Tom Moore, or else songs of her own composition. Here again, she would switch her mood in an instant from a cheerful little folk-song to something poignant and soulful.

Flirtation was now her favourite amusement. Norton bored her and, anyway, it may have been a way of paying him out for his brutality. But his reaction to her behaviour can only be guessed. It is possible that he liked being seen as the husband of such a woman because, when it came down to it, she was his property and no other man could have her. What did it matter that she enacted little dramas with her male admirers, encouraging or neglecting them out of pure whim? Besides, her play-acting was often a sort of joking, such as when she claimed that Lord Chesterfield was so madly in love with her that he always carried her picture close to his heart. Norton knew perfectly well that Chesterfield had scarcely met her. Another of these situations which derived from her impish sense of humour came when she took delight in embarrassing young John Talbot in company, by calling across the room: 'Jack, Jack, for shame! We must not be too familiar in public!' It was not surprising that Talbot had been taken aback, for they had only met once before.

Caroline knew that her behaviour was now provoking whispers of disapproval but it seems that she did not care. Old Lord Holland complained behind her back that she was 'dangerous and indecent for so young a woman' but he could not disguise his admiration for her liveliness. Lady Cowper, Lord Melbourne's sister, wrote to tell a friend that: 'The Sheridans are much admired but are strange girls, swear and say all sorts of things to make men laugh. I am surprised so sensible a Woman as Mrs Sheridan should let them go on so. I suppose she cannot stop the old blood coming out.' But, in fairness she added that: 'They are remarkably good looking girls ... and certainly clever'.[2] Caroline had little to fear from such old Whigs of her grandfather's generation. During the Regency, Society had understood high spirits and the desire to shock people. But there was a clear limit to this tolerance which she should have thought about. Though Lord Holland was a guest in Mrs Sheridan's rooms, Lady Holland never came, because, as a divorced woman, she was not welcome in polite Society. Caroline was probably disappointed not to meet her, for Lady Holland had an enviable reputation for malicious wit. Besides, her exclusion seemed rather unfair.

Caroline liked best of all to talk to artistic men. One of her early friends was Edward Bulwer-Lytton, who was only five years older than herself but had already published two books, *Falkland*, and, in that very year, *Pelham*, which was the most fashionable novel of the season. In this book he introduced himself as the prince of dandy novelists. At many a soirée he could be heard announcing himself as an exquisite with 'fine sensibilities and artificial passions, wearing the orchid of a worldly life'. Caroline did not know what he meant by it, nor whether she was supposed to laugh or take him seriously. But his languorous attitudinizing and outrageous wit were very attractive to her, especially in comparison with her lumpish Norton, who sat scowling in the corner. Luckily for her, perhaps, Bulwer-Lytton was already married, and lived in nearby Hertford Street with his beautiful young wife. Yet she was curiously drawn to him, especially when he hinted that he too was not happy in his own marriage.

Edward Trelawny was very different. He was a splendid man, thirty-six years old, six foot in height, with 'raven black hair which curl[ed] thickly and shortly like a Moor's', black moustachios, and 'a smile which express[ed] good nature, and kind-heartedness'.[3] Trelawny had lived an adventurous life in the Navy but his chief claim to fame was his friendship with the great Romantic poets. Caroline found herself talking to the actual man who, just six years previously, had, with the help of Byron and Leigh Hunt, cremated the body of Shelley on the beach at Spezia. Trelawny spoke solemnly of the occasion: of the corpses too disfigured by water to be recognizable; of their identifying Shelley by a copy of Keats's poems in the jacket pocket; of the Italian quarantine laws against the plague; of the burying in quicklime; of the bonfire on the beach with a few fishermen present; of Lord Byron celebrating Pagan rites; and of how Shelley's heart would not burn, and was saved as a gift for his wife. Then he told her of the war of Greek independence, and how he had arrived at Missolonghi just too late to find Byron alive. Caroline was moved. She felt a deep affinity with these great poets, who had dared to scandalize the world. If only *she* had a cause to die for!

But her favourite new friend was a girl just a year younger than herself. It was soon after her marriage that she had met Fanny Kemble, a young actress whose history was curiously linked with her own. The Kembles, like the Sheridans, were a great theatrical family, indeed, John Phillip Kemble had managed Drury Lane for Richard Brinsley Sheridan; and Caroline's great-grandfather, Thomas Sheridan, had rediscovered Fanny's aunt, the actress Sarah Siddons. Fanny herself had now become famous overnight because her father, Charles Kemble, the part-owner of Covent Garden, had been in such a desperate financial plight that, to save money, he had persuaded her to play Juliet, even though she was completely untrained as an actress. But Fanny was such a success that the fortunes of the Kembles were saved. Her Covent Garden triumph was the talk of fashionable London in the 1829–30 Season, and she was invited as a guest to many a fashionable drawing room, though some people objected to being introduced to an actress, for both social and moral reasons. Caroline had no such objections. It was a delight to her to discover how much they had in common. She told Fanny stories of the old Drury Lane Theatre, of the dramatic triumphs of Richard Brinsley Sheridan, and his friendship with the Prince Regent. In return, Fanny told her of her own girlhood and her meeting with the Prince. As a tiny child, she had been invited to dance in Mrs Fitzherbert's drawing room, and when the Prince of Wales had seen her, he insisted in placing a huge glass bell right over her, so that to the assembled company she had seemed like a little fairy figure.[4] Caroline probably regarded Fanny with envy, for she herself was a natural actress. All her life she sought to display to the public the depth of her own emotions. Even some of her worst quarrels with her husband arose from her boredom with the tedium of their life together, and a need to figure in melodramatic scenes, at whatever cost to herself.

Fanny understood Caroline very well. She would watch her while she gossiped and giggled in London drawing rooms with Bulwer-Lytton, or Trelawny or Harrison Ainsworth, or aspiring politicians, or even members of the aristocracy such as the deaf young Duke of Devonshire, known as 'Hart'. Fanny knew that there were malicious stories circulating about Caroline. It was said that Bulwer-Lytton was her lover, and there were similar rumours about Trelawny and Ainsworth. What made this a matter of concern to her friends, was that Caroline did not seem to care what the sour matrons and sniggering dandies said about her. She would not be cautioned. Her heroes, such as Shelley and Lord Byron, had courted scandal, and she herself seemed delighted to display her disdain for social convention. If her behaviour made her husband jealous, so much the better. Yet Fanny discerned a pathos in Caroline's behaviour, and tried diplomatically to warn her friend to be more discreet. Fanny wrote in her diary that Caroline was:

a splendid creature, nobly endowed in every way, too nobly to become through mere frivolity and foolish vanity the mark of the malice of such things as she is surrounded by, and who will all eagerly embrace the opportunity of slandering one so immeasurably their superior in every respect . . . I feel deeply interested in her . . . with that feeling of admiring solicitude with which one must regard a person so gifted, so tempted, and in such a position as hers.[5]

IX

POETIC AGONY

CAROLINE SOON FOUND A NEW DISTRACTION. Social life was all very well but it did not fulfil her desire for the kind of fame her grandfather had enjoyed. Besides, it was often difficult for her to maintain her drawing-room poise just after a furious row with Norton. None of her friends knew of her treatment at his hands, and even her own family had no idea of the regularity of his assaults. So when she entered yet another fashionable drawing room, and the teasing and flirting began, she was often sorely tempted to blurt out her story to one or other of her sympathetic admirers, if only for the dramatic effect she might create. She never did. She contented herself by displaying a sweetly sorrowful countenance to the more receptive young men, and by deflecting their tender enquiries with hints that she might have revealed a great grief had she chosen to do so. Eventually, however, when even this pastime palled, she hit upon a plan. There was a way in which she might both seek celebrity and tell the story of her sufferings. She would put them into a poem.

When she was seventeen, and still at Wonersh School, she had started a poem entitled 'The Sorrows of Rosalie'. Now, she took it out, dusted it off, and looked at it again. Of course she found it painfully childish, and reflected that a mere schoolgirl could know nothing of sorrow. But she could see how, from the depths of her married grief, she could rewrite it, and shape it to her present purpose.

Her rewritten version of the poem told the story of Rosalie, a simple country girl who meets rich, young Arthur when he tries to buy the cottage she shares with her father. The old man warns his daughter of the temptations of her friendship with Arthur, and reminds her to read her Bible well, but, one night, she runs off with her lover, and the last her father hears of her is the sound of the wicket gate closing behind them. Rosalie and Arthur then live together for a year in a remote cottage, but she cannot persuade him to marry her until after her baby is born. But long before that happens, he deserts her, on the pretext that he does not believe himself to be the father. Rosalie then follows him to the city, and waits at his gate with the baby in her arms. When he comes out with his new sweetheart, he rejects her attempted embrace, and tosses a bag of gold on the ground as payment for her past services. Still carrying her baby, Rosalie trudges back to her father's cottage, only to find that he has died and strangers have moved in. She swoons in the snow, but the new people take her in and nurse her. When she is better, she resolves perversely to go begging through the world. She now becomes utterly destitute, and, because her child is close to dying, steals food to feed him. She is caught but pardoned, because the court recognizes that she stole only to relieve the hunger of her son. Nevertheless, he soon dies of starvation.

'The Sorrows of Rosalie' is largely an exercise in attitudinizing and sentimental rhetoric but it afforded Caroline an opportunity to dramatize many elements in her own situation. Its basic theme is that of a young woman trusting herself to a man, and being repaid with brutality and false-heartedness, just like herself. By depicting the hopeless agony of this helpless girl, she felt she could reveal her own depth of feeling and greatness of soul:

> Wild was my laugh – Oh heartless & unkind!
> Thou suffer! Mayst thou never feel like me!
> Yea, give thy vows of passion to the wind;
> Heaven heard them, though to man unknown they be;
> Heaven sees me shunned by all, betrayed by thee;
> Lured from the happy home where once I smiled;

In publishing 'Rosalie', Caroline was well aware that it would make her even more fascinating to a certain sort of man. In public she might play the part of the glittering socialite, the flouter of convention and bold, facetious conversationalist; but now her admirers would also realize that there was a more profound side to her nature; she was a woman of deep feeling, a lady of sorrows. As such she would become an enigma to them, and even more interesting.

The book came out in 1829, under the full title of *The Sorrows of Rosalie, A Tale with Other Poems.*[1] She included a dedication to Lord Holland, who had always been very kind to her, and whose patronage would help to sell the book, and also an epigraph from Lord Byron, in order to proclaim her Romantic affiliations. To her delight, sales went very well, though the publication and success of her poem probably had more to do with Caroline's aristocratic connections than the intrinsic merit of her verse.

The shorter poems were especially popular, and her friends were never tired of quoting their lines:

> When the sun is shining brightly on a blithesome summer day,
> While others dance and sing, I think of him who's far away;
> Amid the gay I wander on, as sad as sad can be –
> Oh while I think of you, love, do you think of me?[2]

And though she was only twenty-one, Caroline now liked to be thought of as a woman wise in matters of love. She was prolific with advice:

> Oh! love – love well, but only once! for never shall the dream
> Of youthful hope return again on life's dark rolling stream;
> No love can match the early one which young affection
>   nursed –
> Oh, no – the one you loved the best, is she you loved the first.[3]

Caroline never revealed the name of her own first love, and her friends were left to guess whether or not he had been Norton. Meanwhile, she had discovered in herself a richly sentimental vein of feeling, and was pleased to find that its expression was now fashionable among the young Society women who comprised the majority of poetry readers. She realized that she could write such verse with great facility, completely forgetting her grandfather's warning to writers such as herself:

> You write with ease, to show your breeding,
> But easy writing's curst hard reading.[4]

George Norton approved of Caroline's writing career – or rather he did not object to it – because it brought them a useful income. From the proceeds of *Rosalie*, Caroline was able to buy herself a pianola, and when, in the winter of 1828, she discovered that she was going to have a baby, her husband generously informed her that she might pay the expenses of her first confinement from her royalties on the book. When the new social Season came in the following spring, she found that she could now enjoy herself playing the dual roles of authoress and dignified matron. Performance now succeeded flirtation as her party piece. At receptions she was increasingly asked to recite, or sing her own songs, just like Tom Moore.

She also loved to gossip. Theatre talk that Season often turned upon Fanny Kemble's recent triumph as Juliet at Covent Garden. Political chat among the Whigs frequently came round to William Lamb, who they said had just come back from Ireland. In the previous year his wife, Caroline, had died, and he had resigned from the Government. Despite this, he had recently succeeded his father and become the 2nd Lord Melbourne, and his political prospects were transformed. Unfortunately, his name was often dogged by a scandal concerning one woman or another. His morals seemed more suited to the age of his old friend, the Prince Regent, rather than to the respectable politics the new age demanded, and some people thought that the public might no longer be prepared to put up with such behaviour in their leaders. Caroline learned that, while Melbourne had been in Ireland recently, he had been involved in an affair with a Lady Branden which had ended with an unsuccessful action against him for 'criminal conversation', the lawyers' name for adultery. Stories about Melbourne's love-life did not shock her, for she was not prudish like many of the new generation and, indeed, she was probably rather intrigued by what she knew of his amorous reputation. But it is likely that she did not give such tales much credit. After all, in 1829 Melbourne was fifty, and it was almost inconceivable to her that a man as old as that could be involved in a love affair. She probably agreed with her friends that the whole business was a Tory plot to discredit him.

With so many Members of Parliament crowding the small Sheridan rooms that year, gossip inevitably turned to the chances of the Whigs getting back into government. George IV's health was failing, and a new king might mean a new administration. Optimism was also growing among Caroline's Whig friends because the Tories were splitting on the matter of Catholic emancipation. High Tories, such as the Nortons, were in anguish because their erstwhile hero, the Duke of Wellington, was now attempting to bring in an Act to recognize Catholics and Dissenters. One of Caroline's closest confidants was the young Benjamin Disraeli, the author of *Vivian Grey*, a book notorious for its thinly disguised portraits of famous Society figures. Disraeli told her seriously that he had high political ambitions, though it was difficult for her to believe that he would even get into Parliament. He was so un-English, and he presented an extraordinary apparition in Society drawing rooms. When once he came to dine with her, his black ringlets fell to his shoulders, and he was dressed in a black satin-lined velvet jacket, with a scarlet waistcoat, purple trousers with a golden seam and long lace ruffles. He was referred to by some anti-Semites as 'the Jew d'esprit'. Disraeli was particularly contemptuous of George Norton, but Caroline's husband was too obtuse to understand. Once, Norton bored a dinner-table by a long speech in which he praised his own taste in selecting the wine in their glasses. Disraeli agreed out of politeness, but Norton persisted. 'I have got wines twenty times as good in my cellar', he blustered. 'No doubt, no doubt', Disraeli rejoined, while exchanging glances with his fellow guests, 'but, my dear fellow, this is quite good enough for such canaille as you have got today'.[5] Characteristically Norton failed to appreciate the irony.

It was at about this time that Caroline became more aware of the unpleasant fact that she was making enemies. Some women – especially the plain ones – were jealous of her, and even a few men seemed affronted by her intimate flirtatious attempts to charm them. She knew that her quick tongue often gave offence, and that her behaviour sometimes gave rise to gossip. Her sisters frequently warned her that she was indiscreet. For example, Norton sometimes permitted Disraeli to escort her to a theatre or a ball, for he hated such amusements himself, but liked to have his wife shown off. As might be expected, it was soon whispered that Disraeli was her lover. Another alleged liaison was with Prince Leopold of Saxe-Coburg, a widower eighteen years older than herself, and the uncle of the young Princess Victoria. It was true, however, that they were friends, and even when he was elected in 1831 to the throne of Belgium, he remained a good one.

Theodore Hook, the Tory editor of *The John Bull Review*, particularly disliked Caroline, and, on one occasion, succeeded in humiliating her in public. It was at a dinner party given by Sir John McDonald in the early days of her marriage, when Hook was present. He had a 'loud voice and blazing red face and staring black eyes' and manners which Fanny Kemble considered to be less suitable for mixed company in the drawing room than for the after-dinner, all-male drinkers at the table. Hook was famous for his improvised songs at the piano; he could make up a song about anything or anybody at a moment's notice. After dinner at Sir John's, he was persuaded to perform and, when he was finished, made to get up from the piano. Everybody groaned at this, because his comic songs were popular and people wanted another. At this point, Caroline foolishly went and sat herself so close to him that he could not rise, and whispered loudly in her best and most insinuating tones: 'I am going to sit down here, and you shall not come away, for I will keep you in like an iron crow

[bar]'.[6] The company laughed uneasily, and Hook momentarily reddened even more, but then he recovered and sang an extempore song, every verse of which ridiculed Caroline, and ended with a mock tribute to her he termed his 'charming iron crow'. It was her turn to be embarrassed, but, fortunately, she now had enough social poise to remain smiling throughout his performance, though others present had to work hard to hide their discomfort. But the honours had all gone to Hook. Fanny Kemble later wrote that, on the following day, when she was out for a walk with Caroline, she had dared to offer the opinion that, though Hook's sentiments were often misplaced, he was a witty man. Caroline's response was violent. 'Witty!' she had burst out, with her lip and nostril quivering – 'witty! One may well be witty when one fears neither God nor devil.'

More serious was the enmity of such women as Lady Granville, who strongly disliked the flirtation between Caroline and her brother, 'dearest Hart', the Duke of Devonshire. There was ample opportunity for intrigue among the aristocratic country house parties of the day, and Lady Granville dreaded a proposed visit of the Nortons to Chatsworth House. She wrote to her sister, Lady Morpeth: 'I am sorry we are to have an original among us, somebody impossible to like and ungracious to dislike. I am happy to think that Craddock and Walewski are to be with us; a great relief to the sober part of the community . . .'[7] Lady Granville clearly thought that Caroline was a menace, an irresponsible coquette concerned only to fascinate as many men as she could. But Caroline was not as dangerous as many women thought. At that time, she was merely playing with passion.

By the summer of 1829, her life was much happier. She was learning to manage George by a combination of wheedling and flattery. She had become an author, and even her husband approved the fact that she was earning an appreciable part of their income. He now tolerated her Whig friends about the house, for he was only too aware that it was through such friendships of his wife's that his own best hopes of advancement lay. Furthermore, she could look forward to the imminent return from India of her brother Brinsley. Most of all, her happiness was completed by the birth of her first son, Fletcher Spencer Norton, whom she promptly nicknamed 'Penny'. George seemed softened towards her by this event, but, though it drew them together for a time, it also provided grounds for future animosity. Her little boy was pretty with dark eyes and red cheeks, so that the villagers of Long Ditton near Hampton Court called him 'Mossrose'. But when he was six months old, at Christmas 1829, Norton insisted that they should take an open gig when they went down to visit Mrs Sheridan at Hampton Court for the holidays. As a result, the baby contracted such a severe inflammation of the lungs that his doctors thought he would die. In the end, Fletcher recovered, but was sickly for the rest of his life. Caroline never forgave Norton for treating the boy like this, and later told Lord Melbourne that she regarded the incident as positive proof of the insensitive stupidity that characterized all the Nortons.[8]

Despite her crowded and brilliant social life, and her new obligations as a mother, Caroline now began to think of herself as a writer, and filled the late hours with intensive work. This enabled her both to avoid her husband's attentions and also to point out to him what exertions she was making to improve their joint income. Her head was full of writing projects, which she proudly advertised to her family, as Georgiana indicated in a letter she sent to their brother, Brinsley, in India:

> Sunday, January 24 1830
> finished February 8.

> Dearest Brin,
>   I am long in giving the promised account of our doings at Claremont [Prince Leopold's residence near Hampton Court], but have not really had time, owing to the illness of Caroline's beautiful baby – an account of which you will have anon. He is well now ... Caroline has finished her new poem, called 'The Undying One'. She is going to write another poem called 'The Lady of Ringstatten', and she has written two volumes of a novel called 'Love in the World and Love out of the World', which I want her to finish, as prose sells better and easier than poetry. She means to ask £500, and thinks six weeks more hard writing will finish it, and then she intends to write a tragedy.[9]

Caroline never completed the novel, but *The Undying One and Other Poems* appeared at the end of 1829.[10] The title-poem recounts the old story of the Wandering Jew, Isbal, who is condemned from the Cross to live a life without end. The four 'Cantos' (she took the word from Lord Byron) tell in turn of his love affairs with Linda, Edith, Xarifa and Miriam. Unfortunately for Isbal, his sweethearts grow older, whereas he never does, so that his interest in young women begins to be diminished by images of the old women they will become. For their part, the women cannot help noticing his perennial youth. In Isbal's last and most passionate affair, he murders his beloved Miriam, so that he should never see her grow old, and then attempts to join her in death by drowning himself in the sea. As he might have anticipated, the waves keep flinging him back up the shore.

Caroline chose the subject for all sorts of reasons, but especially because it allowed her to explore her favourite theme of suffering. She could put into Isbal's lamentations the words she dare not utter about her own misfortune. And in depicting Isbal's sweethearts, she could shape images of the self she would like to be:

> There was a grace
> Peculiar to herself, ev'n from the first:
> Shadows and thoughtfulness you seemed to trace
> Upon that brow, and then a sudden burst
> Of sunniness and laughter sparkled out,
> And spread their rays of joyfulness about.
> Like the wild music of her native land,
> Which wakes to joy beneath the minstrel's hand.[11]

Caroline had always loved the mystery and romance of the Orient, since the days when she had put on theatricals with her brothers and sisters, and dressed up in a 'turband' for their Turkish tragedies. *The Undying One* enabled her to dress up Isbal, and put him into any number of dramatic situations and exotic settings.

These poems afford an insight into the way she regarded her marriage at that time. Though Norton was sometimes brutal, he was generally sluggish and slow to respond. Caroline liked to imagine scenes so melodramatic that even husbands like Norton had to react. In one such scene, a husband is confronted with his adulterous wife:

> I saw a husband, and a guilty wife,
> Who once made all the sunshine of his life,
> Kneeling upon the threshold of her home,
> Where heavily her weary feet had come:
> A faded form, a humble brow, are hers –
> The livery which the sinful sorrow wears;
> While with deep agony she lifts her eyes,
> And prays him to forgive her, ere she dies![12]

Whether or not such a passage was prompted by adulterous temptations can only be guessed. It is clear, however, that Caroline was

sometimes prepared to goad Norton into a fury, just to get some sort
of response from him:

> She would have given all the store she had,
> That he would be but angry for an hour,
> That she might come and soothe his wounded spirit,
> And lay her weeping head upon his bosom,
> And say how freely she forgave his wrongs:[13]

The Undying One was a success, and the shorter lyrics were even more
popular than the title-poem. Caroline was especially proud of the piece
deliciously entitled, 'My Heart is like a Withered Nut'. But the poem
in the book that became most famous was 'The Arab's Farewell to
His Horse', later retitled 'The Arab's Farewell to His Steed'.[14] It was
later set to music and became a favourite drawing-room ballad in
thousands of Victorian parlours. Caroline did not invent the Arabian
tale. William Beckford had published *Vathek* in 1787, and in her own
time, such authors as Thomas Hope, James Justinian Morier and,
of course, Lord Byron, had produced Oriental romances. But with
'The Arab's Farewell to His Steed', she helped to popularize the notion
of the dashing Bedouin a century before Valentino became world
famous.

The poem tells the story of an Arab so poor that he is forced to sell
his magnificent mare to a stranger:

> My beautiful! my beautiful! that standest meekly by
> With thy proudly arched and glossy neck, and dark and fiery
>   eye;
> Fret not to roam the desert now, with all thy winged speed –
> I may not mount on thee again – thou'rt sold, my Arab steed!
> Fret not with that impatient hoof – snuff not the breezy wind –
> The further that thou fliest now, so far am I behind;
> The stranger hath thy bridle rein – thy master has his gold –
> Fleet limbed and beautiful! farewell! thou'rt sold, my steed –
>   thou'rt sold . . .[15]

The poem is unintentionally autobiographical. In the first place, the
descriptions of the mare remind the reader very much of Caroline
herself. The animal is 'fleet-limbed and beautiful', has a 'silky mane',
a 'proud dark eye' and, most characteristically, a 'rich blood' which
'swells in . . . indignant pain'. Secondly, the Arab may be compared

to Norton in that he is poor and needs the gold of strangers. It was at about the time when this poem was written that whispers started to go round Westminster that Norton was either indifferent to his wife's friendships with other men, or else positively encouraged them for money. Caroline may well have heard the rumours and been shocked by them. Was it possible that Norton hoped to gain from her friendships with the Duke of Devonshire, Prince Leopold and the others? Was he willing to sell her? The evidence from the poem suggests that she could not believe any man – not even Norton – would be so blind to her charms as to trade with them. So, after a moment's temptation, the Arab throws back the gold and gallops off into the desert on his mare:

> Who said, that I had given thee up? Who said that thou wert
>   sold?
> 'Tis false! 'tis false, my Arab steed! I fling them back their
>   gold!
> Thus-thus, I leap upon thy back, and scour the distant plains!
> Away! who overtakes us now shall claim thee for his pains.

Caroline's poems present a dream world of humble cots, laughing children, murmuring brooks, sweet girlhoods, blazes of splendour, kings' courts, time's wings, fancy's dreams, sweet recollections, welcome graves and, above all, romantic agony. Almost invariably, her heroines undergo extremes of suffering and act as mouthpieces for her own self-pity. But such sentiments suited the taste of the time. By 1830, Caroline was quite well known not only as a fashionable beauty but also as a poet.

The summer of 1830 was an eventful one both for the Sheridans and for the nation. Brinsley returned from India, and Georgiana, the most beautiful sister of them all, was married in June to Lord Seymour, heir to the Duke of Somerset. It was a brilliant match, and completed Mrs Sheridan's triumph; she had married all her girls into the aristocracy despite the fact that the Sheridans had barely a penny between them. The only dowry the girls took with them was beauty and brains and, in two of the matches, such talents had gained their rightful reward.

Then, on 26 June, George IV died, and his going necessitated a General Election. And it was now that the political differences between Caroline and her husband began to add to the tension between them. For reform was in the air, and, for the first time since the days of Pitt, a Whig administration was a real possibility. The small house in Storey's Gate was filled with election committees of Caroline's Whig friends, while her husband, George, was down in Guildford trying to keep his Tory seat. In the event, the summer election brought in a Whig government under Lord Grey, with Lord Melbourne as Home Secretary. Caroline's new brother-in-law, Lord Seymour, won Devonshire for the Whigs, but George lost his seat at Guildford. On 5 August, after the election, Caroline wrote to tell Georgiana that Norton had just gone down to Guildford to 'do the honours at a fête-champêtre given in his name and Grantley's'. Her husband had told her that 'although thrown out, he was the most popular candidate' and that people had voted against him with tears in their eyes. It was, she told her sister, his usual mixture of hope, credulity and vanity.

Norton would probably have liked to spend the autumn abusing Caroline's Whig friends to her, but he could not afford to do so, for it was to these Whigs that he now had to look for a job. He even had to keep his wife sweet so that she should make every effort in lobbying for him. But Lord and Lady Grantley and the rest of the Nortons adopted no such attitude. They did not have to disguise it; they hated Caroline thoroughly.

SHERIDAN'S FRIEND

FOLLOWING THE GENERAL ELECTION OF 1830, Caroline's immediate concern was to find a job for George. The Whigs had come in with a policy of cutting back on government expenditure, and it was known that Lord Brougham, the new Lord Chancellor, intended to sweep away hundreds of sinecures, including Norton's little post of Commissioner for Bankruptcy. Accordingly, Caroline started to write around to her grandfather's old friends who were now influential in government, and even to lobby them at dinner parties. Her husband had still not explained their exact financial situation to her but she knew enough to realize that, as he would not work, they must find an alternative source of income. Loyally, she penned begging letters to Lord Brougham; to the Lord President of the Council, Lord Lansdowne; and to the new Home Secretary, Lord Melbourne. Paradoxically, the best argument she could offer for the employment of Norton the Tory was that she was the granddaughter of Sheridan the Whig.

One afternoon in early spring, 1831, she heard a knock at the front door below, and a drawling, masculine voice in the hallway. The maid came up and announced that Lord Melbourne had called. There then entered a tall, clean-shaven man, with the nonchalant, affected manner fashionable in the libertine heyday of her own grandfather. Her visitor was respectful, utterly charming, and profuse with apologies. He was afraid that the time of his visit was inauspicious; he had not forewarned her of his coming; yet he could not help himself, so touched he had been by the mere name of his old friend, Sheridan, in a letter from his granddaughter. Caroline heard hardly a word in the sheer pleasure of his presence. While talking, he held her hand rather longer than necessary, and all the while, his bright, intelligent eyes took in the room. He seemed to view the blue and white furnishings, the pictures, and, above all, her person, with every apparent pleasure. He was invited to sit, and did so with a shower of self-deprecatory irony about his great age, his physical condition and inability to make talk with young ladies. In a moment she found that she was teasing him and, even more surprisingly, he seemed to like it. He was fifty-one at the time and she was twenty-two. The meeting was to transform her life.

Of course she knew something of his history. Lord Melbourne, in 1831, was a man come into his own. Fitted for highest office both by birth and intellect, he had endured the long years of Tory rule, with only a brief taste of power as Chief Secretary for Ireland in Canning's coalition administration. It was not until Lord Grey had formed his Whig Government the previous November, that he had entered into high office at last. So he had only been Home Secretary for a few months when he walked across the park to call on Caroline that spring day.

There then began a conversation which extended over many years. They had much to talk about. For Caroline, Melbourne was a voice from her grandfather's generation, a man of the Regency, civilized, cultivated and frequently profane. His reminiscences included the great literary figures of the Romantic generation. He talked of his marriage to Caroline Ponsonby in 1805, and of his years of misery when, as Caroline Lamb, she had conducted her long and very public love affair with Lord Byron. Throughout the whole painful business he (Melbourne) had remained loyal to his wife. Their only child, Augustus, had been born mentally enfeebled in 1807, and was now the only member of his family living with him. In her later years, Caroline Lamb had been ostracized by the *beau monde*. She had tried to make a society for herself among the artists and poets but had died, in 1828, neglected by all save her husband, who had ceased to live with her but continued to visit her. He had been especially grieved that he was away in Ireland at the moment of her death.

Caroline also learned more of Melbourne's recent involvement with Lady Branden, though perhaps not all of it from his own lips. While still in Ireland, he had formed a close friendship with this beautiful young wife of an Irish peer in holy orders. When Melbourne had resigned as Irish Secretary, Lady Branden followed him back to London where, as in Dublin, he visited her on most evenings. It was said that her husband had actually tried to blackmail him by threatening to make trouble unless he, Branden, was made a bishop. It was when Lady Branden had refused to co-operate in this enterprise that her husband had brought the action against Melbourne for criminal conversation. It had failed because the evidence provided by witnesses proved little more than that Melbourne had sent her some grapes and pineapples. The additional information that a short man had been seen leaving Lady Branden's house in the early hours, was less than convincing to the jury because Melbourne was very tall. Nevertheless, Caroline may have heard the rumour that Lady Branden was still receiving an allowance from him.[1]

What she was soon to learn of the private life of this famous man touched her profoundly with its pathos. His days in London were spent either in business at the Lords, or at his house in South Street. He had no company at home save his servants and Augustus, now a mentally defective young man of twenty-three. Much of his time was spent with Augustus at Brocket, his country house. He read prodigiously, as much for company as for anything else, and his mind, as a result, was so well stocked that an acquaintance described him as being 'saturated with information'. His reading was desultory but very wide in scope. He read history, both ancient and modern, and also the Elizabethan dramatists from whom he could quote long passages. Despite his lifelong scepticism, his especial interest was theology, especially the Christian fathers, and he was an avid collector of dusty folios of religious doctrine.

Melbourne was frank about his physical indolence. He told her he often read in bed until the early hours and rose late. Even after he became a Cabinet Minister, his morning callers were shown into his dressing room where he entertained them while being shaved. His manner to social equals was friendly but informal. He swore a good deal, even in the society of ladies, as was the custom in the Regency days of his youth. When he was a visitor in an elegant drawing room, he would loll about and sometimes put his feet up on the furniture. Caroline noticed that even when he was in the middle of a conversation with his guests, Melbourne would often lose interest and seem to be listening for something else. It was for sounds of Augustus. The young man had to be left on his own at times, and Melbourne was always anxious about him. His special horror was that Augustus might be neglected or ill-treated by servants when he himself was away from home.

This was the man who first presented himself in Caroline's little sitting room at Storey's Gate. At the end of their first meeting Melbourne asked to be allowed to come again, if Mr Norton should consent. Of course Mr Norton consented; indeed, he pronounced himself honoured at Lord Melbourne's interest. So the Melbourne who had been a living legend to Caroline, now became an intimate friend. For the next five years, when they were both in London, he called on her three times a week. He always visited her in the afternoons when he knew her husband would be out. They would spend a couple of hours alone together, and he would leave the house before Norton came home.

Melbourne liked to chat. He would sit next to Caroline on her great blue couch telling stories of Caroline Lamb, Lord Byron and Richard Brinsley Sheridan. Of course there were great divisions between Caroline and himself, of age, income, and social status but these seemed not to matter when they were together. And though Caroline was not surprised to find him an amusing companion she was somewhat taken aback to discover that, for all his years, Melbourne could be a very attractive man indeed. She also sensed that he admired her lustrous hair, her swan-like neck, and the colour coming and going in her cheeks. But it was not only her beauty that delighted him; he also valued her intelligence, wit and tenderness, and these she displayed ruthlessly. She soon realized that Melbourne was both flattered and excited by her obvious interest in him. It was an added advantage that she was called 'Caroline', for that name could still sing to him of an old, lost love. It is likely that she set out to captivate him from the start, for she could rarely resist the temptation to entice any man.

George Norton had taken his 1830 election defeat badly. In the summer of that year he had insisted on Caroline's going with him down to Lord Grantley's place at Wonersh, after which he announced that he was going to retire permanently to the country. He told Caroline that Lord Grantley was willing to make over to them a little cottage on his estate, and he himself had decided to become a country squire. When she demanded to know what on earth she was to do with her time in such a place, he said that she could keep a dairy if she pleased. Caroline was horrified. She detested the Grantleys just as heartily as they did her. The mere thought of country life was death to her and the ruin of all her dreams of social advancement and literary fame. Besides, she knew that if she now went to live at Wonersh she would never see Lord Melbourne again. Outwardly, the move to the country became a joke between herself and her friends but privately she was truly alarmed that Norton was really in earnest about the matter. So she kept on and on, pointing out to him that such a retirement would be the end of all his hopes of advancement as well as her own, until even Norton could see that there was something in her argument. He announced that he would think about the matter while they took their annual holiday in Scotland. So Caroline was obliged to endure another autumn with the Menzies in Perthshire while George thought about living at Wonersh, and he even procrastinated over the New

Year when she spent a few days in Brighton. But in the following spring Melbourne paid Caroline his first visit, and by this time, the first prizes of the new Whig administration were coming through. Caroline's brother, Frank, had already been appointed a Clerk to the Admiralty, and her brother-in-law, Price Blackwood, had been made captain of a frigate. It seemed that there might be something to come for Norton. At once he stopped talking of the delights of a cottage in Wonersh. He had made up his mind. They were to remain in London.

Now began what was to be the happiest year of her life with Norton, for she discovered that there could be compensations even within an unhappy marriage. For example, on 26 April, she was presented at the court of William IV where her charm caused a minor sensation. The new King and his wife greeted her with real affection, for she had been a favourite of theirs since they first knew her as a little girl running round the apartments of Hampton Court. In gratitude, she had written an inscription to the Queen, then the Duchess of Clarence, on the first page of *The Undying One*.

Of course people soon noticed her new friendship which initially brought her considerable prestige. Melbourne occasionally attended her evening receptions and as a result, Caroline swiftly became one of the most influential hostesses in London Society. Her drawing room was a tiny salon frequently crowded with guests wishing to curry favour with the new Home Secretary. Sometimes, however, she found the company of so many mature politicians rather irksome, and could not prevent herself from scandalizing them. At one official engagement to which Melbourne had invited her, she outraged the senior members of the Diplomatic Corps by kicking Melbourne's hat clean over his head.[2] It seems that Melbourne himself was merely amused by the incident, and Caroline found that she could get away with such behaviour simply because she was his friend.

Meanwhile, she was pursuing her literary career with zest. On Tuesday, 31 May her play, *The Gypsy Father*, was presented at Covent Garden. Caroline had great hopes that this piece would establish her as the dramatic successor to her grandfather, but it was poorly received. Fanny Kemble's professional verdict was that the play was full of 'atrocious situations' but she acknowledged that it tugged the heartstrings by making 'one cry horribly'.[3] Caroline was no more successful when she later tried a dramatization of William Beckford's *Vathek*. But though her plays were failures, her poetry was highly regarded in the 1830s. She was twice included in a series of portraits of female poets presented in *Fraser's Magazine* entitled 'Regina's Maids of Honour'. That paper sent round the Irish artist, Daniel Maclise, to sketch her. One of his drawings depicted Caroline at her breakfast-table filling a teapot from an urn, while a portrait of her grandfather, Sheridan, gazes down in apparent approval.

In the summer came the reward for all Caroline's hard lobbying. Lord Melbourne had done his best, and her husband, George, was appointed Recorder of Guildford and a magistrate in the Lambeth Division of the Metropolitan Police Courts. The latter post meant an income of £1000 a year for his trouble of attending court on three days a week between twelve and five p.m. It also meant that he was regularly out of the house. Even this effort was at times too much for him, however, and there were soon complaints about his lack of punctuality. When he heard of them, Norton declared that he would write to *The Times* to defend his reputation. It seems that Melbourne was already apprehensive that he might be criticized for having appointed such a man as Norton, and he wrote to tell Caroline that he would be 'annoyed at having a complaint made on this subject'. He added: 'Pray dissuade him [Norton] from any public exhibition, and urge him gently to a little more activity in the morning. He might surely without difficulty get there by twelve o'clock.' Norton did not write the letter. Yet when a vacancy for another magistrate at Lambeth occurred, he assumed that he should have a voice in the appointment, and said so. By now, Melbourne could barely conceal his irritation and complained to Caroline that her husband seemed to think that the bench was 'to be a sort of pleasant club', and that 'he must have an agreeable fellow to walk with to or from the office'.[4] There was now a tacit recognition between Caroline and Melbourne of what a buffoon her husband was, and she well understood that Melbourne would never have allowed his great name to be linked with such a person except for her sake.

In the spring of 1831, Caroline became pregnant again. Her baby was due at the end of November, and so she planned to spend a lazily pleasant summer with her Sheridan relatives in the country. In July, she went to Maiden Bradley, near Mere in Wiltshire, as the guest of her sister, Georgiana, and her young husband, Lord Seymour (or St Maur). While Melbourne was busy with negotiations to present the new Reform Bill to Parliament, she lazed away her time in a large armchair on the lawn at Maiden Bradley, with Georgiana lying next to her on a 'sopha', a dumb waiter to supply them with wine and biscuits, a beagle puppy at their feet, a pet lamb tied to a stone urn, and a caged parrot put out into the sun.[5] Throughout late July and

August, she wrote to Melbourne almost every other day, in letters which were playful, teasing, tender, and serious by turns. She gave him an account of her days at Maiden Bradley:

Maiden Bradley, July 11 [1831]

Dearest Lord,
I am very dull – how are you? Allow me to give you a description of the way in which we pass our days. Established in what the innkeepers call two 'cheerful rooms' (looking due east) the sun wakes us all at six. We turn our backs upon it and lie till nine, at which time we open our dazzled eyes & dress. We eat our breakfast in solemn silence as is meet & fit in the hall of Seymour's ancestors. After this repast, we females do a little needlework, while Seymour reads Mackintosh. Many times do we inspect our watches, and sometimes order the cook in our despair to produce dinner at a moment's notice! at three is our general hour, and I feel a moment's revived energy when cherry tart appears at the festal board. I am also amused by the act of drinking perry . . .
. . . After tea I am allowed a quiet hour while the young couple caress one another. This, as I am of a social turn of mind, is quite as dull to me as any of the foregoing occupations of the day: and at nine o'clock (or ten at the latest) I am obliged willy nilly to 'retire to rest' as Georgia says it fidgets her to know that Seymour and I are sitting downstairs after she is in bed. He makes a stout fight however & sits up till 12 and I follow his example (when safely lodged in my own room) and remain till 2 or 3 in the morning yawning and scribbling. It is two now, so good night, and recommending the 'day at Bradley' as a model for Brocket Hall.

Believe me ever
Yours very truly
Caroline Norton

Not once in these letters from Maiden Bradley did Caroline speak of love but their intimate tone betrays just how close was the friendship between this pregnant young wife and the ageing politician. She presumes to correct his spelling (in one of his replies he had confused 'despatch' with 'dispatch'); she advises him what to do with Susan, a young girl thoughtlessly taken into the Melbourne household years before by Caroline Lamb, and who now needed to be provided for; she teases him about his amorous inclinations towards a number of

young women (was she not aching to hear his denials?); she tells him
tales of the Seymour household; asks his advice on an alleged portrait
of her Linley grandmother, which had just come to light; archly
reproves him for the coarseness of his observations on the verb 'to
kiss', and enquires after the fortunes of her friend Leopold, the newly
enthroned King of the Belgians, who was just then desperately
attempting to fight off a Dutch army. Norton is rarely mentioned other
than as a private joke and she never refers to the Grantley family
without contempt.

In fact it was Lord Grantley's meanness that brought about a
situation which, for the first time, obliged Caroline's husband to
acknowledge that Melbourne was her special friend and patron. On
4 August 1831, Caroline wrote to tell Melbourne that Grantley had
been guilty of the 'very shabbiest proceedings [she had] ever heard of'
in selling, for sixty guineas, a colt that had always been promised to
her. Even worse, he had tried to bribe a groom to swear that Caroline's
colt had had to be shot, and that the one sold was another animal;
'there has been nothing but swearing, quarrelling, discoveries, & lie
after lie in the nobleman's house'.[6] Melbourne replied offering to give
her another horse. This presented Caroline with a problem for even
she knew that for a married woman to accept such a gift from any
man other than her husband or a relative was a very delicate matter.
She had to ask Norton's permission to accept the animal, and there
was no knowing how he would take the offer. On 12 August she wrote
to Melbourne to tell him the verdict: 'Having enquired of the said
Norton whether I might accept a filly from you, he very graciously
responded that so high was his opinion of your personal merit that I
might take anything from you.'[7]

It is not clear what was going on here. Norton's declaration that
Caroline 'might take anything' from Lord Melbourne may have
signified a collusive acceptance of an improper relationship between
them but, more probably, is a simple measure of his obtuseness and
pomposity. The acceptance of the present worried her relations,
however. When Norton consulted Caroline's new brother-in-law, Lord
Seymour, on the matter, he replied 'with grave caution peculiar to
himself, that he "thought it would be very nice for [Caroline] to have
a horse to ride next spring".' Presumably Seymour felt he could not
tell Norton of his misgivings.

Norton did not accompany Caroline to Maiden Bradley but wrote
to say that he intended to follow her on 9 August. The phrasing of
his note was rather ambiguous and Caroline, who rarely let slip an

opportunity to make him feel stupid, manufactured an embarrassing little scene when he arrived. Of course she wrote to tell Melbourne all about it:

> I must tell you a sentence in Norton's letter announcing his august arrival the following day. Seymour promised to send the carriage for him the last stage to which kindness he thus equivocally eludes. 'I shall start from Frome tomorrow, & hope, by Seymour's kind assistance to kiss you at nine in the evening'!! I was so enchanted at this mode of conveying his gratitude to the noble lord, that I was obliged to read the sentence aloud, much to the confusion of all parties present.[8]

By such means did she and Norton torture each other. She would humiliate him in front of her family or her clever friends, and he would on occasions take a private and brutal revenge.

Some of Caroline's letters from Maiden Bradley sound a more poignant note:

> Dearest Lord . . .
> . . . I trust you are very busy, sending succours to Leopold, as I have not heard from you this morning, and have got into a pernicious habit of expecting your letters at certain intervals and feeling disappointed when they do not come . . .
> . . . I trust the worry and the fagging have not made you ill again. I know it is foolish expecting that you can sit down and write nonsense to me every other day, but promise me that if you are ill you will send a line here, where I do not meet people at every turn ready to give me the last intelligence respecting you; some out of spite and some out of good nature; as I had when you were ill in South St. this spring . . .
> . . . Do not think I am discontented with short letters, it is only when I am entirely left to my own conjectures that I grow anxious; it is sufficient, while I feel that you are so much occupied with graver matters, to hear that you are well and going to spend the ensuing Saturday at Brocket or Chevening, as may be . . .

Towards the end of her holiday, on 26 August, Caroline wrote to Melbourne to report a disturbing event. Seymour had just told her that, between one and three o'clock the previous morning, the house had been burgled, and that some plate, a silver and ebony snuffbox, a bunch of seals, a child's dress and a silver teapot had been taken. The servants had been cross-questioned, but neither the maid, Elizabeth Brady, nor the coachman, John Fluke, seemed to know anything about the raid. Caroline generally trusted her servants but may have had misgivings about Fluke. He disliked her and was too partial to drink. Nevertheless, the missing objects were not found with him. The handyman had also been interrogated but still, at the time she was writing to Melbourne, the culprit had not been discovered. The news of this bizarre little crime disturbed Melbourne greatly, for he perceived that by such a theft, his letters to Caroline might fall into the hands of his political opponents. Only a handful of his letters to Caroline have survived and none of them prove a guilty relationship between them. His real fear, however, was probably that he may have made facetious or even derogatory remarks about colleagues in such letters, and these comments would return to embarrass them all.

In the autumn, Caroline returned to Storey's Gate and social life. Once again her drawing room was regularly filled with politicians returned to Westminster for the new sitting of the House. It was in this room that she first introduced Disraeli to Lord Melbourne. It seems that Melbourne was fascinated by this extraordinary, ringleted apparition before him, a Jew, a Radical and a dandy. He found himself asking: 'Well now, tell me what you want to be.' 'I want to be Prime Minister,' answered Disraeli. Melbourne intimated that he considered this was a most unrealistic ambition for a young man without any influence, and who was also a Jew. He decided that the kindest thing to do would be to discourage him. 'No chance of that in our time. It is all arranged and settled. Nobody can compete with Stanley. If you are going to enter politics and mean to stick to it, I dare say you will do very well, for you have ability and enterprise; and if you are careful how you steer, no doubt you will get into some port at last. But you must put all these foolish notions out of your head; they won't do at all. Stanley will be the next Prime Minister.' At that time, Melbourne's advice was sound; Disraeli had not even succeeded in getting into the House. Nevertheless, Caroline was aware of his talents, allowed him to escort her to receptions, and took a proprietory pleasure in his shining intellect.

The Nortons were much better off now that he had his magistracy, and she was earning money as a writer, so they began to live up to their improved income. They could not yet afford to leave Storey's Gate for something larger, but they could run to having the house redecorated and extended. Soon, the smell of lead paint was strong in the rooms, and provoked Caroline's attacks of morning nausea. More seriously, she feared for the health of her sickly little son, Fletcher, and sent him with his nurse, Mrs Moore, to stay in bracing Margate, while the painters were at their work. George, meanwhile, felt that he could now afford to keep a horse, and purchased a nice little cabriolet, or two-wheeler. When in a good temper, he would sometimes take Caroline driving in the park, idly flicking at the horse with the whip, just to show his style. In November 1831 her second baby was born and, again, it was a boy. Caroline insisted that he be given the famous Sheridan name of Brinsley. Unlike his brother, the child was healthy from the first, and, as he grew, he revealed a cheerful, boisterous nature, that, for a time, gave his mother ample compensation for the unhappiness of her marriage. The whole household was the more cheerful for the presence of the little boy.

Years later, Caroline learned that even when Brinsley was very young, some of her servants had said he looked like Lord Melbourne.

XI

THE WIFE, AND WOMAN'S REWARD

IN THE NEW YEAR OF 1832, Caroline's sister-in-law, Augusta Norton, came to stay at Storey's Gate, and brought trouble with her. When Caroline asked George how long Augusta was staying, he would only say vaguely that it was 'for three or four months'. As a schoolgirl, Caroline always sensed that she had somehow disappointed Miss Norton who had befriended her at Wonersh. The maiden lady had seemed to expect some sort of response from her which Caroline had been unable to supply. Now her crop-headed sister-in-law, who came down to the drawing room in her jacket, short skirt and Turkish trousers, was nothing but an embarrassment. Augusta not only dressed like a man, but behaved like one, and 'astonished and repelled persons who had the usual habits of society'. Caroline could just about put up with her sister-in-law in private, but refused to introduce her to her friends. When Norton demanded that his sister be treated as an honoured house guest, Caroline insisted that people such as Lord Melbourne and Lord Holland could hardly be expected to tolerate for a moment the company of this gauche, opinionated, Tory harridan. He was furious. And when Caroline proposed to go to a reception on her own, he became obstinate and declared that he would sooner 'cut the traces of the carriage than allow [her] to go without' his sister.

The timing of Augusta's visit was especially unfortunate in that it coincided with the climax of the Whig campaign to bring in the new Reform Act. This historic event gave Caroline an opportunity to vie with the great Whig ladies, by turning her own little home into a committee room. After all, though it may not have had the grandeur of Holland House, it was much closer to the House of Commons. Here she supervised groups of Whig ladies writing letters imploring the support of undecided members. Party feeling ran very high, and the opponents of the Bill maintained that its passing would usher in civil war.[1] In the midst of Caroline's preparations sat Augusta Norton, a furious High Tory partisan in a reformist drawing room. While Caroline greeted news of reformist speeches with rapture, and discussed lobbying with her Whig lady friends, Augusta could only quiver with indignation in a corner, or sit whispering Tory animosities with her brother.

Caroline now took upon herself the job of trying to raise support for the Bill among influential figures who had not yet committed themselves. Such a one was Charles Babbage, the mathematician and inventor of an early version of computer who received a note from her:

Saturday, May 2, 1832

Dear Sir,

You will, I fear, think me very impertinent in addressing you, but my sister, Lady Seymour (who is more fortunate in being better acquainted with you), is in Wiltshire, and Seymour in Devonshire, where we wish heartily you could pay him a visit. I don't know whether Lady Seymour's anxiety for Lord John [Russell's] success will weigh with you. She was conceited enough to say to me one day when we were reading your 'Apology' in Mrs Leicester Stanhope's album, 'Mr Babbage likes me!' But whether your imagined preference be great enough to induce you to exert yourself in the same cause as Seymour, I dare not conjecture. All I can say is, that it would be doing a great favour not only to Lord John but to friends of yours who are also friends of his. It is the first year that Georgie Seymour has seemed eager about politics; you will not instruct her so harshly in philosophy as to teach her how to bear a first disappointment?

Not having your name to aid us is as if you made a long speech in favour of Mr Parker – which is not, surely, what you intend; is it?

Pray, pray, do not be angry with me – great anxiety will make one bold, and the last thing I have intended is any disrespect towards you. I know it will be a great disappointment to Georgie, I am certain it will be a great disappointment to Seymour. For myself, I do not say anything but that it is not my first year of anxiety in the cause. Whichever way you decide, let me have one line to say you are not displeased with me. I shall value it as an autograph even if you refuse our petition.

May I get up a petition with many signatures (all ladies) begging you to go down and vote?

With repeated apologies,
Believe me, dear Sir,
Yours very truly
Caroline Norton[2]

On this occasion Caroline was successful; Babbage supported the Bill and, incidentally, became a life-long friend. Such support was crucially important. In the previous March, a Bill introducing reform had been passed by a majority of one vote in the best attended House in living memory, only to be defeated in committee. A second Bill had been thrown out by the Lords in October. Now, in the spring of 1832, the country was poised for the third attempt and the tension was tremendous. The King had reluctantly agreed to create as many peers as was necessary to ensure the Bill's progress through the Upper House. On 4 June, it passed its third reading in the Lords and most of Caroline's friends were jubilant. Characteristically, Lord Melbourne, alone among her Whig friends, was sadly lacking in enthusiasm for the enterprise. He thought the measure would not do much good, and would only raise people's hopes without fulfilling them. By contrast, Augusta Norton announced that the Bill would bring disaster to the monarchy, the aristocracy and the country at large. Caroline's laughter did not improve the lady's temper. After twelve weeks of domestic warfare, Augusta was finally persuaded to leave Storey's Gate, but not before she had become one more of Caroline's virulent enemies among the Nortons.[3]

Caroline's life was now an exciting and demanding one. She was not only a celebrated Society hostess, but also, through her friendship with Melbourne, as influential in politics as any woman could be at that time. Furthermore, she was a successful poet and the friend of many writers and artists. In April her portrait was painted by the fashionable artist, John Hayter, and Tom Moore, then at the height of his fame as a poet and singer, would accompany her across the park to sittings at Hayter's house. But, despite her crowded social life, Caroline was a very affectionate mother and spent much time reading, singing and telling stories to her two little boys. A typical day for her at this time might include a visit to the nursery, family breakfast, morning calls, an afternoon visit from Melbourne, an evening reception, and a dinner engagement. It was not until she returned to the house in the late hours that she had some time to get on with what she regarded as her real work, her writing, and then only if Norton could be persuaded not to insist on his marital rights.

The income she obtained from her scribblings in the late hours was now very necessary to their household economy. Yet working such long hours sometimes made her tetchy and quarrelsome during the day, and contributed to the bickering between them. Their disagreements were often about money, for Norton was mean and she could not have cut a fine figure in Society on the allowance he made her. Then she found a way to finance her social life by taking on responsibility for three fashionable Society publications known as 'scrapbooks'. In 1832 she became the editor of *La Belle Assemblée and Court Magazine*, and she later took on *The English Annual* in 1834, and *The Keepsake* in 1836. These 'scrapbooks' or 'annuals' were addressed to the *beau monde* and were very popular in aristocratic circles. They printed stories, poems, and gossip about the upper classes, and some included illustrations of the latest fashions. Contributors were unpaid. Not even such professional authors as Mrs Hemans and Barry Cornwall received a penny. So, as editor, Caroline had not only to cajole her friends into writing contributions, but then had to sell their work back to them. She found that it was not difficult to do the latter, because people would nearly always pay to see their own names in print, but it was very difficult to get work out of people. Nevertheless, she got Tom Moore, Samuel Rogers, Lord Holland, and her relative by marriage, Charles Phipps, to contribute to one edition of *The Keepsake*, and even persuaded her brother, Richard Brinsley, just back from India, to write a piece on 'The Hindu Girl'. Despite that, she still had to write eleven out of thirty-five articles herself for this one volume. Many of her own pieces appeared anonymously.

Because no contributor was paid, the publisher of a scrapbook volume stood to make a considerable profit, provided that the editor's name on the title-page was sufficiently fashionable to ensure large sales. Caroline's social status had now been enormously elevated by her friendship with Lord Melbourne, and, therefore, she was able to demand relatively high payments from her publishers. She could not at first rival Lady Blessington, who could command £800 to edit an annual, but eventually she asked, and got, £250, while the likes of Mrs Gore were offered only £120 a volume.[4]

Caroline enjoyed editing the scrapbooks, though she probably protested to her friends that she was having to waste her talents on hack work when she might have been composing poetry. She knew perfectly well that the literary standard of these volumes was not very high but it amused her to write little biographical sketches of such fashionable débutantes as Lady Marjoribanks, and to collect Paris fashion plates for *La Belle Assemblée*, which announced itself as 'A Monthly Compendium of Foreign Costume'. Editing also brought her into contact with literary women like herself.

One of these was Miss Laetitia E. Landon, or 'LEL' as she signed her stories. Caroline affected to laugh at this spinster rival, but she was secretly rather jealous of her, and not just because of her reputation as a writer. She knew that Lord Melbourne was friendly with LEL though she could never discover how intimately. No doubt she was often tempted to poke fun at LEL's work to Lord Melbourne, but there was one piece that she dare not ridicule. It was LEL's 'poetical illustration' to the 1832 volume of the *Scrap-book*, in which she addressed the young Princess Victoria, and uttered the wish that 'God [should] keep the crown long from an innocent brow', on the grounds that the young Princess's head would rest uneasy from the first day she wore it. Caroline soon became aware that, though she and Melbourne could laugh about almost everything together, Princess Victoria was the exception. Melbourne would not tolerate the slightest flippancy about this thirteen-year-old girl who was the heir to the throne. Indeed, whenever her name was mentioned, he looked grave.

The scrapbooks took up an increasing amount of Caroline's time in the early 1830s and the discipline of providing matter for them became an increasingly arduous one. Sometimes, she was so short of material that she dashed off stories which were barely disguised bits of autobiography. One example is 'The Templar's Tale', which appeared in *La Belle Assemblée* for 1832,[5] and which tells a tale of courtship, marriage and domestic violence very close to her own experience. Probably she cared little if her friends recognized Norton and herself in the story. The narrator is Dudley deVere, a young lawyer from the Temple (as was Norton, when he had first set eyes on her). While on a visit to the Essex coast, he sees a young schoolgirl, Lucia, and falls in love with her, though she is too young to be approached. Two years pass, and he meets her again in the Zoological Gardens, discovers her identity, proposes, is accepted, and gains her father's permission to marry her. Unfortunately he is plagued by jealousy of Etherington, a young officer colleague of Lucia's father, and involves her in a number of embarrassing and violent scenes. For a while, she shames him into controlling himself but the story moves to a climax when deVere confesses: 'Let me . . . tell of the wicked infatuation by which I blindly alienated from me the purest, the gentlest, and the fondest heart that ever throbbed within the breast of woman'. Etherington asks Lucia to dance with him at a ball, and deVere, in a paroxysm of jealousy, challenges him to a duel. Lucia separates them in the shrubbery, and Etherington leaves. DeVere then relieves his feelings by twisting the neck of a canary that Etherington had given

Lucia, with a degree of 'malevolence which [he] could not restrain'. Later, in a fit of remorse, he realizes that he has become 'a monster of cruelty and meanness'. But it is too late. Lucia's father breaks off the engagement on the grounds that he cannot trust his daughter to such a man.

There are elements of wish-fulfilment in this story. It is significant that it is related by deVere, the Norton figure, who is now consumed with remorse because he has alienated the affections of the 'purest, the gentlest, and the fondest heart that ever throbbed within the breast of woman', by which Caroline meant her own. This remorse is what Caroline wished her husband could feel but which he never did. On the other hand, she clearly wishes that she had had a father who might have prevented her marriage to such a violent man. Unhappily for her, Norton's cruelty was beginning to exceed anything in her stories. In the summer of 1833, shortly before the birth of her third child, he became so brutal that she began to have thoughts of leaving him. On one occasion, she was breakfasting in the morning room at Storey's Gate, looking out over St James's Park while Fletcher, now aged four, played round her feet. Norton came into the room and demanded her chair so that he could look out of the window. Caroline refused, pointing out that, had he wanted that seat, he should have come down earlier. Norton replied by coolly placing the hot tea-kettle upon her hand. She screamed for help but the damage was done. She was severely burnt and scalded. A surgeon was called in from the next house and he dressed her hand, which remained in bandages for some days. Norton, meanwhile, had left the breakfast room simply requesting the servant to 'brush the crumbs away'. He never apologized.[6]

Even in less dramatic moments, Norton was beginning to disgust her. He had taken to smoking a hookah at home, and filling her little rooms with fumes. It was this practice which nearly precipitated a final break between them during the summer of 1832:

> About the same period, a dispute having arisen after dinner, I said I was really weary of my life with the perpetual wranglings; that I had a great deal to do, and would sit no longer with him, but go to the drawing-room and write for a Periodical [The English Annual], of which I had then the editorship; that I only asked him to stay where he was, and smoke there, instead of upstairs. He answered that the house was his, – not mine; – that he should sit in what room he pleased . . .[7]

Foolishly, perhaps, she then went upstairs to the drawing room to write, and, even more foolishly, she locked the door behind her. Norton came after her, smashed it down, pushed the maid out, blew out the candles, and then tried to force Caroline to go downstairs with him. Seeing his mistress assaulted, her manservant risked his job by trying to hold Norton back, while she escaped upstairs to the nursery. There she stayed the night, sharing a bed with the nursemaid. She lay awake trying to think what to do, and finally made up her mind to leave him in the morning.

But, as day came on, she felt sick and giddy and could not get up. Her situation was desperate. She now feared violence at any time and her every impulse was to leave her husband. But she was more than ever dependent upon him because she was in her last months of pregnancy with her third child. Eventually, she scribbled a desperate note to her brother, Richard Brinsley, to ask him to intervene. Even then she tried to soften the story of Norton's violence. She told Brinny that she bore her husband no ill-will, but required him to act more 'gentlemanlike' in his conduct to her or else she must leave him. Brinsley immediately sent a note round to Norton charging him with violence towards his sister. By now Norton was repentant. He replied admitting the incident, but claimed that he had broken open the door 'on principle; thinking it necessary as a husband, to resist such extravagant and disrespectful proceedings' as having any door of his house locked against him. He and Caroline would 'patch up' this 'frivolous quarrel', and he asked her family to 'forget and forgive'. The quarrel was overtaken by events. On 26 August, Caroline gave birth to her third son, William. It was, apparently, a difficult delivery and she made only a slow recovery.

Lord Melbourne continued to visit her, even after her confinement when she was so ill. The maid had instructions to show him upstairs to Caroline's bedroom, and there he would sit on the bed, holding her hand, and trying to distract her with chat about Westminster political intrigue. At first she was too depressed to care much about such matters but Melbourne's company always had a tonic effect upon her, and, as the months wore on, she slowly recovered. Soon she came downstairs to receive him in her sitting room. With the return of her health came a renewed passion for politics. She made no secret to her Tory husband that she exulted in the good fortune of the Whigs. By this political infidelity, she paid him back for his domestic brutality, and her deeper intimacy with Melbourne was, in some ways, revenge for Norton's ill-treatment.

Then came a change in Melbourne's political fortunes. The Prime Minister, Lord Grey, resigned in the summer of 1834, as a result of Lord Brougham's wilful meddling in the Irish situation. On the very day of Grey's departure, Melbourne, who was still Home Secretary, displayed his lack of concern by ostentatiously accompanying a party of ladies on the river. Meanwhile, King William IV had the task of finding a new Prime Minister and, though he was a Tory at heart, the political complexion of the House obliged him to choose a Whig. Of the possible contenders, the King considered Lord Althorp to be too Radical, and he trusted neither Lord Brougham nor Lord Russell. Lord Lansdowne would not serve. Of the senior Whigs, that left Lord Melbourne. The King, therefore, commanded Lord Grey, as outgoing premier, to hand to Melbourne the formal letter of invitation to discuss the formation of a government. Melbourne's natural indolence almost persuaded him against it. He understood perfectly well that, as Prime Minister, he would have less time to watch over Augustus, to pay visits to Caroline, and to read his old play-books and the Christian fathers. What was worse, if he took the job, he would be obliged to spend even more time in the company of his quarrelsome, elderly Cabinet colleagues, or in listening to the constant complaints of King William. But Caroline was naturally ambitious both for her friend and herself, and almost certainly used whatever opportunities she had, when they were sat together on the sofa at Storey's Gate, to try to persuade Melbourne of the splendid opportunity now opening before him. In the end, she was probably rather piqued to learn that it was not she but his private secretary, Tom Young, who had settled the matter. Young was a sharp-tongued, disrespectful and totally loyal adviser to Melbourne. He was probably an enemy to Caroline but, if so, she would have had to admit that he was a good friend to her friend. At the moment of decision, Melbourne explained the matter to Young in this way: 'I think it's a damned bore. I don't know what to do.' 'Why damn it all,' Young replied, 'such a position was never held by any Greek or Roman: and if it only lasts three months, it will be worth while to have been Prime Minister of England.' 'By God, that's true,' said Melbourne, 'I'll go.'[8] He remained in office for five months until December, when he was turned out in favour of Peel and his Tories.

For most of the time during Melbourne's first administration, Caroline was out of the country. In the August of 1834, her Sheridan relatives were planning a trip to the Continent. The Seymours were going, and so was Richard Brinsley, and Helen Blackwood, whose husband was still at sea. Caroline begged Norton to let her go too, but, as she might have expected, he refused to let her go without him. The only solution was to persuade him to go too, even though none of them wanted him as a travelling companion. At first he said 'No', perhaps because he had recently renewed his acquaintance with Miss Margaret Vaughan, a distant cousin rather older than himself. Margaret Vaughan was rich, and Norton had great hopes of inheriting her fortune. She also displayed a 'flattering preference' for him. Yet, despite Miss Vaughan, he agreed to go on holiday with the Sheridans. He appears to have been genuinely jealous of Caroline's close links with her own family. Perhaps he simply wanted to spoil the holiday for them all. Even so, he agreed only on condition that Caroline paid the expenses of the trip for both of them.

During the late summer, Norton still went on making difficulties about the trip. He pretended to be surprised to learn that the party was to start in September and to return just before Christmas. He complained that this would make it impossible for Caroline and himself to pay their annual autumn visit to the Menzies in Perthshire. She was obliged to be tactful for once. She explained that, even though this would be a great disappointment, it was a necessary sacrifice if they were to spend sufficient time on the Continent to make the trip worthwhile. She even tried to enthuse Norton a little by describing the route they would take by way of Calais, Ghent, Antwerp, and Cologne to the Rhine Valley. They were to come home via Brussels where they would call upon their family friend, Leopold, now King of the Belgians.

From the first Norton grumbled, for he spoke neither French nor German and did not like foreigners. He detested the food, and declared that the inns were uncomfortable. He seemed incapable of enjoying anything and did his best to spoil Caroline's pleasure. Later, she included a description of his behaviour in her first novel:

He was continually occupying himself with trivial anxieties which for the time assumed an intense importance. Restless and wretched, he fidgeted about all the little events and minor details of their journey. He spent the first two stages of every day's journey in counting over again the bills which had already been paid, and consulting different estimates of the different rates of currency in the countries they were to pass through. He was always looking for a lost book, or a mislaid paper knife, or an undiscoverable travelling cap: always wondering whether the road they were going was really and actually the best road to the place of their destination, and calculating what hour they would arrive; always abusing the last hotel-keeper and swearing against the bore of the long journey.[9]

Soon he began to complain that he felt ill and there was something wrong with his leg. The Nortons joined the party at Antwerp but they got no farther than Aix-la-Chapelle (Aachen), where George complained that he was lame. So, while her brother and sisters went on with the servants, Caroline was left with Norton. The days at that hotel soon became a nightmare for her, because he insisted that he was very ill and also that only she should attend him. He made her perform the most menial tasks for him, so that, afterwards, she learned that a number of the other guests did not believe that she was really a lady or Norton's wife. This was not surprising because Norton had used the opportunity to humiliate her in public. He made her his 'sick-nurse, valet and chamber-maid'; she was even required to empty his pot.[10] He rarely allowed her to take her dinner away from his sick-room, and, when she did so, he frequently interrupted her meal in the hotel dining room, by sending messages to complain that she was taking too long, or that she was needed to come and change the leeches on his leg. Inevitably, she became ill herself. The German doctor who attended on Norton had warned him that this would happen. He told Norton that his wife needed rest, fresh air and female company. The doctor suggested that Caroline should be allowed time away from the sick-room, and that she might like to call on his own wife and daughter. While she was away, he said, he would send in a *garçon des bains* to wash Norton. The doctor received small thanks for his kindness. Then, one day when Caroline was close to breaking, help came. There was a knock at the sick-room door to admit her brother, Brinsley, who had put aside his own pleasures to come back to keep her company. Curiously, when he was confronted with Brinsley's sharp scrutiny, Norton made a miraculous recovery, and was at least well enough to travel again. Soon the three of them rejoined the party.

Then came the final break between the Sheridans and George Norton. Again it was his hookah which ignited the quarrel. One day the whole party were trundling in their carriages through Germany, with Caroline and George bringing up the rear, when, to relieve his boredom, and probably to irritate Caroline, Norton brought out his hookah and insisted in puffing away at it in their small, confined carriage. Caroline politely asked him to stop smoking but he ignored her. When she found she was becoming nauseous, she pleaded with him to put the pipe away but still he paid no attention. Enraged, she snatched the pipe from his mouth and flung it out of the window. The carriage, by now, was going so slowly uphill that Norton was able to jump out, gather the pieces of his pipe together, and jump in again. Then he seized her by the throat so fiercely that she was almost strangled. In the struggle that followed, she managed to slip from his grasp, scramble out on to the road, and run up to the other carriages imploring protection from Brinsley. The marks of Norton's fingers were still on her throat. Brinsley was terribly angry. He jumped out and stopped the coaches, and then followed a dreadful shouting match between Norton and himself in the middle of the road. After that, the Sheridans refused to travel with Norton any more. They took Caroline further on down the Rhine with them, while Norton was left behind, presumably to complete his recovery.

Caroline loved Germany and the Germans. She always thought of them as a deep-feeling, innocent, simple and noble people, who retained the best elements of the English themselves. Ten years after the trip, she wrote a long poem, *Ehrenbreitstein*, in which she fondly remembered her holiday, and her first experience of Germany:

> But that September who shall tell
> The joy, the triumph, the delight
> Of setting off for foreign lands,
> And travelling on, by day and night?
> Who shall describe how pleased we were,
> The large home party, setting forth
> To bask in sunshine carelessly,
> And seek adventures south and north? . . .[11]

She worked up the piece from the holiday journals and sketch-books she took with her but, even after ten years, she was still able to remember the pleasure of that holiday spoiled only by the presence of her obtuse, resentful husband:

> And then in spite of rattling wheels,
> The long, long letters written home
> To tell of distant Germany,
> To tell how glad we were to roam:
> How all along the vineyard grounds
> The stunted vines like currants grew,
> Not like those married to the elms
> Which our misleading fancy drew.

> How little Nonnenworth was like
> An emerald in a silver setting;
> How stupid one among us was,
> The passports and the trunks forgetting . . .

Ehrenbreitstein is an enthusiastic if undistinguished versification of Caroline's travels in Germany, but one which she dramatizes with the advantage of hindsight. In the poem she presents herself as an innocent, naïve young woman, responding with delight to those same qualities in the Germans, whether they are 'Grand Dukes, Archdukes, blandly kind', or 'peasants beautiful and poor'. These images of her carefree youth then serve as a contrast to the picture she painted of her later self, as a woman of suffering:

> The journal now is locked away,
> The sketch-book opened with a sigh,
> And pictures of the lovely Rhine
> Are gazed at with a saddened eye:
> Because so much that then was joy,
> Succeeding years have turned to pain;
> So much can only grieve the heart,
> That made it beat with pleasure then.

As their holiday came to an end, one of the Sheridans suggested that they should all return to England via Paris. George was no longer with them to spoil the plan, and so Caroline was full of enthusiasm for the idea. Their visit was a triumph. The 'Three Graces' may no longer have afforded a novelty in London, but in Paris they were a sensation, and one of their greatest admirers was the bourgeois monarch himself, Louis Philippe. Henry Greville was an English visitor to Paris at that time and wrote in his diary:

> November 27. – In the evening a good many English came to be presented at the Tuileries – among them the three Sheridan sisters: when they came in the King exclaimed, 'What a batch of them!'[12]

Greville also sat next to Caroline at dinner and observed that 'Her beauty and that of Lady Seymour made a prodigious sensation here.' And Caroline's old enemy, Lady Granville, wrote to her sister, Lady Carlisle: 'I will tell you how Norton behaves in my next. The French are sorry Blackwood goes to the Opera in a skull-cap.'[13]

Meanwhile, George Norton was still recuperating in Germany, and, reluctantly, Caroline wrote to suggest that he should rejoin the party in Paris in December. When he arrived, she had to ensure that he should not meet her Whig friend, Lord Brougham, who had recently abolished George's job of Commissioner for Bankruptcy, and was now out of office himself. Brougham had lately been in London and brought all the gossip from home. He would sit for hours with Caroline, Lady Clanricarde and the Princess Belgioso, telling of how King William IV had dismissed Lord Melbourne as Prime Minister, and how the Houses of Parliament had burned down. No doubt Caroline was avid for news of her friend and loved to listen to Brougham if only to hear the repetition of Melbourne's name.

For some reason, the party did not go on to Brussels as planned. In mid-December, they left Paris for London. The Nortons spent Christmas, as usual, with Mrs Sheridan at Hampton Court.

XII

PUBLIC AFFAIRS

CAROLINE'S POLITICAL INFLUENCE was now at its height, and this fact had not gone unnoticed by the press. In April 1835, *The Satirist*, a newspaper which was beginning to take a lively interest in her doings, reported that, 'Fair Caroline is secretly in extasy [*sic*] at the defeat of the Ministry and the prospect which it opens of her Lamb being recalled to office'.[1] Sir Robert Peel was now the head of a minority Conservative administration, and had already suffered six defeats in the House in as many weeks. There was talk of a possible coalition, between the Tory statesmen, Peel and Lyndhurst, and Lord Melbourne and his moderate Whigs. Enthusiasts for the scheme thought that such a government would act as a stabilizing force, and keep out the Radicals and the Irish. Private talks were arranged between the politicians concerned, and even though Disraeli was still not an MP, Lyndhurst made him his negotiator. To her great delight, Melbourne entrusted Caroline to put his case. So, for a few weeks in March 1835, the little drawing room at Storey's Gate was the very centre of the political world. In the end, Caroline's whispered conversations on the blue couch with Disraeli came to nothing. Melbourne was returned at the head of another weak Whig Government, and remained in office as Prime Minister for the next six years. But nothing could take away from Caroline the pride of knowing the political influence she held at that time. Though it was true that she had married into the aristocracy and had a courtesy title, she was a mere woman, from a family of commoners. But she was now the friend and confidante of the Prime Minister, and a voice in the forming of governments. No woman in the kingdom was more influential than she – not even Lady Holland.[2]

Though political and social life now took much of her time, Caroline was still pursuing her literary career with determination. In 1835, Saunders & Otley brought out her first book of fiction, a 900-page, three-volume work entitled *The Wife, and Woman's Reward*. They gave her £300 for it, and it was the advance payment on this book which had enabled her to pay the expenses of her recent holiday. To her disappointment, sales were not good but she was encouraged when the same firm offered her £500 for a poem about her recent travels. Lord Byron had made travel poetry popular, and there was still a considerable market for it. Curiously, Caroline seems not to have published her holiday poem until *Ehrenbreitstein* came out ten years later.

The Wife, and Woman's Reward consists of two long stories. 'The Woman's Reward' tells of Mary Dupré and her unpleasant younger brother, Lionel. Like George Norton, Lionel has bouts of violent behaviour. In the opening chapter, for example, he deliberately crushes his sister's chameleon in a fit of jealousy. Like George Norton, Lionel hates travel in foreign countries, and misbehaves on holiday.

The other story, 'The Wife', contains a self-portrait in the character of Susan Dalrymple, who, after being jilted, has married Lord Glenalton, whom she does not love. Susan is a wit, and enjoys London social life for a time, but she soon becomes aware of its duplicity, when a designing woman tries to steal away her husband. In the end, Susan makes a passionate appeal to Glenalton, who gives up his mistress, and returns to her. The story is a wish-fulfilment fantasy. Caroline always felt that Norton mistreated her because he could not comprehend her true worth. Glenalton is brought to just such a recognition of his wife's stirling nature. The character of the mistress was probably suggested by Margaret Vaughan, for it was at this time that Caroline first suspected that Norton was having an affair with his cousin. These stories supply characters who may easily be identified with George Norton, Margaret Vaughan and Lord Melbourne, as well as Caroline herself. Far from fearing that the reading public would make such identifications, however, she seems to have revelled in the personal publicity she gained from her stories.

Besides, in the early months of 1835, another member of her family was much more in the public eye. Brinsley Sheridan had started a love affair, and then eloped with the girl in question, just as his father and grandfather had done before him. At that time, Richard Brinsley was admired by all who met him. He was charming, kindly and intelligent, and, with his Irish combination of jet-black hair and blue eyes, he was very attractive to women. His bride was Marcia Grant, the only daughter of Sir Colquhoun Grant, a veteran of Waterloo. Sir Colquhoun was a wealthy landowner, and was living at the time on his estate at Frampton Court in Dorset. On the day of the elopement, Sir Colquhoun must have feared that something was going on, for he left Marcia at Frampton under the special care of his relative, Sir Robert MacFarlane. Somehow the lovers managed to steal away together, and, after it was discovered that Marcia was missing, Sir Robert hurried after them. He turned up suddenly at the home of Richard Brinsley's brother-in-law, Lord Seymour, at Spring Gardens, Westminster, where Caroline and a number of other Sheridans were gathered. She found it an embarrassing occasion. The Sheridans were probably not involved in the elopement, or, if they were, they pretended not to know about it when Sir Robert demanded to be told the whereabouts of the lovers. Sir Robert stormed, and the assembled Sheridans giggled and whispered among themselves. Sheridans were usually noted for their good manners but Sir Robert appeared absurd to them. The situation became even more farcical when George Norton looked in to take Caroline home. In response to Sir Robert's appealing to him as a magistrate and upholder of the law, Norton struck an attitude of injured innocence, declaring that he knew nothing about the elopement and demanding that Sir Robert should trust his integrity in the matter. Sir Robert, by now, felt he was being mocked by the whole pack of them, and retired to report the news to Sir Colquhoun.

Scandal among the upper classes was *The Satirist*'s chief subject matter, and it gave Brinsley's affair a good deal of space. The paper soon spotted that George Norton's statement to Sir Robert MacFarlane was wrong in one significant detail. In accounting for Caroline's movements on the day of Sir Robert's visit, he said he had accompanied her to Lansdowne House and then come on to pick her up at Spring Gardens. In fact, as *The Satirist* pointed out, Norton had escorted his wife not to Lansdowne House but to Melbourne House. The implication was that Norton was conniving in the friendship between his wife and Lord Melbourne but wished to keep the matter hidden. And when it became clear that Richard Brinsley's behaviour had put at risk the pension awarded to his family for his grandfather's service to the country, *The Satirist* printed the following:

> 'Brinsley now will lose his claim
> to Pension,' said his aunt.
> 'What matters it,' cried MELBOURNE's flame
> 'the boy has got a GRANT.'[3]

Then followed a farcical series of events which again resembled the ending of *The Rivals*. Sir Colquhoun challenged Lord Seymour to a duel, but luckily, when they met, no great harm was done and neither was hurt. Sir Colquhoun also brought an action against Richard Brinsley, which obliged him to come back from honeymoon and to appear in the Court of Chancery to answer a summons for abduction. But true to the traditions of Sheridan comedy everything ended happily. Sir Colquhoun was soon reconciled with his daughter and new son-in-law, offered them his blessing and then, within a few months, obligingly died, leaving Marcia heir to all his estates. So Brinsley became the master of Frampton Court, and now had sufficient money behind him to allow him to think of going into politics.

But there was nothing comic about Caroline's domestic life. In the summer of 1835 Norton was so violent after a quarrel that, even though she was pregnant again, she left him. She took her children with her to the Seymours' house for protection. At first, Brinsley refused to negotiate with Norton on her behalf, because he, like other members of her family, did not wish her to go back to her husband at all. But there was little else she could do. She had three small children, was expecting another, and had little money of her own. Her only hope was to patch things up with Norton. So, reluctantly, Brinsley wrote seeking an agreement on her behalf but stipulating that he would not permit his sister to go back unless he was given written guarantees of her husband's future conduct. Norton replied that he was willing to 'make any sacrifice, provided that [Caroline] returned . . . home'.[4] He professed to be glad that his wife's family had scorned him, and avenged her, and 'vowed to treat [her] kindly for the future'. Brinsley Sheridan also used the opportunity to try to improve his sister's financial security. Norton had exaggerated his prospects when the marriage settlement had been drawn up but it might still be possible to get a new financial agreement for Caroline. Sir Robert Ellice was appointed to represent her interests and he tried to persuade Norton that Caroline, not he, should have entire control of their joint family finances. Norton refused. The suggestion did not meet his notions of the dignity due to a husband.

Yet Norton was full of promises that he would change his ways. His letters were pitifully contrite. He wrote to tell her that: 'As there is a God above us, who will judge our actions, I think I have a right to ask you to trust me for the future. If I cannot make you happy let us then quietly and rationally separate, I declaring to the world that the cause of it was not any imputation in you.' He begged her to write to him at once with 'complete forgiveness' and a 'real pardon'; he implored her not to crush him; and he ended: 'I go on my knees to you! Have pity – have compassion on me.'[5] The dramatic element in Caroline's nature always thrilled to this little scene they acted out after their quarrels. Norton played the naughty child, she the forgiving mother; and for once she had the power to punish him, by withholding her forgiveness. In practice she always forgave him in the end, for there was little else she could do.

The Sheridans did not believe Norton's promises to reform but Caroline was obliged to pretend that she did so, and returned to Storey's Gate. On the second day, Norton beat her again. He seemed to be entirely unaware that his actions were dangerous to a woman in the last weeks of pregnancy. In August, she suffered a miscarriage, and in the 'very severe illness which followed the agitation and misery to which [she] had been exposed', she became very ill. This time she took refuge at Brinsley's London home. Norton did not seem to mind. He simply told her that he was not prepared to pay for the nurse who looked after her.

There followed an uneasy truce. Norton spent most of his days now with Margaret Vaughan, and defended his increasingly frequent visits to her by pointing out to Caroline that his cousin was rich, and that he might become her heir. Caroline was still not sure whether they were having an affair but she was very aware that Margaret Vaughan hated her and was poisoning her husband's mind against her. In the autumn, he went off as usual, to the Menzies in Scotland, but there was no suggestion this time that she should go with him.

She spent much of the winter with the Seymours at Maiden Bradley. Now she was worried about her boys, especially the eldest, Fletcher, who was six years old, and had been frail almost from birth. In the early weeks of 1836 she took them all home to the empty house at Storey's Gate, while Norton was still in Scotland. Even when he did return, he was almost always out at the court or seeing Margaret Vaughan. By this time, Caroline and George Norton were no longer living as man and wife. They simply kept house together for the sake of the boys. But it became even more important that they should keep up a family home when Fletcher became ill again, this time with 'scarlatina' (scarlet fever). He was ill for many weeks during which time she feared he might die. Caroline spent whole days with him in the nursery. When he began to get better she tried to cheer him up by promising him a holiday in the country. She told him she would take him down to Frampton Court, in Dorset, at Easter. She knew that Brinsley and Marcia would welcome the boys and herself, though not, of course, her husband. That was a small matter, however. The holiday would cost them nothing, and that was the only thing Norton cared about.

Fletcher was thrilled by the thought of their holiday and he now made rapid progress. He had never seen Frampton Court and wanted to know all about it. She told him that, at Frampton, there was a great park to run in, trees to climb and even peacocks who ran about and spread their wings to show their feathers to little boys. Fletcher could hardly wait to go.

CHAPTER

XIII

AT FRAMPTON COURT

CAROLINE NEVER DID TAKE HER BOYS TO DORSET. On the evening of 30 March 1836 a closed carriage turned off the Dorchester road, through the gates of Frampton Court. There were no children inside, only Caroline and her maid. At Peacock Lodge, she glimpsed her friend, the gatekeeper, bowing a welcome, but, in her misery, she could barely raise a hand in acknowledgement. As the carriage rolled up the gravelled drive, it was pursued by the melancholy cries of peacocks now hidden in the dusky plantations. The horses clattered on, past the imposing double-flighted staircase to the front door of the great house, and turned through a low brick archway into a gravelled courtyard at the rear. Here, the driver pulled his team round the gently playing fountain and came to rest before a huge door above which was inscribed the word 'Salve'.[1] A bell clanged within the house, and a servant came to help her down, while another went for his master. Soon Richard Brinsley and Marcia came out to meet her. They were puzzled because they could see no children in the carriage. But, after looking closely at her face, Brinsley waved away her attempts to explain, and led her into the house. He was not satisfied till he had sat her down on a great couch and she had taken some refreshment. Only then was he willing to hear her story.

She told them that she and Norton had parted again. This time, however, he had left her. What was more, he had taken the children with him. She could still hardly believe it, because she had always assumed that, whatever else happened between them, Norton would allow the boys to remain with her. William was not yet two years old, Brinny three and a half, and Fletcher six, but with very poor health. She could not understand how even someone as unfeeling as Norton could deprive such delicate little creatures of the daily care of their own mother. He had, until two days previously, talked with approval of the boys going with her for an Easter holiday to Dorset. Then after a visit from Margaret Vaughan, he changed his mind. Eighteen years later she published an account of that day:

He never opposed in any way my plans for the Easter, but, on the contrary, urged me, now we were friends, to overrule my brother's objections to receive him, and get him also invited [to Frampton] – in which attempt I did not succeed. On the day previous to that I was to leave the town, I returned from my drive, and found Miss Vaughan had called in my absence, and remained closeted with my husband for some time. Lord Melbourne was with him when I came in, and they were talking together. After Lord M. left, Mr Norton talked discontentedly of the appointment, and angrily of my not getting that and pecuniary interests arranged for him. He also said Miss Vaughan had told him, if he himself were not noticed by my brother, he ought not to submit to my going to his house with my children. I said nothing should prevent my going to my brother; that it was Mr Norton's own fault that he was not on terms with my family; that the doctor had ordered change of air for the older child, who was recovering from scarlatina; and that I should give my servants orders to refuse Miss Vaughan admittance to my house, as she laboured always for mischief, in spite of my patience with her. We parted angrily – Mr Norton to dine with the chief magistrate, Sir Frederick Roe, and I to dine with Lady Mary Fox. We spent the evening together at a party at Lord Harrington's,[1] and returned home together. The dispute was then renewed, whether under the circumstances I should go to my brother's. Mr Norton's last words were – 'Well, the children shall not, that I have determined;' and as he entered the house he desired the servant to unpack the carriage (which had been prepared for starting), and take the children's things out, for that they were not going. He then went up to the nursery, and repeated the order to the nurse ... the sole observation I made on this occasion, when the nurse asked me 'what she was to do?' was, that 'Mr Norton's orders must be obeyed'. I neither braved him with useless words, nor complained.[2]

After this dispute, Caroline tossed on her bed all night, reliving the painful scene of the previous evening and going back over other quarrels, brutalities and humiliations she had endured in her years with George Norton. Slowly, the morning light whitened the windows of Storey's Gate. Now she had to decide what to do. Should she go to Dorset without her children, or should she stay with them in the home which had become hateful to her? She had to get advice. As always, she relied on her family. She rose early. The children's nurse, Martha Morris, helped her to dress and then let her out of the park door before seven o'clock. She walked up the Horseguards on her way to consult the Seymours at their house in Spring Gardens, just off Trafalgar Square. St James's Park was misty and mysterious at that hour, full of blurred ominous shapes, and almost deserted. She passed by the back of 10 Downing Street. Though she knew that it was unlikely that Melbourne would be there so early, she was tempted, perhaps, to knock at the door in the hope that she might see him. If so, she resisted the impulse. Melbourne had recently seemed embarrassed by her visits. So she kept on for Spring Gardens, where Georgiana was amazed to receive her so early in the morning.

She stayed with the Seymours till twelve o'clock. They were furious to hear that Norton would not let the boys go on holiday with her. Most of the morning was spent discussing what she should do. They debated whether she should collect the boys now and simply drive off with them to Frampton, or whether she should stay on at Spring Gardens until Norton relented. It seemed unlikely that, if she took the boys down to Dorset, Norton would follow them and take them back by force. Caroline knew, however, that she must not give him the opportunity of rightfully claiming that she had deserted him. But when she was just rising to go home to see to her sons, there was a new development. Seymour's manservant came in bringing terrible news. A hackney coach had been seen at the door of the Nortons' home, with the children being bundled into it with their luggage. It had driven off, he did not know where. When she heard this, Caroline, in her distraction, wanted to rush back to her house on foot, and it was all Seymour could do to persuade her to wait a few minutes for the chaise. He then went with her to Storey's Gate. When they got there, the servant's words proved true. The children were gone.

This was the story she told her solemn-faced brother, Brinsley, who sat with her on the couch at Frampton Court. She may have passed over her immediate hysterical reaction to the news, when she had run from room to room in her house, shrieking at the servants to find the boys, but she described carefully how, after she had got over the shock, she had searched London for them, calling at every address connected with Margaret Vaughan. Later she wrote to Melbourne to tell him about it:

Frampton [Postmark: 2 April, 1836]
He has taken my children from me! – You thought me causelessly

irritated in the morning, when he said Miss Vaughan had advised me not to take Spencer out of town [in] such weather. I knew my fool better than you – I saw that some one had meddled in my home. In the evening he picked a quarrel with me about nothing, & then said the children shouldn't go, & forbid the servants to obey my orders. Next morning, while I went to consult Seymour, he put them all into a hackney coach & sent them to Miss Vaughan who sent them to a house agent, and after 4 hours search & baffling, – when I did find them, this agent refused to let me see them, and called in the police! I could hear their little feet running merrily over my head while I sat sobbing below – only the ceiling between us, and I not able to get at them! my little merry Briney! & poor Spencer who had been so ill and was to be so carefully muffled up to go down with me to the sea – all dragged about in damp hackney coaches to get to some place to hide them from their mother . . . I came away without being able even to kiss them & say good bye – if they keep my boys from me I shall go mad.

She added a postscript. Her footman, who had remained loyal, had just sent her a note, saying that Norton had been going among the servants enquiring whether they had ever seen any undue familiarity between his mistress and her author friend, Mr Fitzroy Campbell, or 'any other gentleman who comes to the house'. As Melbourne was one of the 'other gentlemen' Caroline presumably thought he should be warned. She ended her letter on a bitter note, with the reflection that this was the holiday originally intended to calm her down and do her good, whereas Norton's behaviour was very likely to kill her.

Her attitude to Melbourne was now becoming resentful. However unreasonably, it seemed to her that he was, perhaps, partly responsible for the trouble in which she found herself. She also felt that he was not standing by her now that she needed help, and showed signs of casting her off altogether. His visits to Storey's Gate had recently been less frequent, and he had not written immediately to Frampton to give her any sign that he felt for her suffering at the loss of the children.

By 4 April she still had not received a reply from him so she wrote again. She said that she was awaiting a letter from Norton's lawyer, Sir William Follett, which would tell her whether or not her husband would grant her a divorce. If he refused, then she would ask their clergyman, Mr Barlow, the rector of the Duke Street Chapel, to negotiate a separation for her. On the other hand, she said, she might simply give in and return to Norton unconditionally. Her reasons for this were threefold: in her heart she knew that Norton would never agree to any of her terms; she could always leave him again if things got worse; and, above all, by returning, she would get her children back. This last was her greatest priority. If, however, Norton would not give her access to her boys, she said she would abduct them, and take refuge with her friend, Leopold, King of the Belgians. At the end of the letter, she could not resist complaining about Melbourne himself:

> I was looking thro some papers last night for N's own letters . . . and I could not help smiling . . . at the reflection how very small a portion of our very own short lives a single interest is permitted to stand forward and obscure others . . . here is a man, who was mad to marry me at eighteen, who turns me out of his house nine years afterwards & inflicts vengeance as bitterly as he can by taking away the children who were the offspring of that long desired union & cursing me thro' them. And here am I, appealing to you with a mournful conviction of my own folly to try & feel as much for me as you did when you 'could not think what had become of me because I had not written for three days'. Well, well, it is all a folly perhaps . . .'[3]

Of course, she knew that Melbourne would dread the publicity attendant upon the break-up of her marriage. And, very soon, Norton published news of the event to the whole of Society. On 1 April he inserted a newspaper advertisement announcing that Caroline had left his house, and declared that he would no longer be answerable for her debts. As might be expected, this acted as a signal to the editors of the satirical papers to step up their campaign against Melbourne.

Even so, when he eventually replied to her at Frampton, she was dissatisfied with the tepid tone of his letters. There was she, writing once, perhaps twice a day, and pouring out her feelings on paper, whereas he answered only seldom, and when he did so, his words were studied, and guarded. What she could not forgive, was that there was nothing in his letters to let her know that he missed her as much as she did him. Perhaps Brinsley tried to get her to see sense about this. There were good reasons why Melbourne could not be more forthcoming. After all, he was Prime Minister, and had many duties to attend to and official letters to write. It was no good Caroline complaining that, until recently, Melbourne had always made time for her. Melbourne could not write what was in his heart, in case his letters fell into the wrong hands and were used against him. Legally speaking, every letter that Caroline received was her husband's property, because, under the law, a wife's possessions passed to her husband when she married. For this reason, Norton was entitled to seize Melbourne's letters, and even to pass them over to his Tory friends if he wanted to.

Melbourne's first letter to Frampton was a model of caution. It was addressed from Panshanger, where he was taking a holiday:

> April 6th, 1836
>
> I hardly know what to write to you, or what comfort to offer. You know as well as I do, that the best course is to keep yourself tranquil, and not to give way to the feelings of passion which, God knows, are too natural to be easily resisted. This conduct upon his part seems perfectly unaccountable, and, depend upon it, being as you are, in the right, it will be made ultimately to appear, whatever temporary representations may prevail. You cannot have better or more affectionate advisers than you have with you upon the spot, who are well acquainted with the circumstances of the case and the characters of those with whom you have to deal. You know that I have always counselled you to bear everything and remain to the last. I thought it for the best. I am afraid it is no longer possible. Open breaches of this kind are always to be lamented but you have the consolation that you have done your utmost to stave off this as long as possible.[4]

Caroline then received more news from some of her former servants at Storey's Gate. Apparently, Norton was employing private detectives to make enquiries about her friendships with various men. She learned that they had cross-questioned the staff about the visits she had received from Fitzroy Campbell, John Trelawny, Harrison Ainsworth and even the Duke of Devonshire. No doubt they were also interested in her sittings with Benjamin Haydon, the portrait painter, who quite openly declared that he was in love with her. Clearly, Norton was now seeking any scrap of evidence to try to prove that she had committed adultery, though he had no clear idea with whom.

Melbourne's next letter, dated 8 April, was very bitter about Norton:

> It is vain to rail, otherwise I could do so too: but it was at all times easy to see that it [Norton] was the most dangerous and

ill-conditioned creature possible, and that there was nothing that might not be expected from such a creature of folly and malignity . . .[5]

What she wanted most from Melbourne, however, were not observations on Norton's character, but sentiments of affection and words of advice. These Melbourne long withheld. And when, eventually, he did suggest a solution, his words outraged her. She was astounded to read that he actually advised her to go back to live with a man he himself considered to be 'a creature of folly and malignity':

> April 10
>
> Never, to be sure, was there such conduct. To set foot on that sort of enquiry without the slightest ground for it! But it does not surprise me! I have always known that there was there a mixture of folly and violence which might lead to any absurdity or any injustice. You know so well my opinion that it is unnecessary for me to repeat it. I have always told you that a woman should never part from her husband whilst she can remain with him. This is generally the case; particularly in such a case as yours, that is, in the case of a woman of lively imagination, fond of company and conversation, and whose celebrity and superiority has necessarily created many enemies. Depend upon it, if a reconciliation is feasible there can be no doubt of the prudence of it. It is so evident that it is unnecessary to expatiate upon it. Lord Holland, who is almost the only person to mention the subject to me, is of entirely that opinion.
>
> Yours
> Melbourne[6]

Caroline stayed on at Frampton for nearly the whole of April, trying to work out what to do. During that time, Melbourne persisted in his opinion that she should return to the very husband for whom, in the same letters, he could not conceal his contempt. On 19 April he wrote to say: 'If, for the sake of the children, you think you can endure to return to him, you certainly will act most wisely and prudently for yourself in doing so.'

Then came a development which amazed her. One day, towards the end of the month, there was a knock at her door and the servant announced the arrival of Mr Barlow, her clergyman from London. Barlow was still acting as an intermediary between herself and her husband, and she may have hoped that he brought good news, perhaps even a familiar request from Norton for her forgiveness. But Barlow's news was of a very different kind. Far from suing for peace, Norton now claimed that she had committed adultery, and was about to bring an action against her supposed lover for 'criminal conversation'. The man named was Lord Melbourne.

Oddly enough, this possibility seems never to have occurred to Caroline. She would not have been surprised had Norton named Trelawny, or Haydon, for she had flirted with these men in public, probably to make him jealous. But she never seems to have anticipated that he would accuse Melbourne. There are several possible reasons for this. One is that Norton may have colluded originally in her relationship with the Prime Minister. It is more likely, however, that Caroline so admired Melbourne's intelligence, imagination and ability, that she could not conceive how any person, not even one as obtuse as Norton, could have the impertinence to criticize a being so immeasurably superior to himself. Nevertheless, had she thought about it, she might have admitted that her husband had some grounds for suspicion. After all, Melbourne had been making private visits to her three times a week for the last five years, and the Tory press had been printing gossip about their friendship during that time. Even Caroline's family had suggested that she should be a little more discreet in the relationship. Yet she persisted in arguing that the allegation was a preposterous one. After all, Melbourne was nearly thirty years older than her, and the Prime Minister. She did not even know for sure that a Prime Minister could be tried in court.

But, when she had more time to think about it, she was appalled by Norton's allegation. Perhaps for the first time, she began to perceive how their friendship might disgrace Melbourne and bring down his government. She could not bear to think of the worry and embarrassment she had brought him. Her only refuge was the hope that her husband would not really go through with the action, and would cry off when he had forced sufficient concessions from her. In late April, she wrote to Melbourne again:

> Barlow has been very kind; he is going to try & see Norton tomorrow and I have written a few lines to Norton that Barlow may read to him. I have of course not mentioned you, I am supposed, & will to the last possible minute appear ignorant of this new accusation . . .
> I recoil from this burning disgrace, with an agony, which is

perhaps triumph to those who inflict it, but I will yet hope it may not be . . . N is unwilling, most unwilling himself to bring you forward. Grantley, & perhaps other Tories have urged him to do so . . .

I perceive your enemies join mine. Do nothing till you hear from me tomorrow, & for the present suppose us to be on the point of reconciliation. We have time before us. I think Barlow will do good. I dare say even now, all may end without scandal . . .[7]

But Melbourne did not agree that all would be well. The tone of his letters became more despairing, and more virulent towards her husband. He wrote to say of Norton: 'You seem to me to be hardly aware of what a GNOME he is. In my opinion he has somehow or other made this whole matter subservient to his pecuniary interest.' For Melbourne was now convinced that Norton had selected him as co-respondent simply to get the highest damages possible. He felt that whether or not Norton really believed his allegation to be true was beside the point. His Tory brother, Lord Grantley, and his Tory guardian, Lord Wynford, may have egged him on for their own political reasons, but money, not politics, was Norton's motive.

Caroline was never so much alone as during that Easter at Frampton, surrounded by her family. She knew that her affairs formed the only topic of conversation among her relations but, whenever she entered the dining room, Brinsley, Marcia and her mother would break off their talk and turn to something else. She tried to absent herself as much as possible, and spent long hours walking the gravel paths, and standing on the little balustraded stone bridge.[8] Perhaps she fancied that she caught some faint image of her children's faces in the water. For their loss was still her greatest grief and overshadowed even her concern for Melbourne. What made things worse was that she did not know for sure where they were, only that they were among strangers who did not care about them. For Margaret Vaughan had never liked children, and, as for the Grantleys, they were too cold and selfish to treat anyone with kindness. Caroline was dreadfully worried about Fletcher, who needed nursing, and she dreaded that William would cry for her every night. But it was Brinny for whom she was most concerned. He had a fiercely loyal nature and would never allow anyone to criticize her without protesting; she guessed that Margaret Vaughan would beat him for it. Then, she heard from a servant that the boys had been sent down to Lord Grantley's place at Wonersh. They seemed further away than ever.

At night she withdrew soon after dinner and sat up late in her room writing letters. To her mind, everything now depended upon whether Norton would drop his charge. She still believed that a trial was unlikely, if only because she could not imagine a Prime Minister being tried in open court. And there were still negotiations going on, with Mr Barlow talking sweet reason between the parties. But, ominously, Brinsley advised her to appoint a legal adviser, so she retained her lawyer uncle, Sir James Graham. Towards the end of the month, she could endure the smothering peace of Frampton no longer and decided to go to London to see Barlow, her Uncle James, and even her husband if he agreed. She hoped it was still not too late to persuade Norton to call off his action.

XIV

SCANDAL

FOR SEVERAL YEARS before her flight to Frampton, Caroline had been a favourite target for *The Satirist* newspaper. At first, it had hinted that she was the mistress of Captain Thomas Duncombe, a good-looking young dandy with a weakness for fighting duels; then, for a short time, it had made insinuations about her friendship with the Duke of Devonshire; but finally, all its innuendo was directed to her friendship with Melbourne. The previous spring, when Caroline had been pregnant again, and, at the same time, awaiting the publication of her book, *The Wife, and Woman's Reward*, *The Satirist* made great fun with her in their issue of 3 May, suggesting that Melbourne had an interest in both productions:

A REVISE

'When will the work be finished you are now engaged about,'
    said MELBOURNE; 'when, I mean, will it, fair CAROLINE
    BE OUT?'
'Within a week or two, I hope,' she quietly repeats,
'You'll see me free of Proof and press, revised and bound
    in sheets.'

The paper followed up this line with a review of the book which implied that Melbourne was indeed the father of Caroline's child:

Mrs Norton's New Work, 'The Wife', is thought to contain some passages of her own life, veiled of course for prudent reasons, with a large share of fiction. The present Premier, during his late retirement from office, was kind enough, it is said, to look over the loose sheets, in order that the work might receive the finishing touches which his Lordship's judgement suggested. The fair Caroline has reasons to be proud of the Premier's condescension.

There followed in the summer months a series of scurrilous verses, more or less indecent, all suggesting that Caroline and Melbourne were lovers. The writers especially loved to pun on Melbourne's family name, which was 'Lamb':

THE WOLF IN LAMB'S CLOTHING

'Lord MELBOURNE, Tom, has proved to me, by favours
  without end,'
said CAROLINE'S fond hubby, 'an invaluable friend.'
'Indeed', quoth DUNCOMBE, judging well the sheepish
  statesman's fleece,
'Take care the Lamb prove not the Wolf to your domestic
  peace.'[1]

A LAMB-POON

'Though it for ever my renown may blot,
I'll still stand up, dear CAROLINE for thee,
For, Oh! How oft (the marriage vows forgot!),
Hast thou consented to lie down for me.'
                    MELBOURNE Downing Street[2]

REFORM

'It's cold,' quoth NORTON, 'very cold indeed,
'Mongst other things pray MELBOURNE, do reform it.'
'If of reform,' said he, 'you stand in need,
the shortest way, dear CAROLINE's to warm it.'[3]

In July, the paper recycled the joke about Melbourne's alleged paternity:

'Norton's new work is to be dedicated to Melbourne – is it not?'
asked Lady Tullamore. 'Yes', replied Mrs Lane Fox, 'and it is, I
hear, now lie-ing in sheets awaiting only the leisure of the
publishers to present it to the world.'

And though, soon after these pieces appeared, Caroline miscarried and was very ill, *The Satirist* still continued its fun:

MELTING MOMENTS

How comes it, gentle Melbourne, pray
  That when the tide of love runs high,
Men turn their eyes upon the clay,
  Instead of gazing upon the sky?
While in that hour of tender mirth,

To our more gentle sex 'tis given
To turn our backs upon the earth,
And lift our pious eyes to heaven!

The treatment accorded to Norton had changed as time went on. At first he was depicted as an affectionate buffoon, who had remained blithely unaware of his wife's liaison with Melbourne, while the cuckold's horns sprouted on his head. Alternatively, it was implied that, far from being simple, Norton was cold and cunning, and had known all about Caroline's affair with Melbourne from the start. Indeed, it was said that he had sold his wife to Melbourne, in return for various well-paid jobs.

'Melbourne really ought to do something more for Norton', observed Lord Edward Seymour to the ex-editress of the Court Journal. 'Upon my word' responded Caroline sarcastically casting a glance at the os frontis of the Lambeth Street Dogberry, 'I think he has done quite enough'.[4]

Another opinion of Norton, promoted by some papers, was that he was a typical member of an amoral, sensual, upper-class set, led by Caroline's brother-in-law, Edward Lord Seymour, or 'Noddy' as his friends called him. Seymour himself was characterized in *The Satirist* by having said that polygamy was unnecessary and expensive because: 'by taking the wives of our friends and neighbours we save the trouble of their keep you know'.[5]

It was such publicity appearing throughout 1835 which probably began to frighten Melbourne off. Nevertheless, Caroline's decision in late April 1836, to return to London from Frampton, was partly brought about by the hope that he would see her again. After much begging on her part, her brother conducted her back to his town house in Grosvenor Square on the 22nd, and she stayed there for some weeks. Her position was now a most peculiar one, for she was a gentlewoman with no home to go to. Of course she knew that her relatives, the Sheridans and the Seymours, would offer her hospitality indefinitely, but she was too proud to accept more than a temporary home. Besides, she sensed she would soon become an embarrassment to them. Their friends and guests read the newspapers, and many might now not be willing to meet her socially. So she decided to remain with Brinsley and Marcia at Grosvenor Square for only a brief time, during which she would find out whether or not Norton was going to go ahead

with his case. If he agreed to withdraw, she would have to decide on
what conditions she was prepared to go back to him. If he persisted
with his action, she would take up residence in a small select hotel, so
that she might evade the world. Even to do that, she was obliged to
borrow money from her brother, for she had none of her own.

In the meantime, the faithful Brinsley wanted her close to him, so
that she might consult him about every letter that came. The chief
go-between with Norton was Mr Barlow, though Colonel Stanhope
was also trying to get him to see reason. One day at the end of April,
Barlow came round to see her directly after talking to Norton. He sat
with her for nearly two hours, to tell her how he had been received.
Norton, apparently, had declared that he would neither read a letter
from her, nor have it read to him. He behaved, said Barlow, like an
ungovernable child, and 'foamed and stamped, & rambled from one
accusation to another so that it was impossible to make out what he
wanted or who he meant to attack'.[6] Brinsley, meanwhile, had been
to see the famous barrister, Dr Stephen Lushington, who, even though
he was ill, had agreed to act as counsel to her uncle and legal adviser,
Sir James Graham. Brinsley told her that Lushington had acted as
counsel for Queen Caroline in her divorce trial in 1820, and had also
represented Lady Byron in her separation proceedings with the poet.[7]
Despite all her troubles, Caroline probably felt a thrill of pleasure at
the thought of this flattering connection with women in cases of such
distinguished notoriety.

In late April, she paid another uninvited visit to Melbourne, at
Downing Street. Again he was appalled at her sudden appearance in
that place, and she was made very aware that she had become a
profound embarrassment to him, both personally and politically. But
she had felt that she had to see him once more, if only to break the
dreadful news that she was now quite sure that Norton would go
ahead with his action. Shortly afterwards, she wrote Melbourne a
note:

> I will not deny that among all the bitterness of this hour, what
> sinks me most is the thought of you – of the expression of your
> eye the day I told you at D[ow]n[in]g St – the shrinking from me
> & my burdensome & embarassing [sic] distress . . .
>   . . . God forgive you, for I do believe no one, young or old,
> ever loved another better than I have loved you. I 'trust to truth
> and you' . . .
>   . . . I don't much care how it ends. I have always the knowledge

that you will be afraid to see much of me – perhaps afraid to see me at all. I have always the memory of how you received me that day . . .

. . . I will not write again, because you seem to dread it. I'm sorry to have been a vexation to you . . .[8]

Of course she did write to him again, just before she left Grosvenor Square, to tell him that Barlow had still not heard that Norton would withdraw his action, but that, anyhow, she had made up her mind to go back to her husband if he would have her, so that she might see her 'poor boys' again.

This decision, to return to the man she detested, is a measure of the pain Caroline felt at the loss of her children. Once, when she learned that they had been brought back to London, she loitered in the early morning outside the house where they were kept, and Brinny was just able to give her 'a little crumpled letter, which he had had in his pocket a fortnight', before Norton's servant intervened.[9] As a result of this incident, the boys were sent off again to Wonersh, and one day she went down there with the intention of stealing them away. But, as she explained to Lord Melbourne: 'I failed. I saw them all; carried Brin to the gate, could not open it, and was afraid they would tear him to pieces, they caught him so fiercely. And the elder one was so frightened he did not follow.'[10]

On another dreadful day, she was cross-examined by Lord Melbourne's defence lawyer as part of the preparation of his client's case. No doubt she also thought that she was helping to defend her own reputation at the same time. In the event, she was deeply upset by this barrister. Naturally, he asked her questions which probed at every weak spot in Melbourne's defence. He wanted to know about her meetings with Melbourne, their intentions, motives and propriety. Caroline was deeply shocked by the cross-examinaton. She had assumed that she would be treated as a gentlewoman whose obvious innocence had been affronted. Instead, she was asked what she thought were coarse, and insinuating questions, and treated with what seemed like open contempt. She had barely been accorded the courtesy appropriate to a lady. It amazed her to discover that this lawyer actually thought that she might be guilty. She complained to Melbourne, who replied:

South Street, June 9th, 1836
I do not wonder at the impression made upon you. I knew it

would be so, and therefore I was most unwilling to have the interview take place at all. All the attorneys I have ever seen have the same manner: hard, cold, incredulous, distrustful, sarcastic, sneering. They are said to be conversant with the worst part of human nature, and with the most discreditable transactions. They have so many falsehoods told them, that they place confidence in none.[11]

Melbourne, during this time, had become ill with worry. He had little appetite and could not sleep. He told Caroline in a letter, that, as a result of Norton's action, he now suffered more intensely than he had ever done before. He went on to assure her, however, that his concern was not for himself or the political consequences of Norton's action, but because of the anxiety and solicitude he felt for her. Later she heard that he had taken to his bed and remained there during the last two weeks of May. As the June days passed, and it was announced that the action of Norton versus Melbourne would be heard on the 22nd of the month, she learned that he still kept to his bed, and sent apologies to official meetings and receptions on the grounds that he was too ill to attend.[12]

Caroline sensed now that Melbourne was in a panic, and she shared his concern. For the unthinkable was about to take place; an action for adultery was to be brought against a Prime Minister in office. It was only when this realization became public that the tone of even the Tory newspapers began to change. Previously, the friendship of Caroline and Melbourne had been a joking matter; now, the increasing likelihood that the Prime Minister really would go on trial, made the business much more serious. For example, as recently as Sunday 15 May 1836, *Bell's Life in London* had predicted an action for crim-con 'against a Noble Lord not very low in the Administration for being NORTY with a lady'. By 22 May, however, the same paper gravely reported the 'severe indisposition' of Viscount Melbourne, and assured its readers that: 'We understand his Lordship treats with contempt the rumours respecting his supposed intimacy with a fashionable "Blue-Stocking".' On 5 June, the same paper announced even more solemnly that an action was to be brought against Viscount Melbourne by Mr Norton 'to recover damages for crim.con', and that the damages were to be set at £10,000. The trial, it commented, would put an end to speculation: 'The proof of the pudding is in the eating'.

Caroline's grief for her children did not diminish her awareness of the gravity of the situation for Melbourne and his government. She had been brought up in a political family, and understood the significance of the impending trial for the Whig Party. And she perfectly understood that, though Melbourne was genuinely concerned for her in the matter, he was right to be even more alarmed for himself and his government. But she may not have appreciated what was his chief anxiety in the case. This concerned the hundreds of notes he had dashed off to her during their six-year friendship. These letters might have meant trouble for him, not because they contained evidence of an adulterous relationship with Caroline (Melbourne was far too old a fox to put that sort of thing on paper) but because, in the guise of light-hearted gossip, they included many indiscreet remarks about his political friends, which could have undermined him if made public. The trouble was that Melbourne could not remember what he had written about his colleagues. That is why he was in a panic. He knew that ridicule of fellow Cabinet Ministers was just as likely to bring down a government as evidence of sexual impropriety. He was so worried about it all, that he went to the King and talked of resigning. But William IV would not hear of such a thing. What was more, the Duke of Wellington, who had challenged his own mistress to 'publish and be damned', told Melbourne that he himself would never have resigned on such a matter, and would not join any Tory faction that aimed to profit from it.[13] But still Melbourne was racked with gloom.

In mid-June Caroline moved from her brother's house to Hill's Hotel, 18 Spring Gardens, Westminster. She now went out very little during the day, and then only to see her lawyer, or her family. Much of her time was spent writing, either for her annuals, or else letters to her friends. One of her new friends was Mary Shelley, the widow of the poet and the daughter of the philosopher, the late William Godwin, and his first wife, the feminist Mary Wollstonecraft. Godwin had recently died and his civil list pension had died with him, leaving his second wife almost penniless. The Godwins and the Shelleys were names still so scandalous that there were few in these increasingly strait-laced days who were sympathetic to the plight of this old woman. But Mary begged Caroline to try to get an extension of Godwin's pension to take in the remaining life of his widow, and, despite all the troubles which she was facing, and the fact that she was reluctant to ask Melbourne any favours, Caroline made time to write to ask him to do something for Mrs Godwin. In this she was partly successful, for though he told her that pensions could not be transferred, Melbourne saw to it that Mrs Godwin was given a small annuity from the King's bounty.

Caroline Norton seated beneath the portrait of her grandfather,
Richard Brinsley Sheridan

Richard Brinsley Sheridan, painted by J. Russell
(*National Portrait Gallery*)

Frampton Court, Dorset, the home of Caroline's brother, Richard Brinsley Sheridan

Queen Victoria's adored first Prime Minister,
William Lamb, second Viscount Melbourne,
painted by John Partridge (*National Portrait Gallery*)

Caroline Norton; a detail from
a painting by Frank Stone (*National Portrait Gallery*)

Sidney Herbert, painted by F. Grant c. 1847
(*National Portrait Gallery*)

Mary Shelley, painted by Richard Rothwell c. 1840
(*National Portrait Gallery*)

Memorial window to Fletcher Norton in Frampton Church, Dorset,
presented by his mother

Caroline also continued to dine out, though her invitations were fewer, and came chiefly from relatives or very old friends. The Sheridans and Seymours were totally loyal to her. Far from acknowledging Caroline's social notoriety, her brothers and sisters always included her among their guests, and made a point of letting it be known beforehand that she would be present. Such a gesture amounted to a public declaration of faith in her innocence. They took the view that if other guests chose not to come to their houses because Caroline was to be present, then that was their misjudgement. Of course, these evenings were still an ordeal for Caroline, for, as the date of the trial approached, she knew that her relationship with Lord Melbourne was the chief topic of conversation in every drawing room she entered. But she held her head high, and pretended not to notice the frequent coldness of her reception, or the whisperings that started in the corner when she turned away. She probably much preferred the intimate dinner parties of another new friend, the barrister, Abraham Hayward. Here, most of the guests were people of artistic rather than social distinction. It was, perhaps, a mistake for her to go to such dinners, for they did her reputation no good. This was because, as a result of the scandal about her, Hayward did not feel that he could invite any other ladies. So, when Caroline arrived late, dressed in pink, 'with a black lace veil and her dark hair drawn smoothly back',[14] she was often the only woman at the dinner-table, and the men sitting round the table were obliged to compete for her teasing attention.

Yet, beneath her dining-room levity, she was aghast at the plight she found herself in. It seemed to her that she had thrown her life away, and now found herself in a situation in which she might go down to history as the scarlet woman who disgraced Melbourne and brought down the Whigs. She was often angry with herself because she seemed incapable of discretion. Even now she had learned nothing, and would always take the opportunity to create a drama between herself and a man. She loved the shared intimacy of a lifted eyebrow, a whispered confidence, or a moment of outrageous flirtation. But she reflected bitterly that, in the end she had to pay, and so did her intimates. Melbourne knew that now. She remembered his horrified face, when she had seen him during her last uninvited visit to Downing Street. She had written to him afterwards: 'If you knew all the struggle it was to go to you at all – all the pain it was to say it to you – all the hopelessness with which I set out – your manner would have been kinder than it was.'[15]

As the date of the trial approached, so her terror grew. Now she kept to her room at Hill's Hotel, spending the daylight hours scribbling more notes to Brinsley, Georgiana, Barlow and, especially, to Melbourne. Her comfort was that a verdict of 'not proven' for Melbourne would vindicate her own reputation. But daily, the consequences of a 'guilty' verdict became more enormous in her mind. It seemed to her that, if she became responsible for the fall of the Melbourne Government, she would be the most scandalous woman in history.

At this dramatic moment in her life, Caroline may have been struck by the resemblance between the events in which she found herself involved, and the plot of her grandfather's most famous play. *The School for Scandal* was prophetic for her. At the end of Act IV, the flirtatious Lady Teazle ('Tease-All') is discovered in a strange man's room, while her husband looks on in horror, and the rest of Society with delight. Though Lady Teazle's only real fault has been indiscretion, everyone now believes her to be guilty of infidelity. In a moment, she has lost her reputation.

When the play was first performed on the night of 8 May 1777 at Drury Lane, it was said that passers-by were startled by a great shout followed by a burst of applause louder than had ever sounded from a theatre. The screen had fallen on Lady Teazle. The theatre audience understood, however, that she was not really an adulteress but a vain, rash, foolish young wife. It was the climax to Richard Brinsley Sheridan's masterpiece. After the performance, he went out into the drunken, scandalous darkness of the London streets, howling and shouting in his ecstasy. To quieten him, the nightwatchman knocked him down and locked him up.

Perhaps Caroline saw the omen in the tale. Her grandfather had already written her story, and now he was laughing at her.

All the long day, while the trial was taking place, Caroline stood at the window at Hampton Court or walked the paths, seeing nothing but memories of her past life. At times she was aware of the anxious glances of her mother, or of the attentions of servants with their gentle enquiries about her welfare. But her mind was not on them, nor on ancient rooms and gardens. She had spent the day with visions from the past: her mother's white face when she returned from the Cape in her widow's weeds; George Norton burning her letters; Lord Melbourne on the sofa at Storey's Gate; and little Brinny, torn screaming from her arms at Wonersh Park.

She sighed, and shuddered. The June day was nearly done, and the courts of Hampton now entirely in shadow. Her brother had promised to let her know the outcome of the first day, but neither he nor his messenger had arrived. She could not understand it. The judge would surely have adjourned the proceedings by six o'clock, and it would take a swift rider only an hour to get there. It was half past seven now. She heard her mother call her for dinner.

The two women sat alone as darkness gathered in the room. Caroline could hardly eat a thing, but pretended to do so, to please Mrs Sheridan. She took no wine. On several occasions she started up at the fancied beat of a horse's hooves, but still nobody came. After dinner, they sat on either side of the fire. Though it was June, Mrs Sheridan had had one lit. At first Caroline pretended to sew but, soon after the candles were brought in, she gave up all pretence and simply sat. Her mother did not irritate her with talk, though both wondered why Brinsley did not come. And there they sat, till long after the clock sounded midnight.

XV

VERDICTS

IT WAS NEARLY MIDNIGHT at the Westminster Court of Common Pleas but the onlookers had kept their seats all day. The ushers had placed candlesticks along the tables but Lord Justice Tindall could see little into the dark well of the court, and only sensed the presence of the public by the chattering or sighs of disapproval. He could hardly see the foreman and so repeated his question. Was the jury prepared to retire to consider its verdict? He was sure that they would ask for an adjournment until the next day.

They did not. The judge could not easily make out what was happening on the jury benches but it seemed that the foreman had risen as if unsure what to do. He was bending over the other members and listening to their whispered replies. This moment of indecision started a burst of coughing and muttering in the courtroom. The event also seemed to have communicated itself to those outside the court, for doors opened to squeeze in yet more dark bodies, and the draughts they admitted set the candles guttering along the benches.

The foreman coughed and cleared his throat. There was, he said respectfully, no need for the jury to withdraw. He paused and raised the volume of his voice. 'It is my duty to say that we have agreed a verdict for the defendant.'

There were shouts of 'Bravo' and 'Good old Melbourne' from the courtroom, as well as hisses and groans from the Norton supporters. At once the judge directed the police to bring before him anyone who behaved improperly, but this did not prevent more shouting and booing when the news reached the street outside. It was soon over. The hour was too late for the mob to have their fun. Lord Tindall retired exhausted. Charles Dickens went off briskly to write his piece for *The Morning Chronicle* and Serjeant Talfourd hurried after him, no doubt hoping to discuss the day's events over a glass of wine. Richard Brinsley Sheridan left as quickly as he could. He still had to take the news to Hampton Court.

When Sir John Campbell was able to get out, past the proffered handshakes of his swollen band of admirers, he had been in court for twelve continuous hours. He thought it best to go to the House of Commons at once, for he knew that it would still be sitting, and his Party leaders would expect to consult with him. When he arrived, he found that the news of his victory had preceded him, and he was greeted with a roar of approval and the waving of order papers from the Whig benches. The Party had triumphed. Melbourne was saved, the Whig Party was saved, the Government was saved, and it was Campbell who had done it. That was their verdict. For the first time he sensed the full significance of the result he had secured. He felt, like the Duke of Wellington after Waterloo, 'not knowing so great a victory had been achieved'. Even the ranks of Torydom on the opposite benches could scarce forbear him a rather thin cheer. In the lobbies the Tories were now openly saying that it had been a dirty business from the start, and God forbid that their political hopes should depend on such a case as this. They said that if Wynford and Grantley had encouraged this court action, then they had done the Tory Party no favours. Campbell smiled. It was the greatest triumph of his long political career. Later, Lord Malmesbury was heard to say that: 'Melbourne had had more opportunities than any man had had before and had made no use of them'.[1]

A junior solicitor had left the courtroom that night with a more romantic vision of events. This young man, who was one day to become Chief Justice Bushe, trudged through the dark streets of the West End until he came to No. 2 Storey's Gate, where he stopped, 'looking with curiosity at the house, speculating over the dramatic incidents of the day'. There was a light burning in the upper bedroom, for George Norton was still in residence; but there was no light in the first-floor sitting room. And among the geraniums on the balcony, he saw no slim young figure, leaning out to smell the summer blossoms in St James's Park.

A hand fell on his shoulder. 'What does this mean, Mr Solicitor?' came a gruff voice, and he turned in brief alarm. It was Lord Melbourne. The Prime Minister looked fit and well. His manner was jocular. Clearly, the verdict had, at a stroke, restored him to health. Together the two men looked up a moment at the darkened house, and then turned to walk towards clubland. Bushe had difficulty in keeping up with his tall companion, for Lord Melbourne was bounding with good spirits. He knew that the case would do him no harm, indeed, it would merely add to his reputation as a cheerful old roué.

Now he could see how he might yet win through to become the first Prime Minister of the new Queen's reign.

Caroline awoke with a start in her chair, to find her mother had risen. There had been a sound from the courtyard below. It was the gate. A horse clattered across the yard. Caroline rose, and Mrs Sheridan held up her candle to see the door. There was a sound of voices below and then of footfalls on the stair. For an age, two pairs of boots sounded along the corridor, till the far door opened to reveal another candle held aloft. It moved towards them, some feet in the air, till the feeble flames united in fighting off the gloomy reaches of the room. The servant stood back and a messenger hurried forward. It was Brinsley. Melbourne was not guilty.

Caroline turned away, her heart singing. He was not guilty. And if he was not guilty, then, surely, she was not guilty. No-one could blame her now. She could go about again without a stain on her character. Norton would have to give her her children back. But she would not have to live with him. She could become a free and independent woman, living her own life as a writer. Everything was possible now that she had regained her reputation.

But England was asleep. Before Caroline had woken in the morning, respectable professional men would have read *The Times*, or *The Morning Chronicle*, and reflected that old Melbourne was lucky to have got away with it. But their wives were more interested in Caroline. As they read of the goings-on at Storey's Gate, they were almost unanimous in their verdict. She was a scandalous woman.

Was Caroline guilty? No-one ever saw her in bed with Melbourne but, as the judge remarked, that was not a requirement in a successful action for adultery. Furthermore, she and Melbourne had had ample opportunities for an affair, they both detested Norton, and they were very fond of each other. Melbourne is unlikely to have had any moral scruples in the matter, because he was a relic from the promiscuous Regency period. Besides, he had had a number of love affairs before he ever met Caroline.

Yet Melbourne made a solemn declaration to his defence counsel, that he was innocent of any impropriety with Caroline, and he repeated this statement years later. This must bear some weight because, though not a believer in God, he had a strong respect for the truth. His testimony seems to be borne out by the letters that passed between them in future years, for never once do these suggest that they had been lovers in the sexual sense. Indeed, though her letters reveal a growing realization in Caroline that she had been in love with Melbourne all the time, they also assume a common knowledge between them that they are guiltless. For example, in June 1836, the very month of the trial, she wrote to Melbourne to say: 'I will not vex you further. I will wait, (with what calmness I can, after three weeks daily suspence [*sic*] & discomfort) and hope that *what was not* cannot be proved.'[2] It is difficult to understand why she should write 'what was not', if they both knew that it was. Of course she might have written this deliberately, as a 'plant', hoping that George Norton would seize the correspondence and be confronted with apparent evidence of their innocence, but this seems unlikely. Caroline was not that sort of a schemer.

Despite her admiration for Romantic poets, she was no rebel against accepted modes of thought. Indeed, her problem was that she was essentially conventional though not respectable, and because of this, she was at odds with the spirit of the age. When Melbourne first met her, she was full of life but looking for masculine sympathy. This he could supply. For her part, she offered him company, admiration, gaiety and affection, and he probably settled for these. She was also something of a tease but he had to put up with it. The relationship flattered them both. Caroline luxuriated in her intimacy with such a great man, whereas Melbourne, who liked to cultivate his reputation, was not averse to being seen so regularly in the company of this pretty, witty young woman. Inevitably, as the years went on, something else developed between them. It was a passionate, intimate friendship. Caroline could never shake it off.

They were probably innocent of adultery. Caroline was astonished to find that, after the trial, public opinion still condemned her. Her response was something of a paradox. She decided that, if in the face of the evidence people persisted in treating her as a scandalous woman, in the future she might just as well behave like one.

PART TWO

A Woman's Life

XVI

A Woman Waiting

It was very quiet in the Mayfair sitting room where the sixty-nine-year-old Caroline Norton dozed in her wheelchair. When she awoke, the room was dark; there were few sounds from the Chesterfield Street outside, and only the occasional rustling of the parakeets in her aviary. She guessed it was noon. While she had slept, her old servant had covered the birds and drawn her curtains. From the kitchen below, she caught the chink of plates and the familiar smell of roast dinner. Her cook had been instructed to make a special meal that day to welcome her guest.

But he had not come! The disappointment came rushing upon her. He had written to say that he would be arriving that day, and she had calculated that, if he had taken the overnight train from Stirling, he should certainly have been with her by that time. She could only guess that he had been delayed at the House of Commons. His letter had hinted that there were great matters impending. Perhaps the Prime Minister, Lord Beaconsfield, had offered him a government post, or even a seat in the Lords. She assumed that this was the reason why he was calling on her. He would be flushed with success, and wanting someone to tell. Why else would he want to see an old woman such as herself?

Her servant came to draw back the curtains, and to tell her that dinner would soon be ready. Once again the faces of old friends peered out at her from their heavy frames on wall and mantelshelf. Here was Disraeli, now Lord Beaconsfield. It was in her company that he had first proclaimed his ambition to become Prime Minister, and she remembered how, in kindness, Lord Melbourne had tried to put him off. The room was full of the pictures and books she had collected during the forty years she had lived in Mayfair. Norton had not let her take a thing from Storey's Gate, so most of the furniture had come from her uncle, Charles Sheridan, or her mother at Hampton Court. Among the bric-à-brac her eye sought out the picture of her friend, ever boyish in his homespun tweed. A sigh escaped her while she sat there, waiting.

*

Caroline first came to live in Mayfair in October 1836, just a few months after the trial. She could not bear to go on living with her mother at Hampton Court. For a few days in June of that year, just after she had heard that Lord Melbourne had won, the Sheridans were euphoric, but a reaction quickly set in, and she became depressed. After all the excitement came – nothing. She had nothing to do but wait to learn what provision Norton would allow for her and her boys. She had expected a communication from him immediately after the trial but it seemed he was in no hurry, and it was all a question of solicitors' letters. So she had to sit about at Hampton Court through the dusty July days, while her mother suffocated her with kindness.

At first she paid little attention to anyone, for her mind was still racing with the great events she had lived through. But when at last she was able to focus upon her mother's words, she discovered that Mrs Sheridan, even at this late stage, was beginning to voice her doubts. Caroline wrote to tell Lord Melbourne that her mother had urged her, 'if it be true, what is alledged [sic] – to inform Brin & Seymour of the fact, – to be sincere with my own friends [and to] consider that a false defence will only aggravate my case'.[1] She was startled to discover that her mother doubted her, and became very angry about it. For a time, the atmosphere in the apartment was difficult.

Then her rage gave way to lassitude. Hampton Court began to oppress her with its size and gloom. She fretted for her boys. By late June she had not seen them for three whole months but they were always in her thoughts, and she was full of forebodings that they were being ill-treated by the malicious Miss Vaughan, or the cold-hearted Grantleys. It seemed outrageous to her that her husband would not let her have her boys at once, especially as William was only a baby, and needed his mother urgently.

But still Norton did not write to say when she might have them back. Even Melbourne rarely wrote, and she dreaded that he had cast her off for good. What is more, the realities of her curious position now began to be apparent to her. She had no money, and no prospect of having any until Norton made her an allowance. She was living on the charity of her mother, and, when she needed a little pocket money, she was obliged to borrow it from Brinsley. All these things conspired to depress her. She complained of feeling 'ill and weary', and, by the end of July, she wrote to Lord Melbourne that she had 'spit blood twice, for two or three days at a time, this last fortnight'.[2] She began to convince herself that she would soon succumb to the family disease of tuberculosis in a dramatic deathbed scene. So she began to cough. No doubt she reflected with grim satisfaction that they would all be sorry when she died, her mother, George Norton, and, above all, Lord Melbourne.

She would have felt more cheerful had she enjoyed a little company at Hampton Court, but she soon became aware that her mother rarely invited guests to their rooms, and, when she did, only very old friends. If they went out, it was only ever to their relatives, the Sheridans and the Seymours. Caroline soon realized that Mrs Sheridan was apprehensive of the reception her daughter would get. At first she was incredulous at the idea, for she still assumed that Melbourne's acquittal would restore her own reputation, but now her mother's doubts began to prepare her for the thought that many Society matrons might regard her as unfit company for their daughters. She was indignant. Melbourne had lost nothing at all by the trial, because he was a man, but she, who had not even been given the chance to tell her side of the story, was now under a shadow. She became convinced of this after several difficult evenings running the gauntlet of guests at her relations' houses. At one such reception, she met an old friend named Douglas Kinnaird, who told her that he had recently attended a dinner party, where he had 'caught' a dislike for her from the assembled company. There had been 'much abuse and fault-finding' of her.[3] The patronizing tolerance extended to her by more liberal-minded Whig families was probably even more upsetting to her but she had to learn to endure it. Once she joined a house party at Cresselly, near Tenby, where another guest, a Miss Fanny Allen, wrote an account of the visit to her niece:

> You will not guess whom we are meeting here today, so I may as well tell you. You know we are not fastidious in the morals of our lady friends from examples of the Countess Guiccioli [one of Byron's mistresses] and Mrs Norton is our expected guest – Lady Cawdor has just gone, but says she should have no objection to meeting Mrs Norton at all. Though the trial revealed a mode of going on that was rather strange and not altogether respectable, her guilt or innocence she put out of the question.[4]

Caroline had gone to Cresselly with her half-uncle, Charles Sheridan, and it was he who rescued her from Hampton Court. He was a bachelor, aged forty, with literary ambitions. He had long wanted to take a house in the West End of London but needed company. He now suggested to Caroline that she should join him at 16 Green Street, and that they should also offer a home to her handsome twenty-year-old brother, Charlie. Her Uncle Charles had a private income but he was proud to have published a translation of the Romaic songs, and now wanted to set himself up as some sort of writer. He pointed out that, if Caroline joined him, she could go on writing her scrapbooks and poems, and so make an income for herself. They would scribble in adjoining rooms. Caroline was also aware that Green Street was at the centre of fashionable London, and only a few steps from South Street, where Lord Melbourne lived. She forgot her cough at once, and accepted the invitation.

They moved into Green Street during the autumn of 1836. From the first, Caroline delighted in her new-found existence, despite the fact that a Mayfair address was no help to a woman trying to restore her reputation. For the area was not only the home of the aristocracy, but had long been recognized as the haunt of prostitutes. It took its name from the annual fair held behind St James's Palace, which dated back to the days of Edward I, but which had become a noticeable nuisance during the Restoration. By that time, fine ladies and gentlemen playing at pall-mall in the park, or walking to their elegant homes along its northern boundary, were beginning to object to the continued presence of footpads, drunks and whores, so Charles II put the fair down, though, for a brief while under James II, it was permitted to return for two weeks each spring. When the fashionable streets and squares were laid out in the eighteenth century, they were called after local aristocratic landowners, such as Sir Thomas Bond and Lady Berkeley, but the area still took its name from the old May Fair. By the turn of the nineteenth century, the fair had again been suppressed and London's most fashionable quarter had been fully developed into the grid of terraces and piazzas bounded by Piccadilly, Park Lane, Oxford Street and Regent Street. Mayfair was now the unrivalled urban haunt of Society people, but, even so, this most elegant quarter was highly favoured by the demi-monde. When Thomas Shepherd built a new market place on the old fair-ground site, to serve the growing needs of the area, it soon became a centre for prostitutes as well as tradesmen. During Caroline's lifetime, one street alone, South Street, housed not only national figures such as Lord Melbourne and Florence Nightingale, but also 'Skittles' Walters, the most famous courtesan of the century.

Caroline cared nothing about the doubtful reputation of the place. Her spirits had soared again after leaving Hampton Court, and by the autumn of 1836, she had regained not only her confidence, but the recklessness that had got her into trouble with Melbourne. She thought it was amusing that the neighbourhood was full of brothels, and persisted in trying to persuade her friends that Mayfair was a suitable residential area, even for a woman living on her own. She argued that it did not matter that there were 'fie-fies' (or prostitutes) in the street provided that a respectable lady was not mistaken for one. When Mary Shelley wrote to say that she was thinking of taking a house in Mayfair, but was rather doubtful, because as the widow of the 'scandalous' poet, she had to be careful of her reputation, Caroline reassured her:

> With respect to your house in Berkeley Street, I think it would be most childish to give up a good and cheap house because a fie-fie had lived in it, which, I suppose, is the English of the 'associations'. My uncle says he never heard of such an objection, but he is not the best person to ask. If it is any satisfaction to you to know that they thought to deter me from taking a house in Hereford Street by telling me that there were two houses of that sort in the same street, and that I obstinately persist in thinking of the neighbourhood as good as when the houses do not acknowledge themselves (as in Grosvenor Square), you have that bright example before you. I really think these sorts of objections are absurd, and if you consider them otherwise, you will never get a small, cheap, and pretty house at the West-end of town, for such houses are the natural prey of such persons; and ever and anon they hire them, and put parrot's cages and geraniums in the balcony which they paint light green.
>
> But if you act discreetly and modestly (that is, if you paint the rails dark green, and don't buy a parrot, and are contented with two geraniums inside the drawing-room) the barrenness of virtue will be apparent, and the house will be as good as if its face was built out of the sorrowful and remorseful bricks of the Millbank Penitentiary.[5]

It was only when all the bustle of moving to Green Street was over that Caroline was able to take full stock of her situation. It was an entirely unprecedented one for a woman of her class. She was notorious. Her quarrel with her husband had received unrivalled publicity and had been presented to the entire nation in sensational terms. She would never consent to return to him, nor would he have her back. Yet, because Norton's action had failed, he could not divorce her on grounds of her infidelity; while because she had returned to him after their parting in 1835, she was advised that she would never get a divorce on grounds of his cruelty. She dare not even apply for a formal separation, because her lawyers told her that if she succeeded, it might later prevent her from obtaining a divorce in Scotland. There was nothing she could do but wait. She had to wait for Melbourne to signal that it was safe for their friendship to begin again, and for Norton to tell her how he would support her, and when she might see her boys. These men would decide the pattern of her life.

Then something in her rebelled. She decided to try to force events. The time for waiting was over. She was tired of being 'Old Sherry's' granddaughter, and wanted to be regarded as a woman in her own right. The only question was how to go about it.

· Her answer lay in writing. In those first days of her independent life, Caroline sat for hours at her desk in Green Street, scribbling furiously. To earn money, she started a poem entitled: *A Voice from the Factories*. She also wrote many letters. One was to Norton, demanding that he make some decision. Another was to Melbourne, because she missed him terribly and wanted to see him again. She had to get some answers from these people so that she could plan her future. It was not unlike creating a character in one of her books, and it occurred to her that, if she could get her way, she could make up her own story in any way she pleased.

XVII

STRANGER AND FRIENDS

CAROLINE NEEDED FRIENDS. In the weeks after the Melbourne trial, many people in Society stood poised to decide upon her reputation. It was, therefore, very important that she should be seen in Society, enjoying the confidence of influential figures who were not members of her immediate family circle. Her first impulse was to look to Lord Melbourne.

It was not just that a signal from him would obtain her acceptance again in many drawing rooms. She was desperate to see him. Melbourne had been her most intimate friend for more than five years, and she was used to talking to him almost daily. No-one could comfort her as he could, and she hungered for his companionship again. She had no doubt that, as soon as all danger of scandal was over, he too would want to resume their regular meetings. The only question was when.

So, in her last days at Hampton Court, and later in her study at Green Street, she dashed off letters almost daily to him, in the perfect assurance of their sympathetic reception. Her family advised her to stop writing to him but she paid no attention. She wrote about her wretched health, the conduct of the trial, her longing for her boys, and the prospect of a divorce in Scotland. She wanted his advice on how she should 'shape her own fate', and said that she wanted him as an adviser rather than her brother and uncle. But she got no answer to her letters until late June, while she was still at Hampton Court, when he wrote a letter which she considered kept her 'at arm's length' because it was 'written coldly & scoldingly'.[1] Melbourne now suggested that it would be better if they did not correspond, at least for a while. It was then that she first began to fear that he wanted to drop her, just as he had cast off Lady Branden years before. She received the letter when she was ill, and made the mistake of responding that she could, if she wished, publish his correspondence. His reply has not survived but he obviously reacted strongly to this hint of blackmail, and she quickly answered to assure him that, of course, she never *would* publish his letters; she only said that she *could*. The rest of her note is full of reproach:

there is hardly a man on earth who would not have written a kind word when the trial was over & asked how I was . . . but no one either in the past or the future will have loved you more earnestly, more completely – & I may say more steadily than the woman whose threat of passion you pretend to fear – and who has been made to appear a painted prostitute in a Public Court before a jury of Englishmen – for the sake of acquaintance with one who did not think it worth while to ask after her.[2]

He did not reply. Daily she looked for his letters but none came. She even suspected that her family was hiding them, but they assured her it was not so. Throughout July, when she was coughing blood, they tried to comfort her with the old arguments. Lord Melbourne, they said, was a man with great responsibilities, many worries and much to do. She must not expect him to find time to write to her. There was some truth in this, for 1836 was a difficult year, and Melbourne had a lot on his plate. The King was ill; there was an economic depression and consequent working-class unrest; people were badgering him to allow the Dorset 'martyrs' to return from Australia to their homes in Tolpuddle; there were problems about the poor law, troubles in Ireland and the ever-present threat of Russian expansion in the Middle East. Despite these good reasons for Melbourne's failure to write, Caroline did not accept them as adequate. Melbourne had always found time for her in the early days of their friendship, whatever was going on in the world. She guessed that the true reason for his silence was that she had become an embarrassment to him, and he wanted to drop her. She made up her mind that she would not let him do it.

So she began a campaign to force him to acknowledge her. Almost every day the letters arrived at Melbourne's private house in South Street, to remind him of her sufferings, of the sacrifice she had made for him, of his own duplicity, of their past friendship, and of how ill she was. She was perfectly sincere in these sentiments but the letters are also performances. For example, she added a footnote to her letter written on 8 july:

Pray do not write harshly – pray do not! I had rather be forgotten. I have not deserved it – and it kills me.[3]

Fanny Allen had once said that she was 'a very fine actress, scarcely inferior to Grisi', and she liked writing different parts for herself.

Besides, she knew her man. In personal matters, Melbourne was soft-hearted, and she understood how such a pathetic appeal would agitate him. Sometimes she liked to hint that death might soon separate them, so that his refusing to write now was an opportunity missed:

> The day will come, without anticipating it, when one of us may no longer communicate with the other. Forbidding me to write after being in the habit of hearing from or seeing you so constantly, gives me a feeling as if you were dead, & adds one needless misery to what I am enduring.[4]

While still at Hampton Court, she wrote to tell him that she dreaded the night, while she sat alone in her room, imagining him at some splendid reception. Even when she tried to sleep, she was troubled by dreams in which the Nortons or Miss Vaughan were trying to poison her little son, Brinny.

Such pathos would have melted a colder heart than Melbourne's, and he surrendered over the letter-writing. He seems to have determined to breeze it out. In late July, Caroline received two cheerful, friendly letters from him, in which, writing sometimes like an elderly solicitor, sometimes like a family doctor, he tried to stick to practicalities. He regretted that he could offer her little advice on what to do about the children but he was very clear that she should accept no less than £300–£400 as an annual settlement from her husband. He said that he had often thought of sending her money himself but had not liked to do so, because her feelings had been so 'galled' by recent events that they were very 'sore and sensitive'. Then he expanded upon their future relationship, in words that were intended to soothe, but in effect, filled her with despair:

> As I trust we are now upon terms of confidential and affectionate friendship, I venture to say that you have nothing to do but express a wish, and it shall be instantly complied with. I miss you, I miss your society and conversation every day at the hours at which I was accustomed to enjoy them; and when you say that your place can be easily supplied . . . you know well enough that there is nobody who can supply your place.[5]

The subtext of this letter was, of course, that he would try to be a good friend to her at a distance but that she must never expect that they would become regular companions again.

Still she persisted, and continued to write to Melbourne in the autumn, after she had moved to Green Street. Now she reported news which she knew would frighten him. Apparently, Norton had ordered that their youngest child, William, should be known by his second name, Charles – presumably so that he should not bear Melbourne's Christian name. What was worse, Norton had

asked all the servants whether they had not remarked my poor Brin's likeness to you – they said 'yes; he is more handsome and cheerful than the other children, & he had [sic] got something of my Lord's manner; especially for a day or two after he happens to see my Lord, he's very like'. Well isn't that enough to convince you – didn't you think all along that he was his child? Now mark the answer of a servant to a man who is called a gentleman. 'No Sir, we none of us thought it, because the Mother would never have let a joke be made about the likeness, if there had been a reason for it.'[6]

This news seems to have scared Melbourne off for a long time, and his letters became rare events, though she continued to write to him almost daily. In the early months of 1837, he reluctantly gave way a little and permitted her to visit him once or twice at South Street but the visits were not a success. He was so resolutely affable, that her great weight of feeling for him seemed absurd and out of place. He was clearly determined to keep her at a distance. When she begged him to visit her in Green Street, he intimated that he was overburdened by official engagements which kept him out late. She wrote to him on 6 March:

I have always had the greatest horror of your thinking I was more forward than I should be, and what between that fear & other feelings, I have . . . done exactly the things I should not . . . You lay to my charge the seeking you whether you desired it or not.[7]

To shame him, she copied out the words of one of his old letters to her, written years before:

I have been in despair today at not seeing you but I know it is a long way and a difficult operation – and if you can continue to call, the later the better, as a number of people come to me for one reason or another.[8]

With the passage of time, the loss of his company seemed increasingly unendurable, especially when kind friends regaled her with stories of his attentions to other women. Caroline had the odd feeling that, while she felt desperately old at twenty-nine, Melbourne was growing younger again. She could not prevent a bitter tone creeping into her letters:

> If I could find a man of the present day who could write & read, & who did not carry a comb & a box of pink lip-salve in his coat pocket I would not trouble you – but there are none such.[9]

She now became increasingly resentful:

> I looked to you for protection – for kindness – for sympathy. I perceive nothing but shrinking & a vague desire to be rid of me all together ... They bid me be quiet and put a card for some party in my hand. But it will not do. That was part of my life – and it will not make a life itself. You will drive me mad, and for my madness you may thank yourself ... Stay away or come – choose your own way ...[10]

During the first hard winter of her independent life, Caroline had come to understand two things about Melbourne. She discovered, to her surprise, that she really was in love with him, and also that he was fast becoming a stranger.

She attempted to compensate by finding new friends. She gave one or two little dinner parties at Green Street, and, like Lady Caroline Lamb before her, supplied the absence of more fashionable guests with the company of writers. Tom Moore came, and he introduced her to Samuel Rogers, the author of the poem: *The Pleasures of Memory*. She also made friends with two 'literary lawyers': Abraham Hayward, who became her legal adviser for many years, and Thomas Talfourd, MP, who had assisted Sir John Campbell to defend Melbourne.

She also had reason to be grateful to two women for their support and companionship. With the exceptions of her mother and sisters, Caroline had never before thought of cultivating friendship among other women. Her object had been to attract men. Furthermore, the men she knew had always been scornful of the idea that women might be friends with one another. It was, perhaps, typical of Norton that he had persistently denied the possibility of friendship among women but even such a comparatively civilized man as Lord Melbourne had observed that it was rare for women to be kind to each other.

Yet, at the very height of Caroline's notoriety, one of the most fashionable women in London, the young Duchess of Sutherland, had gone out of her way to befriend her. Immediately after Melbourne's trial, many aristocratic families were deciding whether or not to favour Norton, and Caroline might have lost her place in social life altogether. At this very moment, the Duchess had insisted in taking her out in her carriage, and had driven round Hyde Park at the most fashionable hour for such parades. She continued to be a good friend long after that. Caroline repaid her with a dedication in her poem 'The Dream', which came out in 1840:

> But thou gav'st me, what woman seldom dares,
>   Belief – in spite of many a cold dissent –
> When, slandered and maligned, I stood apart,
> From those whose bounded power, hath wrung, not
>   crushed, my heart.
>   . . .
>
> Then, then, when cowards lied away my name,
>   And scoff'd to see me feebly stem the tide;
> When some were kind, on whom I had no claim,
>   And some forsook on whom my love relied,
> And some, who might have battled for my sake,
> Stood off in doubt to see what turn 'the world'
>   would take –
>
> Thou gavest me that the poor do give the poor,
>   Kind words, and holy wishes, and true tears;
> The loved, the near of kin, could do no more,
>   Who changed not with the gloom of varying years,
> But clung the closer when I stood forlorn,
> And blunted Slander's dart with their indignant scorn.[11]

At the other end of the social scale from the Duchess of Sutherland was Mary Shelley, with whom Caroline became much more intimate at this time. In 1837, Mary was forty years old, and living alone with her son, Percy. She had very little money, and earned a living by writing, and by editing the works of her husband, whom she represented not so much as a man of flesh and blood but as an angel. This was, perhaps, to counteract the scandalous reputation attaching to his name even fifteen years after his death. Mary was still paying the price for his outspoken atheism and alleged promiscuity. As a result, she had still to pretend not to hear malicious whispers about him, when she was announced in a Society drawing room. For Caroline, Mary was not only an older, wiser friend, who had learned to cope with social ostracism, she was a direct link with the great Romantic poets. For her part, Mary Shelley admired Caroline deeply. When Edward Trelawny confessed to her that he was fascinated by Caroline, she replied in a letter:

> [I do] not wonder at your not being able to deny yourself the pleasure of Mrs Norton's society. I never saw a woman I thought so fascinating. Had I been a man I should certainly have been in love with her.[12]

Caroline was also curious about Mary's mother, Mary Wollstonecraft, author of the *Vindication of the Rights of Women*. In this matter, Mary was, perhaps, a disappointment, for her mother had died only ten days after her birth, and, therefore, she had no personal recollections of her. Nevertheless, she intrigued Caroline by her account of her mother's heroic life. Caroline's attitude to Mary Wollstonecraft was ambivalent. On the one hand, she could not approve of this woman who had advocated equality between the sexes, and lived openly with a man not her husband. Yet, the more she learned of Mary's story, the more her heart went out to her, in sympathy for her courage, truthfulness and sheer goodness.

Mary Shelley and Caroline soon combined forces again, in another attempt to get a pension for old Mrs Godwin, Mary's step-mother, and widow of William Godwin, the author of the *Enquiry Concerning Political Justice*. When William IV died in 1837, the tiny annuity she received from the King's bounty died with him. In lobbying for Mrs Godwin, both these women took a risk. Since the death of her husband, Mary had worked hard to overcome much social disapproval and to make a new life for herself and her son. She could ill-afford to use up what social tolerance she now enjoyed, in defence of the interests of a poor and undistinguished old woman, not even her own mother, whose only claim to fame was that she had married the prophet of anarchistic communism. Caroline also had something to lose in pleading the case. To do so, she had to test the patience of Lord Melbourne even more, by writing to him on behalf of Mrs Godwin, at the very time when she did not want to ask him for favours. Despite this, she and Mary did their best for Mrs Godwin. Caroline not only petitioned Melbourne, but also coached Mary in the art:

> As to petitioning, no one dislikes begging more than I do, especially when one begs for what seems mere justice; but I have long observed that though people will resist claims (however just) they like to do favours. Therefore, when I beg I am a crawling lizard, a humble toad, a brown snake in cold weather, or any other simile . . . which would be the most natural attitude for petitioning, but which must never be assumed except in the poodle style, standing with one's paw bent to catch the bits of bread on one's nose . . .
> My meaning is, that if one asks at all, one should rather think of the person written to than one's own feelings. He [Melbourne] is an indolent man – talk of her age and infirmities; a patron of all genius – talk of your father's and your own; a prudent man – speak of the likelihood of the pension being a short grant . . .; lastly, he is a great man – take it all as a personal favour.[13]

She might have admitted to her friend that she already had long experience of petitioning Melbourne on her own behalf but with little success. His friendship was a personal favour she seemed to have lost herself.

XVIII

A DREAM OF CHILDREN

MUCH MORE IMPORTANT THAN HER FRIENDS were her children. After the verdict for Melbourne at the trial, Caroline assumed that Norton would have no excuse left for keeping them from her. On 26 June 1836, she wrote to him from Hampton Court, asking about his intentions and reminding him that she had not seen her children in six months. At that time, it did not occur to her to doubt that Norton would let her have the boys; she was concerned only with the practicalities of when and how. She suggested in her letter that Fletcher, the eldest, should remain at his school, and should divide his holiday time between Norton and herself. But she argued that it was important that the two younger ones should live with her while they were small: 'I merely wish to have the few first years of their lives at my disposal.' She added that, when she had him at home, she would be able to give Brinsley special help with his nervous stammer.

The reply did not come for weeks, and then not in Norton's hand but in an official letter from his solicitor. She learned that he had agreed that she might see her children briefly but only in his lawyer's chambers. Caroline was appalled. It seemed outrageous to her that her husband expected her to talk to her little boys in the offices of the very men who had recently been trying to prove that she was an immoral woman. What is more, it soon became plain to her that he was trying to enforce an even more serious condition. He would only let her see the boys if she was prepared to sign an undertaking to accept the very small allowance he proposed to make her. By these means he hoped to limit his financial liability for any debts she might incur. Should she not agree to this, he threatened to sell off her personal possessions. She had, of course, left her home so abruptly that she had taken hardly anything with her. Norton still possessed most of her clothes and personal effects, and, as she pointed out in a letter, he had in his house many gifts made to her by her family and friends on her marriage, and books and other things that had belonged to her father.[1] She perceived, quite correctly, that he was now trying to use her children and possessions to blackmail her.

Caroline was determined not to put up with such treatment, and consulted her lawyers to find out precisely what rights she had, as a mother, in the future of her own children. Their answers startled and dismayed her. She discovered that the laws of England allowed the separated mother no rights at all in her children. Authority over the offspring of a marriage rested entirely with fathers. Mothers did not even have a right of access. They had to rely on the mercy of their husbands.

Such dreadful information might have broken Caroline's will, so that she agreed to Norton's blackmail. It did not. She wrote to her lawyers:

> allow me to repeat clearly, emphatically, and decidedly, that I refuse all communications on any but that one subject – my children. They may bereave me of my beloved boys (since the law allows it), they may drive me mad, or wear me into my grave by the slow torture of that greatest of sorrows; but while I have control of my reason, and strength to guide my pen, I will sign nothing, do nothing, listen to nothing, which has reference to any other subject – till it is decided what intercourse is to be allowed me with my children.[2]

Eventually, Norton permitted her to see the boys but only for a half-hour meeting at Brinsley's London house in Grosvenor Square. Even then, he insisted that two of his female servants were present, probably to act as spies. The meeting was not a success, for Caroline and her boys could hardly speak for crying.[3] She was later allowed to see them again, in St James's Park, and this time the solemn-eyed little Fletcher managed to whisper to her that he had previously tried to get the servants to pass her a note but they had refused. After this meeting, as the September days passed, she resorted to walking the London streets to try to snatch glimpses of them in their usual haunts. At last, in desperation, she simply entered Norton's house while he was away, and walked up to the nursery to see her children. It worked once, because his servants were too dumbfounded to prevent her, but the next time she tried it, the manservant refused to let her in.

Then she heard that the boys were to be sent to Lady Menzies, at Rannoch Lodge. They were to go up to Scotland by the east coast packet. She wrote to Norton and begged that she should be allowed to say goodbye to them but she received no reply. Somehow she discovered that they were to embark on the *Royal Windsor* from St Catherine's Dock and, even though she had influenza, she rose from her bed and waited on the dock while the passengers boarded the boat. The boys did not come. She went home miserable and feverish, and it was only later she learned that they had sailed on the *Dundee*, with their uncle, Lord Grantley.

Caroline was exhausted and became ill. For weeks past in Green Street, she had been working long hours at her poem *A Voice from the Factories*.[4] Its success was essential to her future as a writer, and the task had helped to take her mind off her children. In October 1836, the poem was accepted by Messrs John Murray. It was published anonymously, at her request, for she was still smarting from recent publicity. She dedicated it to Lord Ashley (Anthony Ashley Cooper) who later became famous as the reforming Lord Shaftesbury, and had just started his campaign to restrict working hours in the textile industry to ten a day.

She had read the report of the Sadler parliamentary committee of enquiry into working conditions in the industry, and she was deeply disturbed by its references to the children in the mills. The subject seems to have had a special appeal to her because of her situation. Visions of little children doomed to labour from dawn till dusk at their spinning and weaving machines became entwined in her imagination with images of the faces of her own children, while the features of cruel overseers took on the lineaments of her husband or Lord Grantley. Sadly, *A Voice from the Factories* is not so much a poem as an argument. Caroline knew nothing about the life of textile mills; she had probably never been in one, and, what was worse for the quality of her writing, probably never understood that she was deficient in this matter. Rather than conveying the sights, sounds and smells of mill life, she was intent on applying 'serious poetry' to contemporary events. The effect is solemn and rhetorical.

In her dedication she declares that child labour is 'an evil which it behoves Christian law-givers to remove', and the fifty-nine stanzas which follow proceed to argue the point. Her opinions, however, may be considered rather self-contradictory. As a Radical and a Romantic she contemptuously dismisses the argument of the 'British Senate' that excessive child labour must be allowed, in order to maintain the 'unalienable RIGHT OF GAIN', but she also accepts as fact the notion that the world will always have 'its Rulers and its ruled', and that 'some must own and some must till the land'. She thought that this system was justified because some men are cleverer than others. Unfortunately, the argument for authority based on intellectual superiority became an increasingly difficult one for her to maintain in her long dispute with her husband. This was because, even though she claimed to believe that men are superior to women because they are more intelligent, it was plain to everyone who knew them, that Norton was stupid and she was not.

Much of the polemic of *A Voice from the Factories* seems dated and tedious to the modern reader but the passage about the little high-wire walker in the circus has both feeling and observation. This was partly because, though Caroline had never been in a mill, she almost certainly had visited a circus, and also because the helpless plight of the wire-walker aroused her mother's instincts and reminded her of Brinny at the mercy of Miss Vaughan:

> See the Stage-Wonder (taught to earn its bread
> By the exertion of an infant skill),
> Forsake the wholesome slumbers of its bed,
> And mime, obedient to the public will.
> Where is the heart so cold that does not thrill
> With a vexatious sympathy, to see
> That child prepare to play its part, and still
> With simulated airs of gaiety
> Rise to the dangerous rope, and bend the supple knee?

> Painted and spangled, trembling there it stands,
> Glances below for friend or father's face,
> Then lifts its small round arms and feeble hands
> With the taught movements of an artist's grace:
> Leaves its uncertain gilded resting-place –
> Springs lightly as the elastic cord gives way –
> And runs along with scarce perceptible pace –
> Like a bright bird upon a waving spray,
> Fluttering and sinking still, whene'er the branches play.
> . . .

> What is it makes us feel relieved to see
> That hapless little dancer reach the ground;
> With its whole spirit's elasticity
> Thrown into one glad, safe triumphant bound?
> Why are we sad, when as it gazes round
> At that wide sea of paint, and gauze and plumes,
> (Once more awake to sense, and sight, and sound,)
> The nature of its age it re-assumes,
> And one spontaneous smile at length its face illumes?[5]

What with her fever, the emotional reaction to completing her poem, and grief at the loss of her children, Caroline now became really ill and took to her bed. As she lay there, she had the curious sensation that her children were near. Later, she wrote a poem about it:

I was alone but not asleep;
Too weary and too weak to weep;
My eyes had closed in sadness there,
And they who watched o'er my despair
Had placed that dim light in the room,
And deepened the surrounding gloom
By curtaining the few sad rays
Which made things present to my gaze:
. . .

And while I darkly rested there,
The breath of a young child's floating hair,
Perfumed and warm, and glistening bright,
Swept by me in the shrouding night;
And the footsteps of children, light and quick
(While my heart beat loud, and my breath came thick),
Went to and fro on the silent floor
And the lock was turned in the fastened door
. . .

Those light steps drew more near my bed;
And by visions I was visited
Of the gentle eyes which I might not see,
And the faces that were so far from me . . .[6]

By November 1836, she had heard nothing from the boys, whom she presumed to be still in Scotland. She dreaded Christmas without them and, as there seemed no reason for her to stay in London, she accepted an invitation from Brinsley and Marcia Sheridan to go down to Frampton Court, even though the place seemed gloomy with memories of the previous Easter. After Christmas she left Dorset and drove up to Wiltshire, to spend the New Year with the Seymours at Maiden Bradley. Georgiana and her family were kind, but did not understand how to comfort her in her grief. They tried to avoid mentioning her children, for there was little they could say to help. Caroline usually made a point of retiring early, in order to give them all a break from her problems. She sat up late in her room, writing poems and letters to her friends. Then, one day she had some news which excited her. Margaret Vaughan had died. Caroline learned that she had left George Norton all her Yorkshire estates and £200 a year. It was not the money that concerned her, it was the thought that the worst influence on her husband was now removed and that, therefore, Norton might change his mind about letting her see the children. This new hope brought her back to Green Street at once.

But there was no progress, only the start of a dreary exchange of letters between Norton's solicitor and her own. Both she and Norton had precise objectives. By holding out the possibility of regular access to the boys, he was trying to get her to accept as low a settlement as possible, and an additional agreement that she would settle her own debts. On the other hand, she would not make any financial agreement until she was granted access to her children. The money or the boys, it was a question of which came first. In September 1836, he offered her £150 a year, which figure her advisers told her was far too low. She refused it. In October, he suggested £143 per annum, plus the £57 she received under her father's will, making a total of £200. Again she said no, but this time more because the access he was suggesting was inadequate, rather than because of the paltry nature of the sum he offered.

So Norton tried another approach. He placed advertisements in several newspapers to announce that he would not be responsible for Caroline's debts. Of course, as a lawyer, he knew that the announcement had no legal force, because the law said that he was responsible, but he must have thought it worth a try. Meanwhile, on 26 October, Caroline wrote to her solicitors to reaffirm her rejection of his offers. She well understood that, because he would refuse to pay her tradesmen's bills, she would need to change her custom frequently, and that she would have much 'mortification and impertinence' (or tradesmen's rudeness) to endure. She was also resigned to the fact that Norton would never let her have her books, literary papers and other personal possessions. Even worse, he would not even hand over the clothes she had left at Storey's Gate, though he knew that Caroline had very little money with which to buy replacements. Nevertheless, she persisted in her refusal. He would obtain no agreement without regular access. On 6 November, she wrote to her solicitor from Frampton, still arguing that, whatever her husband said, she believed that, as a mother, she had a natural claim on her children, and should have them to live with her for a part of each year. She added that she feared that the climate of Scotland was too sharp for the chest of her more delicate child, Fletcher. But Norton simply would not consider such arguments, and there the matter stood at Christmas.[7]

It was not until the following March that she received some definite news, and then it was that her youngest child, William, had been ill during the winter in Scotland. It now seemed to her that the health of all the children was at risk, and she went at once to Norton's chambers, to beg him for some agreement which would allow their children a place of safety. When she saw him he was curiously amenable, even jovial, and, to her disquiet, she sensed that he was sexually excited by her presence. She had almost forgotten that once she had controlled him through his sensuality, and the temptation was to try to do so again. He was now all sympathy. Margaret Vaughan's influence seemed to be wearing off. He even told her that he was moving into Green Street, to be near her, and he did so. On 13 March he wrote to her from No. 30, to acknowledge her 'long suffering and estimable spirit'. He promised to bring the boys down from Scotland, if only she would accept the £200 a year he offered. Of course he reserved the right to set certain conditions to Caroline's access. The boys were to live with their nurse, a young woman who, by coincidence, was also named 'Caroline', and who had cared for them over the previous winter. Caroline protested that this still would not do, and, after more negotiations, he gave in and agreed that she could have them all the time. Rather tactlessly he wrote to say that this would mean a 'sad parting [for them] from little Cary'. Caroline was still unclear about the exact details of what arrangement he was proposing but she was desperate for her children. Against advice, she agreed.

But on 15 March, he wrote to announce that he had changed his mind. He now said that, even if she agreed to the £200 a year, he could not allow unlimited access 'until [he saw] . . . a certainty of [the children] being brought up with the strictness [he] required'. It would have been laughable had it not been so enraging. He was now setting himself up as the moral arbiter of her conduct! Furiously, she replied and objected. On 16 March he declared that he 'must consider these negotiations at an end'.

It was stalemate. Caroline now realized that he had never intended her to have the boys but had used the possibility of it merely to persuade her to enter into a financial agreement much against her interest. After years of marriage to him, she was only beginning to plumb the depths of Norton's cunning. She was furious:

I hope there will one day be a tribunal to which mothers may appeal from such inhuman cruelty and perversion of all rights of nature! meanwhile, I renounce the vain attempt to work upon feelings of justice which do not exist in your heart.[8]

These thoughts set her mind racing. After all, there *was* such a tribunal at Westminster, and it might be prepared to listen to arguments about natural justice for mothers. Even if she could not change her husband, she could change the law.

XIX

CAMPAIGN AND QUARREL

CAROLINE'S PLAN WAS AN AUDACIOUS ONE. It seemed to her that, if she herself believed the laws concerning mothers and children to be inhumane, then others might do so too; and if she could persuade Parliament of the justice of her views, then she might get such laws altered. Success would mean that she would regain her children, and incidentally help thousands of other mothers as well.

Such a task was not impossible because, unlike almost all other women at that time, Caroline had some political influence. She had many friends in both Houses of Parliament, and liked to think of the Prime Minister as one of them. Her brother-in-law was an MP, and her brother was planning a political career. A number of her grandfather's old friends were still active in public life, and the name of 'Sheridan' still counted for something in the Whig Party. She was a celebrated political hostess, and knew how to go about lobbying politicians. What was more, her husband was a lawyer, and during the long tedious days when she was first married, she had often passed the time by browsing through his law-books. She could write and speak well. Few women were better equipped to conduct a political campaign.

Furthermore, the struggle for social justice was very much part of her family tradition. She had been brought up in the beliefs of John Locke, and the conviction that the Glorious Revolution of 1688 had created the ideal constitution. Her radical grandfather, Richard Brinsley Sheridan, had opposed the Divine Right of Kings, absolutism, and all form of tyranny. Throughout his long parliamentary life, he had fought for oppressed people, including slaves, common seamen and Catholics. He had believed in justice for all. Caroline now began to consider how far that revolution, which had proclaimed the Rights of Man, had also established rights for women, especially mothers deprived of their children.

The results of Caroline's research astounded her, for the situation was far worse than she had suspected. It was not just that, in nineteenth-century England, a married woman had no say over her children, and could not own property. She *had no existence in law*.

A married woman was not a person at all. Sir William Blackstone, the great jurist, had explained the matter: 'in law husband and wife are one person, and the husband is that person'.[1] When she married, a woman's property was transferred to her husband, so that she ceased to own even her 'paraphernalia', as the lawyers called her clothes and personal effects. This ruling had significant implications in a case such as Caroline's. She and Norton might both sign a document which recorded that she would accept a very small annual allowance in return for regular visits from her children, but he knew perfectly well that he was not obliged to honour this agreement, because his wife was not a legal person, and therefore could not make such contracts.

In the 1830s, the law still maintained that either the husband was the same person as his wife, or else he was her legal protector, like a parent and a child. Had Caroline asked her uncle and legal adviser, Sir James Graham, how such a monstrous fiction had come about, he would have been obliged to refer her to mediaeval times, when the only kind of property was land, and owners were obliged to follow the King's banner in war. Of course a woman who had inherited an estate could not ride to war herself, and therefore, on her marriage, the obligation immediately became her husband's. He thus became the effective owner of the estate, and, in later times, the actual owner.

But Caroline was not so concerned about property as her children. If such a legal situation could not be changed, then she recognized that she would always be at Norton's mercy in this matter. He could let her see her children or not, as he wished. He could take them away entirely, and there was nothing she could do about it. He could beat them, starve them, neglect them, or give them over to a mistress, and still she had no right to intervene. This state of affairs was based upon the view that fathers rather than mothers should have the ultimate authority over their children, because men were intellectually and morally superior to women. It was a doctrine that Mary Wollstonecraft had opposed in the *Vindication of the Rights of Women*, by arguing that women were not just creatures of emotion, created solely to minister to the desires and needs of men, but moral, and therefore, rational beings. It followed that they were entitled to equal rights under the law.

It would have been convenient if Caroline could have used these arguments but she was prevented from doing so because she did not agree with them. Indeed, she always professed to believe in the innate superiority of men:

The wild and stupid theories advanced by a few women, of 'equal rights' and 'equal intelligence' are not the opinions of their sex. I, for one (I, with millions more), believe in the natural superiority of man, as I do the existence of God.

The natural position of woman is inferiority to man. Amen! That is a thing of God's appointing, not of man's devising. I believe it sincerely, as a part of my religion. I never pretended to the wild and ridiculous doctrine of equality.[2]

And because she could not employ the argument that sexual equality demanded equal rights, Caroline had to fall back on the assertion that there were 'natural rights' peculiar to mothers. These 'natural rights', she thought, entitled women to a special consideration in law when the guardianship of their children was considered. This was an argument she was to repeat many times in her campaign for infant custody. She even tried it out on Norton, and wrote to tell him that 'whatever the law may be . . . nature [had given her] a claim' on her children.

For she had not given up hopes of changing his mind, and regularly wrote to him through her solicitor. It was a lonely business. In the spring and summer of 1837, she spent most of her time at 16 Green Street on her own. Her Uncle Charles was very kind but he preferred to eat at his club on most evenings, while her brother Charlie was often out until the early hours. She passed many long days and evenings alone, but these times were not unpleasant to her, for she was learning the solitary discipline of the professional writer. Sometimes a friend, such as the Duchess of Sutherland, would call to take her out driving, and sometimes her brother or sisters would come with an invitation to dinner. In March, Brinsley and Marcia even took her on a brief trip to Paris. But these were exceptions. Her days were spent largely at her desk, editing her vanity books and writing her poems but also conducting her tireless campaign to get her children back.

After a two-month break, Norton wrote again on 19 May 1837, to suggest that they should meet alone to settle their affairs. Caroline refused to see him at the house he had just inherited from Miss Vaughan, No. 1 Lower Berkeley Street, but reluctantly consented to call at his new address, 10 Wilton Place, just off Knightsbridge. She did not want to meet him alone, especially since she had sensed his renewed interest in her at their previous meeting, for she was aware that the law did not admit that a husband might rape his wife. She also knew that it gave Norton pleasure to play cat and mouse with her, especially in places where she could not call for help. And even though she feared he was merely up to his old game of trying to extricate himself as cheaply as possible from their marriage, she was more alarmed when he hinted at times that he yearned to have her back and sobbing for forgiveness in his bed.

The interview was distressing and embarrassing. Norton broke down and begged her to forget the past and to return to him. He suggested that they could leave town together and go to his new estate at Kettlethorpe in Yorkshire. He said that, if she consented, she could see the boys again in a few days. Caroline was amazed at this sudden change in him, and strongly tempted by the thought of seeing her boys. She decided 'to make a raft out of the wreck and drift back [to] a comfortless haven', and reluctantly fell in with his suggestions, provided that, when she went to Yorkshire with him, he guaranteed immediately to get the boys down from Perthshire, where they were still living with Lady Menzies. He agreed. Then there was a hitch. He wrote to say that he would have to get permission from Lord Grantley, his brother and head of the family, if he were to sign a new settlement for themselves and the boys. He begged Caroline to write to Grantley to gain his favour. He signed his letter: 'Your poor old worn out Georgie'.

Caroline rightly suspected that if all these efforts depended upon Grantley's good-will they would be bound to fail, because he had not got any. Grantley's lack of human kindness was conspicuous even among the Nortons. He barely spoke to his wife or his brother George, and never disguised his loathing for Caroline herself. Despite this, George went down to Wonersh to explain matters to his brother, and wrote to Caroline to say that all seemed well. Grantley had promised to come up to London to talk to them both, and, after that, George said, the boys would be brought down from Scotland.

She waited and waited, until a note arrived from Norton on the evening of Saturday 27 May, confessing that Grantley had still not come but insisting that his brother's permission was essential before, 'in the infinite mercy of God', he and Caroline could plan their future. In this he was correct, because Caroline now wanted a formal financial agreement between them, and it was Grantley who held the purse-strings. Two days later, Norton wrote again, to suggest two possible plans. They could either resume their married life, or else separate, with an agreement which allowed Caroline access to the boys. In either case, he said, she might 'confidently leave it to [him] to make every arrangement' about money and the children.[3] He begged her to tell nobody about their negotiations, not even her brother Brinsley, because these were not matters for third parties. Though she was desperate to see the boys, Caroline took exception to this request, and protested bitterly that it was unreasonable when every detail of their affairs was being submitted to *his* brother.

Then Norton began to raise more difficulties. He complained that she still seemed to distrust him, and added that, on re-consideration, he now thought it unwise to bring the boys down from Scotland to London, during the summer. He suggested that it would be better for their health if she went up to see them at Rannoch Lodge. At this, Caroline's patience snapped, for she perceived that once again, she was being played with. She could guess what sort of reception she would get from Lady Menzies, and the mere prospect of the journey to Perthshire wearied her. On 30 May, she complained to Norton that, whereas he professed concern that a sea-trip might exhaust the boys, he thought nothing of suggesting a 500-mile journey for her:

> Altogether it does not amuse me that any human being should have the heart so to play upon the affection and sorrow of another as you do on mine . . . It is most barbarous . . . to renew my hope, my anxiety, and my restlessness, only to destroy me by inches, as you are doing! . . . I really did believe you – I really did think you were sending for the boys, and that against all others could say, to warn me not to hope.[4]

On getting her note, Norton invited her to call on him at Wilton Place the next day but she was so upset that she went round that evening. Her appearance was so distraught that even he took pity on her. He softened his tone and assured her that the boys would soon be in London.

On Thursday 1 June, Caroline received an extraordinary rambling letter from him, accusing her of double-dealing because, that afternoon at his office, an action-attorney had presented him with a bill on behalf of her dressmaker, a Miss M. It seems that he was especially upset because he had assumed that, in merely holding negotiations with Caroline, she would hold off her creditors. He complained that he had kept his side of the bargain and sent for the boys. It was true that he had not done this as soon as he had promised but this was because he said he had been obliged to spend much of the previous day at a sale, waiting to bid for a silver candlestick that had belonged to Margaret Vaughan. He hinted that Caroline herself might profit from his efforts, for he had also bought a mosaic table which might, one day, be hers, 'if you behave yourself as such'. He cautioned her either to return to him, or swiftly to accept his new offer of £500 a year, before he was tempted to spend the money on furniture for his new home at Kettlethorpe. He ended:

Pray Mrs Brown, how many chairs have you got – also tables? Have you e'er a dining one? Pray come on Friday night; bring all you have got, and we'll be married on Christmas day. Your affectionate intended, Greenacre.[5]

These curious words were familiar to Caroline and the newspaper-reading public of the time, for they had recently received great publicity in a court of law. They had been written in a note from a man named James Greenacre to Hannah Brown, a servant. He had enticed her to an empty house, murdered her for her money, and then made off with his fancy woman. He had been arrested, and hanged on 2 May. Norton's fascination with the Greenacre story is another clue to his nature. Like Greenacre, he himself was a violent, passionate man, who derived sensual pleasure from meeting a desperate, vulnerable woman in an empty house.

In reply to his letter she wearily pointed out that she was not responsible for the serving of Miss M's bills, and that all these difficulties could easily be overcome by allowing her to see the boys, from whom she had now been separated for fifteen months. She ended: 'Let me know if Grantley is come, for I am hungry for the children'. So these interminable negotiations went on.

Yet Caroline hated having to beg Norton for the privilege of seeing her own boys, and was keenly aware that, even when she did so, he might remove them again at a whim. What she wanted was a change in the law to guarantee a separated mother the custody of her young children. Having formulated this realistic aim, Caroline set about considering how best to persuade MPs of the justice of her case. She hit upon the idea of writing a pamphlet, and decided to research case histories of separated mothers who had tried to keep their children with them. She felt confident she could do this, both because of her knowledge of the law, even though it was amateur, and also because of her friendship with a number of lawyers who could help her.

Other people were less enthusiastic. When Caroline told her mother what she proposed to do, Mrs Sheridan was horrified. She said that pamphleteering was an 'indelicate' activity for a lady, and added that

Caroline's name had already enjoyed far too much publicity. Publishers were no more encouraging. Caroline approached several with her pamphlet but they all declined to publish it, chiefly because she referred to actual cases in her text, and they were afraid they might lay themselves open to prosecution. Eventually, John Murray agreed to help her, but only on strict conditions. In the summer of 1837, he brought out 500 copies of: *Observations on the Natural Claim of a Mother to the Custody of her Children as affected by the Common Law Right of the Father*, for private circulation only.[6]

The argument of the pamphlet was simple. Caroline contended that, in broken marriages, all children below the age of seven should be placed in the care of the mother, and that the fate of older children should be determined by the Court of Chancery rather than the father. Hitherto, she said, the law had been chiefly concerned to protect property in such cases, when its true task was to safeguard the innocent people involved:

> The fact is, in this 'commercial country', as it is eternally called, the rights of property are the only rights really and efficiently protected; and the consideration of property the only one which weighs with the decision made in a court of justice. I do not mean that they decide unjustly in favour of the rich, but that where there is no property law fails; as if it was for that, and not for men, that laws were made.[7]

During the next year, Caroline's life became deeply involved in the struggle for an Infant Custody Bill, and, to this end, she became close friends with two ambitious, radical lawyers. In 1837, Abraham Hayward QC was the thirty-six-year-old editor of *The Law Magazine*. He cultivated literary interests, and had published a translation of Goethe's *Faust*. He was a hot-tempered, sharp-tongued man, but also an entertaining companion and an affectionate friend. His dinners in the Temple were famous, both for their food and witty conversation. His guests included: Lockhart, the biographer of Burns and Scott; Lord Macaulay; the Reverend Sydney Smith; the popular novelist, Henry Bulwer; and, later, Caroline herself.[8] Hayward soon became her lawyer, friend, and ally for life. Because he hated his first name, 'Abraham', she always called him 'A'.

It was Hayward who had introduced her to Serjeant Talfourd, a vigorous forty-two-year-old lawyer, who had just been re-elected as MP for Reading. He was even more literary than Hayward and had written a tragedy, *Ion*, of which he was inordinately proud, and which had recently been staged by Macready with great success. His friend Charles Dickens had dedicated the *Pickwick Papers* to him, in gratitude for his efforts in promoting a Copyright Bill. He was a friend and admirer of Charles Lamb, and through him had met both Wordsworth and Coleridge. He had promoted many good causes in both the courts and the House, and had led the campaign to get the pillory abolished. He had also acted as a junior counsel for the defence in Norton's action against Melbourne. Caroline soon realized that, in him, she had a splendid champion to fight for mothers' rights. She wrote enthusiastically to Mary Shelley:

> I do not know Mr Talfourd personally, but I asked Mr Hayward (who seems a great friend of his) to request him to undertake the task. I hardly hoped for such prompt acquiescence; and if I had to choose from the whole House of Commons, I could not choose a man whose talent, good feeling and weight with the House would give a better or so good a chance of success. He has the printed proof of my pamphlet.[9]

As might have been expected, Caroline's friendships were not unnoticed by the Tory press, and, within a short time, *The British & Foreign Review* was implying that Talfourd was the lover of this 'she-devil', as it called her.[10]

On 1 June, Caroline's pamphlet came out, and she excitedly wrote to Mary Shelley to give her an even more exciting piece of news: 'Tonight Talfourd ("blessed be his name for that same, and a crown of glory to him", as the Irish say) has given notice of a motion in the House of Commons to alter this law'. The parliamentary campaign had begun.

With all this excitement, Caroline might have forgotten the cause of it all, which was the loss she felt of her boys, but their absence was a continual ache in her heart. Then suddenly Norton informed her that they were at last on their way to London, on the steamer from Leith. She would see them within a few days. She was so excited that she gave up all efforts towards economy and hired a smart little carriage, so that she could drive them round London. On 13 June 1837, she dared to send it round to Norton's new house at Wilton Place, with orders to collect them. Then she waited in her little sitting room in Green Street, in an agony of apprehension. Within a few minutes, she heard the vehicle returning, and went to the door. They were there. Her three children looking grave and frightened sat behind the coachman in the open carriage. She flew to greet them.

She had dreaded that they might have been ill-treated and half-starved by Lady Menzies, but the appearance of Fletcher and William reassured her. Brinsley, however, looked like a 'perfect skeleton' and seemed to be growing crooked, so that she made up her mind to get a doctor to look at him the following day. She was prepared to pay for the best, and chose Sir James Brodie, who had been surgeon to William IV. Meanwhile, she was apprehensive that her boys might have forgotten her but she need not have feared. After a brief shyness, they started to chatter away to her, as she later explained to a friend:

[Brin] is very merry . . . The little one is the sharpest little fellow you ever saw, & speaks as fluently as I do. They were very happy at returning but cannot understand going away in the evening.

The eldest & youngest have purses full of sixpences, and talked of little else for two hours. Brin's private fortune I have not yet heard mentioned, so I am in great hopes I have one son who does not resemble his Father in thinking money the object of life.

I have no more to say except that I feel very sad, and still miss a child, for this sharp talkative little being, does not seem to me my fair fat baby. They grow up in such a moment![11]

These feelings of sadness came over her in the evenings, when the boys went back to sleep at their father's house. But her days were a delight, and, during the bright June mornings, she drove with her children through fashionable London, to see the sights from the carriage. So she became absorbed in her domestic bliss and nothing else seemed real. When Talfourd contacted her about the conduct of the Infant Custody Bill she told him that it was no longer a matter of personal concern to her. Her quarrel with Norton seemed to be over, so there was no need for the campaign. With that, Talfourd lost interest in the business himself, and allowed the Infant Custody Bill to lapse in the Commons.

XX

THE RIVALS

MEANWHILE, Caroline was still trying to mend her broken friendship with Melbourne. He was not encouraging. He never attended her little Green Street dinner parties, and rarely replied to the letters she wrote during the spring and early summer of 1837. For this he may be forgiven. Caroline's letters were laced with resentment and jealousy, and replying to them must have seemed a profitless enterprise to a man with so much on his mind. But Caroline was not one to suffer in silence, and wrote to tell him: 'I have been in despair all day at not seeing you . . . it breaks my whole life at not seeing you.'[1] She liked to contrast her own lonely life with his glamorous one, and counted all his friends as her personal enemies. She complained: 'You parade yourself among my acknowledged & open foes [in] a circle of flattery and intrigue',[2] which charge he might have denied by admitting that his friends now rarely gave her a thought. Such a response, however, would not have comforted Caroline, especially as she was consumed by jealousy of his women acquaintances. She was very vulnerable to the gossip of her own kind friends, and convinced that Melbourne had taken Lady Hester Stanhope as his mistress. She declared that: 'There are insults women are slow to forgive – and I think yr connection with Lady Stanhope is one'.[3] By this time, Caroline was a great embarrassment to Melbourne, and it is not surprising that he resisted her appeals that he should help her regain her place in Society. When she begged him to get her an invitation to the house of his sister, Lady Cowper, he declined, though he did not tell her that his relations had refused to meet the woman who had so damaged his own reputation.

But Caroline was tenacious, and in letter after letter she begged him to meet her again. Sometimes she complained of being lonely, for her uncle and brother were out most of the time. Sometimes she reported she was ill, and said it would comfort her to see him.[4] Sometimes she tried to entice him, by hinting that she had mysterious secrets to tell, and assuring him that there would be no scene. She suggested that he should call for tea with their mutual friend, Edward Ellice. Melbourne did not rise to any of these baits. He dreaded the publicity that might be provoked if he was caught paying Caroline secret visits.

Nevertheless, it seems to have dawned on him that if he could only find a respectable way of meeting Caroline just once, he could use the opportunity to get her to understand that everything was over, and that they could not resume their past intimacy. His opportunity came when Caroline's Uncle Charles invited him to dinner. This kindly man had noticed her growing unhappiness, and had asked her if it would help if he invited Melbourne. Charles Sheridan was of the opinion that it was 'ridiculous for [their] acquaintance to be at an end because of the past'.[5] Both Caroline and Melbourne jumped at the opportunity, but of course for different reasons.

Soon after, on an evening in late spring, Lord Melbourne and Edward Ellice dined with Caroline and her uncle in Green Street. There are no records of the occasion, but it may be assumed that, after dinner, Sheridan and Ellice contrived to leave the other two alone. This was the first private conversation between Caroline and Melbourne for over a year, and he used it to settle two important issues between them. First, he made it plain that her hopes of a renewal in their daily friendship were quite impossible. He refused to listen to plans she had made for secret meetings between them. His reasons were compelling. They were a marked couple, and he occupied a great office of state. His political career could not have withstood any new scandal, and the future of the Whig Government rested with him. On the subject of money, however, he was more accommodating. He understood that Caroline was concerned not only for her own future, but also for that of her son, Brinsley. Norton seemed to suspect that Melbourne was the boy's true father, and because of this, Caroline had long feared that one day Brinsley might be disinherited. To allay her fears, Melbourne seems to have promised her some sort of settlement, both for herself and her boy. He kept this promise but it caused Caroline a great deal of trouble afterwards. Throughout the discussion, Melbourne was at pains to resist Caroline's weeping and pleadings. If the tone of later letters is anything to go by, he was kindly but did not encourage her. He wanted them to be neither lovers nor enemies but friends. They had fought the wars of love together, and rancour must not separate them now.

Caroline, however, still hoped that, as the effects of the trial wore off, Melbourne would be bold enough to resume their passionate friendship. And she was encouraged in this hope on the very morning when she first saw her boys again. She had just ushered them into her sitting room, when there was a tap at the door and her maid Sophia brought in a large bouquet of carnations. They were from Lord Melbourne. It was a moment of bliss. In daydreams she depicted future years with her boys living at home with her, and Lord Melbourne calling again for afternoon visits, just as he used to do. Perhaps this might have come about but history interrupted. In that same month of June 1837, Melbourne fell in love with somebody else.

It was only slowly that Caroline learned of this, and at first she dismissed it as unbelievable. Reports about his friendships with Lady Hester Stanhope and the novelist, Emily Eden, still worried her, for these women had much more opportunity to see him than she did, and he was never averse to flirtation and female flattery. But since their meeting, she was fairly confident that Melbourne had not involved himself deeply with anyone else. Indeed, his life was pathetically lonely. Of course, he frequently attended formal receptions as a part of his duties but afterwards he would go home to his house in South Street, with no family to greet him other than his half-witted son. She knew that he still sat up on most nights, reading old plays or books of church history.

Yet Caroline had developed such a sensitivity towards Melbourne that, even at a distance, she could sense a change in his mood. The whisper of his name in a drawing room was sufficient to alarm her, and a ribald remark about him in a newspaper could set her mooning for hours. Now she sensed a change in him, and this impression was reinforced on the few occasions when they met by a new coolness on his part. He seemed affable enough, but this only emphasized his detachment. For many weeks she could not account for these signs. Then slowly she realized the truth. The whisperers and scandal-mongers had been right after all; the impossible had happened. Melbourne had fallen in love with the new Queen.

It seemed an incredible thought to her, especially as Melbourne had always been so irreverent about the monarchy. He had described the three previous occupants of the throne as 'an imbecile, a profligate and a buffoon'.[6] But his attitude changed immediately on the death of the 'buffoon', William IV, on 20 June 1837, when, that same day, he waited in the Red Salon at Kensington Palace, where the Privy Councillors were to swear allegiance to the new sovereign. At a signal, the doors opened to admit a young girl, less than five feet tall, dressed entirely in black, and 'quite alone'. Victoria was conducted to her throne by the Royal Dukes, and received oaths of loyalty from members of the Council. It was then that Melbourne first heard her precise silvery tones ring out, and his heart was filled with admiration. From that time, his position as Prime Minister allowed him to see her almost every day. They met each morning for an audience, and again at dinner, and he often went riding with her in the afternoons. He advised, amused, and (privately) adored her. People said that he was a changed man when in her company. The Regency cynic was gone. He never blasphemed, lolled about, put his feet on the chairs or told indecent stories. He became a kindly, respectable uncle, with just sufficient humour to make his conversation delightful to the earnest girl. But his new manner was not a piece of acting. When out of her presence, if he spoke of the young Queen, his eyes would often fill with tears. He was besotted with her. That day in the Red Salon there began what has been called 'one of the romances of history'.[7] It lasted three years.

Melbourne's passion seemed unnatural to Caroline. She did not understand how a man of fifty-eight could be enthralled by a girl of eighteen, quite forgetting that in previous years it was her own youth and freshness which had charmed him. But there was no doubting that he had found another young girl to adore. And Victoria was taken with him. He must have seemed a romantic and tragic figure when he told her of his marriage to Caroline Lamb, of his rivalry with Lord Byron, and of his sad life with Augustus. Victoria dared not ask him about his friendships with Lady Branden and Caroline, but she discussed them with the Duchess of Sutherland. She was in awe of his experience of life, and believed he had much to teach her. Soon she became very possessive about him, and privately jealous of the women he knew. When he dined with the elderly Lady Holland, she confessed to her diary on 15 February 1838, 'I WISH he dined with me!'[8] No doubt she was even more envious when she heard that Melbourne paid an occasional visit to the youthful Mrs Norton.

Caroline heard the Court gossip from her friend, the Duchess of Sutherland, and she was mortified by the news of Melbourne's romance. But she dare not complain in her letters. A Queen was beyond criticism, and besides, she knew that he would never have permitted a word against her rival. Yet she clung firmly to the conviction that Melbourne was still hers by right, and she took consolation in the thought that this eighteen-year-old girl would soon find another, younger man. In this she was right but, in the meantime, Melbourne was determined that his old and new loves should not meet. He had a horror of the scandalous Caroline being presented to the pure young girl who was now his darling. So he used his authority as Prime

Minister to prevent her presentation at Court. It was his most disloyal act towards her, and greatly put back her hopes of becoming received in Society once more.

1838 was Coronation Year, and by the spring London was 'raving mad' about it all.[9] In May the Queen gave the first of three state balls, and these were followed by two levées and a concert. The aristocracy flocked to these events, and also to the hundreds of receptions, dances, and social gatherings given to celebrate the Coronation. The Sheridans and Seymours were among those invited to royal occasions but, as she had not been presented to the Queen, Caroline was not. So on many an evening when London Society was gathered together, Caroline stayed at home in Green Street. Of course she went to the private parties thrown by her relatives, and she attended the great Coronation Ball given by her old friend, Lord Lansdowne. Even when she was invited to such events, however, she was often faced with barely concealed hostility. Public acceptance of her had now become something of a Party matter, with the Whig families acknowledging, and the Tories ignoring her at receptions. But hostile treatment brought out courage in Caroline. She went wherever she was invited, and pretended not to notice the slights she received. After all, most of the men liked her.

The young Queen thought that Coronation Year was 'wonderful', and she was grateful to Melbourne who had been responsible for many of the arrangements. But Victoria was now openly jealous of his friendships among other women, and admitted that she could not bear to see Caroline's beautiful friend, the Duchess of Sutherland, Mistress of the Robes, sitting next to him at table and taking up his attention. Victoria so much forgot herself that one day she blurted out that she hated his regular visits to Holland House, and that she had a much greater affection for him than ever Lady Holland had. Melbourne was a master of tact. He merely smiled kindly and 'bowed assent'.[10] In fact this elderly roué was touched by the young girl's devotion but he was far too adroit to let it be an embarrassment to them both. Nevertheless, their passionate friendship was now a matter of public comment.

Throughout this time, Caroline continued to write to Melbourne, but though she constantly complained of his friendship with Lady Stanhope, she well understood where his affections were truly fixed. In February 1838, she included an oblique comment on the Queen when she wrote to complain that Lady Hester and her husband, a 'rank Tory', had twice been invited to dine at the Palace, while her own loyal Whig relatives, the Seymours, had never once received an invitation. She could not bear to think of him seated at dinner between her two rivals, the Queen and Hester Stanhope. In February 1839, she allowed her resentment to show in her indiscreet comments on a similar occasion: 'Here is a little family reunion for you, the Queen, & the woman you never made a doubt has been yr brother's mistress, (if she hasn't also been yours) . . . whom everyone mentions as your mistress, and wonders at your thrusting her on the Queen'.[11] It is not clear of which woman she was more jealous but she well knew it was safe for her to castigate Lady Hester, while she must not criticize Victoria.

Lord Melbourne's sixtieth birthday was on 15 March 1839 and Caroline sent round a present of two dozen claret glasses to South Street. She also put in a bitter little note to explain that they had been ordered the previous year, before she and Melbourne had become 'such very distant acquaintances'. But she was sympathetic, because she had learned from the newspapers that he was now in serious political trouble. The Jamaica Bill was going badly, and it was thought that if the Whigs could not get it through, the Government might fall. As for the Queen, she was appalled at the thought of losing Melbourne, and she deliberately made her Whig sympathies clear by making it plain that, even if Tory men came into government, she would accept no Tory ladies into her Household. This 'bedchamber plot' amounted to a miniature constitutional crisis in the relations between the Government and Crown, and was sufficiently serious to persuade the Tory leader, Sir Robert Peel, to hold off for a while to consider the situation. Melbourne saw his chance. He called together the Whig Parliamentary Party including those who had felt that it was time for them to leave office. He then produced from his pocket a letter he had received from the Queen in which she told him how she had resisted taking Tory ladies into her Household. His account of the situation now put the matter into a new light for his colleagues. For he saw the romance in it. According to him, this brave young girl had risked much to save the administration, and it was a matter of gallantry and patriotism for his colleagues to support her stand. They were convinced. The Whig Government soldiered on, and Melbourne resumed his idyll with the Queen.

His hold upon office was not merely an expression of his political tenacity, however, for he knew that when he lost it, he would lose his daily companionship with Victoria. But not everybody felt that this would be a bad thing, and the friendship between the monarch and her Prime Minister soon became very unpopular. One reason was because of their treatment of Lady Flora Hastings. It had been noticed in the Court that the figure of this poor young girl had recently become very swollen, and the gossips were whispering that she was pregnant. The Queen, who was already showing signs of prudery, insisted that Lady Flora should be medically examined, and Melbourne went along with this. It seems that, once again, he thought that he was defending the purity of the young Queen from unwholesome contact. Of course the whole Court knew about the business and, as might be expected, Lady Flora's family were furious at what they considered to be an affront to her reputation. When it was discovered that she was not pregnant, but cancerous, there was outrage even in Court circles, and the general public soon got to know of it. At the Ascot meeting that year, Victoria and Melbourne were hissed, and there were cries of 'Mrs Melbourne'. Lady Flora died on 5 July 1839, an object of universal sympathy. Her sad story confirmed many in their view that the friendship between the Queen and her Prime Minister was too close, and not in the national interest.

Melbourne too was aware that he could no longer keep the Queen to himself. In May 1839 she was twenty years old, and a consort had to be found for her. King Leopold, her uncle, was anxious that she should meet her two Saxe-Coburg cousins, the Princes Ernest and Albert, and they arrived on 8 October. The day after, Victoria wrote to Leopold from Windsor:

> Ernest is grown quite handsome; Albert's beauty is most striking, and he is amiable and unaffected – in short very fascinating . . .[12]

She had fallen in love with Albert. For a while, Melbourne put up a fight against the marriage by making facetious jokes, as when he told her that Germans smoked, and, what was worse, never washed their faces. But then his attitude changed. It seems that he had begun to recognize the fact that he would not be with Victoria much longer, and that she would need a new guide in her life. So he told her that he considered Prince Albert to be a 'very agreeable young man', and, when the marriage settlement was discussed, tried unsuccessfully to have him given precedence over the Royal Dukes.

He also began to prepare the Queen for his departure by deliberately playing up the old Regency cynicism, which he knew she disliked. For example, when she subjected him to a gushing speech about Albert's views on chastity, and added that she would never have married a man who had had an affair, Melbourne replied that every man should be allowed an affair at least once. This remark annoyed her, as he knew it would, and he provoked her even more on another occasion. It was when she told him that the thing she liked best about Albert was that he paid no attention to any woman but herself. Melbourne considered the matter and then replied coolly: 'That sort of thing is apt to come later'.

Victoria and Albert were married on 10 February 1840, and Melbourne was almost overcome with emotion during the ceremony. This event, and his inevitably changed relationship with the Queen, removed his last objections to Caroline's appearing at Court. She was presented in May by her sister, Lady Seymour. Caroline was very nervous, presumably because she feared an unsympathetic reception from the Queen. She trembled as she curtseyed before the throne in her 'Isle of Wight lace over white satin', while balancing her headdress of 'wreaths of lilac flowers, with pearl piquets intermixed, and plumes of ostrich feathers'.[13] But she need not have feared. The Queen displayed nothing more than curiosity towards this woman she had heard so much about. Afterwards, Victoria discussed the presentation with King Leopold, who told her something of Caroline's story:

> It was a very generous feeling which prompted you to see Mrs Norton, and I have been too much her friend to find fault with her.
> True it is that Norton freely accepted her, and she was very poor, and could, therefore, hardly venture to refuse him. Many people will flirt with a clever, handsome, but poor girl though not marry her; besides, the idea of having old Sherry as a grandfather had nothing very captivating. A very unpleasant husband Norton was, and one who had little tact.
> I can well believe that she was much frightened having so many eyes on her, some of which, perhaps, not with the most amiable expression.[14]

But the Queen was a new bride, and her thoughts were soon on matters other than her Prime Minister's friendship with Mrs Norton. As for Melbourne, his idyll was over; for Caroline, a rival was gone.

XXI

INFANT CUSTODY

VICTORIA'S CURIOSITY AT THE PRESENTATION was not solely because of Caroline's friendship with Lord Melbourne. By 1840, Caroline had become famous. To understand how this came about, it is necessary to return to June 1837, when she was reunited with her boys in London.

The end of that holiday came abruptly. Norton told her that he had to go down to Wonersh for a short visit, and that, though the boys might continue to see her daily, they had to go home at nights, where his sister, Augusta, would be responsible for them. Augusta arrived on 18 June. A few days later, Caroline discovered that the five-year-old Brinsley was feverish, and he begged to be allowed to stay the night with her. She dared not keep him. That evening she took him round to Norton's house in Wilton Place, where she was met by a stony-faced Augusta. At the door, Brinsley started to whimper that he wanted 'to go home with Mamma', but Augusta seized hold of him, and attempted to pull him into the house. Caroline instinctively held him back, and a fearful row broke out, with both women tugging at the child and screaming abuse at each other. During the shouting-match that followed, Caroline made the mistake of screaming that she had never had any intention of going back to Norton.[1] Eventually the sobbing children were dragged in by shame-faced servants and the door was shut with a bang. The next morning, an anxious Caroline was on the doorstep early to collect the boys, but she found that the servants had orders not to let her in. So she kept hammering at the door until, at last, the footman was obliged to open it. As soon as this happened, she tried to push past him and force her way inside. She was frantic because she could hear the children crying out for her in an upper room. But her way was barred, first by the servant, then Augusta, then by Norton himself. He seems to have made a sudden return from Wonersh, perhaps because Augusta had sent for him. Together, the Nortons and their servants manhandled Caroline out of the house. The following day, she was covered with bruises 'as though a cartwheel had gone over her'.

The quarrel had all happened so quickly that Caroline had not had time to take in its implications. But it was plain to her that, once again, Norton was preventing her from seeing her children. All she could do was to send her servants to spy on the house. Soon, she found out that the boys had been sent to Wonersh, so she hired a carriage and followed them. Next day, Lord Grantley, who had been away from home, arrived at Wonersh Park to be told by his butler that Mrs Norton had forced her way in, and was sitting in the nursery with her boys. Grantley marched up the stairs and burst in to find her seated, with William on her lap, and the two older ones standing close. When he ranted at her, she simply refused to leave. But when he ordered two of his servants to wrench William from her, she immediately let go, for fear that the boy should be hurt. These servants then bundled her out of the house, and Grantley leered triumphantly down at her, while she trudged away along the drive. When she returned home, she became ill from grief and rough treatment, and had to go to bed.[2]

Then began a struggle for the children which lasted many years. Caroline now understood that the reunion in June was only a brief armistice. What made matters worse was the memory of her shameful part in discouraging Talfourd from going on with his Infant Custody Bill. He had originally given the House notice of the Bill in February, and it was printed in May, but when Caroline had told him she was no longer interested, he had withdrawn the second reading in the summer. His feeble explanation to the House was that he did not intend to press this 'subject of delicacy and importance' at that time. Caroline's shame was further compounded by public criticism of her own part in the business. Soon after Talfourd's speech, *The British & Foreign Review* said that the Bill had been withdrawn simply because Mrs Norton had got her children back and now had no use for the reform. It suggested that she had planned the entire campaign merely to solve her own domestic problems. The writer, Harriet Martineau, agreed with the *Review*. She always took the view that Caroline's reforms were never undertaken to help other women, but purely for her own selfish ends. In this she was unfair, but there is no doubt that Caroline's *original* motivation was self-interest.

One of her good qualities, however, was persistence, and she now encouraged Talfourd to renew his campaign in the House of Commons. She herself helped public discussion along by publishing another pamphlet on women's rights. It was called: *The Separation of Mother & Child by the Law of Custody of Infants, Considered*,[3] and she worked harder at it than anything else she had written. She read through countless court reports to obtain evidence, and this research convinced her more than ever before of the need for a change in the laws affecting a mother's right to see her children. One of her discoveries was that the present law was deeply anomalous. For example, if a woman had an illegitimate child, nobody could challenge her right to it until it was seven years old; whereas a child born within wedlock was entirely the responsibility of its father. He could take it away from its mother whenever he wished. In one case Caroline investigated, a man named Skinner had removed his children from his wife and given them to his mistress to look after. Nobody could stop him. A father could take his children by force, 'even should they be infants at the breast', and he could, afterwards prevent their mother from seeing them. Caroline discovered that no court was willing to intervene in even the most blatant cases where children had been removed from mothers, and no court was willing to consider the reasons for marriage-breakdown when deciding the future of the children. Judges argued that they had no power 'to order that a woman should have occasional access to her children, [even] though she could prove that she was driven by violence from her husband's house, and that he had deserted her for a mistress'. But Caroline could not refrain from pointing out with some bitterness, that though the law allowed a girl of fifteen or sixteen to 'give [herself] away' in marriage, it considered her too young to choose whether she should live with her mother or father. She concluded that such a situation could not be accounted for: 'unless indeed the laws are made for men alone'.

Despite this, Caroline noticed that courts did sometimes regard children's interests as paramount, as when they refused to force those over fourteen to return unwillingly to their fathers, and also when they removed children from fathers considered to be immoral or irreligious. So she could argue in her pamphlet that there was already a precedent in which the interests of members of the family other than the father were considered by the courts, and that these should be extended to include the mother. She pointed out that it was the mother who 'endure[d] for nearly a year a tedious suffering, ending in an agony which [imperilled] her life', and that most men recognized her instinctive relationship with her child. Such suffering established a 'natural law' to which a mother might appeal. In Caroline's view, only a few men were so debased that they defied this natural law in order to wreak an 'unmanly vengeance' on an innocent mother. If the law recognized a mother's rights, it would benefit not only her, but her children too, because young children needed a mother's care. Removing children from their mothers was an act of inexcusable cruelty, as she knew from personal experience.

> It requires but little imagination to conceive the effect upon a woman's heart, of suddenly snapping the tenderest of ties, and depriving her of the sweetest and most continual occupations; or to picture to oneself how dreary must be the silence of her day! how bitter the perpetual recurrence of the hour devoted for years to her goodnight visit to her nursery! how wearing the nights of fitful sleep, disturbed by the indistinct, yet heavy consciousness of sorrow! how maddening these bursts of intense longing to be with her children ... And this is a grief which does not wear out, or go by like other sorrows – it is the torture of a life-time: Why should any man have power because he is offended, to inflict the torture of a lifetime.[4]

Cruelty always moved Caroline to indignation:

> ... A man does not purchase a wife as he would buy a fine blood-mare, or a hound, to continue a race of animals and then be got rid of, her offspring remaining his undoubted and undisputed property. He chooses a companion; a thinking, acting, reflecting being; one, if a mother, is the mother of immortal souls, and accountable to God for the trust. That man may afterwards repent the choice he made and become discontented with it, but his discontent does not transform the woman into a cypher or slave; it does not reverse and alter every right and purpose of her existence; it does not, or rather it ought not, to change her from a wife and mother into a thing as helpless, useless and blighted as a scathed tree.[5]

Once again she had rested her case upon the idea of 'rights', but this time the tenor of her argument suggests that she had been reading the work of her grandfather's old friend, Edmund Burke. Rights, she argued, are 'either Natural or Artificial ... if Artificial, the Law has the same power to adjudge the custody of infants, that it would have in case of any other artificial right; if Natural, the law has no power to order children from their mother, since by nature the rights of both parents are co-equal'.[6] Whether they were founded upon convention or nature, parental rights were the same for both parents. Talfourd was so impressed by her words that he quoted her pamphlet copiously in the House.

Caroline started to write her pamphlet in Green Street, in the autumn of 1837. She now spent most of her days there, working at her desk. Such hard, purposeful living always raised her spirits. She scribbled her poems and pamphlets in a great rush, and posted them off to John Murray. He was helpful and generous. In addition to paying her, he would sometimes send her free copies of the books he published. Among them was *Don Juan*, by her hero Lord Byron. To Caroline's great surprise, she hated it. She had been disposed to like anything by her grandfather's old friend, but Byron's cheerful libertinism grated on her. She told Murray that the effect of reading the poem was 'like hearing some sweet and touching melody familiar to me . . . suddenly struck up in quick time with all the words parodied'.[7]

One day she received a new proposal from Norton. After the dreadful scene in the summer, he had packed the boys off to Scotland again, and placed yet another advertisement in the press to disclaim responsibility for her debts, though, as Abraham Hayward had pointed out, this was a 'useless insult, as he would not be liable if he made her a proper allowance'. Norton now suggested that, as they were unable to come to agreement about children and finances, they should each appoint a referee. He nominated Sir John Bayley, son of a famous judge, and one of his counsels during the Melbourne trial. But when Caroline chose Thomas Talfourd, Norton quickly changed his tune, and said that there should be only one referee to represent them both, and that this should be Bayley. Against Brinsley's advice, Caroline agreed.

So began the involvement of the Bayley family in Caroline's affairs, which resulted in something which would have been farce, if so much human misery had not been attached to it. Sir John Bayley started work in November 1837, and, from the first, tried hard to get an agreement between the parties. Initially, he was very suspicious of Caroline, having been told by Norton that she was a 'tricksy, worldly, revengeful' woman. To his surprise, he encountered a beautiful young mother, grief-stricken at the loss of her children and desperate to see them again. Sir John's gallantry was roused.

From Caroline he learned that Norton had been a most violent and cruel husband, and that there was 'nothing he [had] not attempted short of murdering' her. Bayley tried to calm her. He assured Caroline that he wanted to be a friend to them both, and promised to ask Norton to bring the boys down from Scotland as an earnest of good intentions. Norton agreed, and on 30 November, told Bayley that he had instructed that the boys should be sent down on the *Dundee*. Sir John was delighted by what seemed immediate progress, but was rather taken aback when Caroline told him not to trust anything Norton said. Her instinct was right; the boys never came. Sir John was dumbfounded. He did not know how to proceed with a man who did not keep his word. As a result, on 2 December, he wrote to Norton and declined to act further for him, though it seems he was still willing to represent Caroline.

She felt vindicated by this episode. A respected barrister, who had been appointed by her husband, had now examined her case, and had changed sides. For his part, Sir John was infuriated by Norton's conduct. He now believed that Norton was not a man of his word. He had broken his promise to bring the boys to London, and also an agreement which would have allowed Richard Brinsley Sheridan to buy back his sister's personal effects. In fact, Norton had changed his mind suddenly, when he realized that Caroline's note-books might furnish evidence of her meetings with lovers. When Caroline learned of his motives, she remarked dryly to Bayley that if she had had an affair, she was hardly likely to have left notes on it. Despite these irritants, Sir John still worked hard to get an agreement, but just when he thought he was succeeding, Norton backed out again. He pretended to think that Caroline was leading an immoral life which made her unfit to see the boys. He loftily demanded further proofs of Caroline's 'improved conduct'. It was as if he considered himself to be her schoolmaster. Caroline quietly assured Bayley that, though her husband represented her as 'a shameless, impudent, painted creature – a sort of strolling actress at a fair', she lived very quietly at home, with her uncle and brother.

Caroline had almost given up hope now. Worn out with grief and worry, she went down to Frampton Court once more for Christmas 1837, and wrote to tell Sir John that the journey, the cold, and the misery had 'knocked [her] up'. She said she was wearing out fast, and would soon give no one any trouble. But he replied cheerfully that he was going to have one more try to get an agreement, and that he had high hopes. He said that he had completed a draft agreement with Norton, and they had sent it to Lord Wynford, Norton's uncle, whose assent would have to be obtained. On 21 December, Wynford withdrew his last objections, though Caroline suspected this was only because he wanted to stop her publishing her husband's letters, which were so objectionable they would have embarrassed the whole Norton family. Over the New Year, she allowed herself to dream that she would soon see the boys, but then Sir John wrote again to tell her wearily that Norton had raised yet more objections, and refused to pay her more than a derisory £400. Bayley had had enough. But he did not want to give up without retaining Caroline's respect:

> I am most anxious that my character should stand clear with the world, particularly as I came into the negotiation as Mr Norton's friend, and have been driven, by a sense of justice, to turn my back upon him . . . I did believe Mr Norton, and that must be the excuse for the misery and disappointment which you have endured at my hands. Let me stand well with your own kind, considerate, and consistent family, and I can easily bear the rest![8]

For a while, it seemed that Talfourd might be more successful than Bayley. Caroline had lobbied hard for his Bill among her political friends, and initially the omens looked good. It was true that there was not much parliamentary interest in the measure, and only 108 of the 656 MPs turned out when it first came before the House, but it was passed by 91 votes to 17. Talfourd had not requested government support, and had to rely upon cross-party votes to get the Bill through. He must have been pleased, therefore, to win those of Disraeli, by then a Tory; Charles Villiers, the Whig; and the Radical, Daniel Harvey. Ominously, however, there were powerful names among his few opponents, including the historian, Grote, and the future Lord Chancellor, Sugden. Caroline was especially stung by their arguments, because these assumed throughout that any woman separated from her husband must be guilty of adultery. Even when Lord Mahon proposed the amendment that access to children should not apply to women guilty of 'unchastity', the Bill's opponents continued with this line of argument, though it was of no apparent interest to them if husbands were adulterers. Sugden also argued that the slightest relaxation of the marriage laws would turn 'even those who had hitherto been most faithful and devoted wives and mothers, into a dangerous menace to society'.[9]

It was this kind of argument that swayed the few lords who turned up to debate the Bill. Caroline wrote to explain matters to a friend: 'You cannot get Peers to sit up till three in the morning listening to the wrongs of separated wives. They are disturbed by the preposterous importance set by women on the society of their infant children, and doubtful of the effect of such a claim on the authority of the heads of families.' But she was still hopeful at this stage, because she understood that the lords would let their legal experts settle the matter for them. Unfortunately for her, she had made an enemy in Lord Brougham, who believed, perhaps correctly, that she had used her personal influence to get him sacked from Melbourne's Government. He was determined to oppose any measure that she was associated with, and made a brilliant speech against Talfourd's Bill, arguing that legal hardships were necessarily inflicted on women in order to protect the family unit. The Lords threw the Bill out, and the cause seemed hopeless.

Queen Victoria was crowned in June 1838, but that same month brought only humiliation to Caroline, after Norton published yet another advertisement, this time in several newspapers:

> Whereas on March 30, 1836, my wife, Caroline Elizabeth Sarah, left me, her family, and home, and hath from thenceforth continued to live separate and apart from me, etc . . .

He was attempting by this advertisement to signal again to Caroline's creditors that he would refuse to pay her bills, but this did not prevent a livery-stable keeper from bringing an action against him for non-payment of £142. It was the cost of the phaeton Caroline had hired to drive the boys about in London the previous summer. The case was heard before Lord Abinger, an old friend of Norton's uncle, Lord Wynford. Unfortunately for Caroline, the case once more paraded her marital troubles before the public, and that did not help to restore her reputation. Whole columns of newsprint invited their readers to consider just *why* Norton was unwilling to pay his wife's debts, and the whole story of her friendship with Melbourne was dragged out again. At the outset, Caroline's lawyers hoped to introduce Norton's letters into the evidence. These notes included more than one statement by him that he did not really believe Caroline had committed adultery. Their publication would have gone a long way towards clearing her name. But when Sir John Bayley, who had been called as a witness by the plaintiff, tried to have Norton's letters read out in court, there was an objection from the defence. It was upheld by the judge, Lord Abinger. He had made little pretence of impartiality throughout, and now he scolded Sir John for trying to produce evidence which, he said, could only have been obtained when he was acting as Norton's legal adviser. Abinger also berated Caroline for trying to help the plaintiff against her own husband, and ended by acidly reminding the jury that it was not obliged to consider whether Mrs Norton had been turned out of her house for adultery. Norton won.

Caroline was so incensed by this failure to have her case put in court that she announced she would write to *The Times* about it. Her friends begged her not to do so, and, as for Melbourne, the last thing he wanted in Coronation Year was for the whole matter to be repeated. His hands were full enough with political problems and the arrangements for the Coronation. He could barely conceal his exasperation that yet again this 'sobbing, moaning, and complaining woman' should seek the centre of the stage, when he wanted all eyes to be on the Queen. He was well aware that, if Caroline wrote to *The Times*, then Norton would reply and the correspondence would go on until the editor's patience ran out. This he told Caroline. Reluctantly she agreed not to write to the papers, but she made it plain she only did so for his sake:

> young, childless, defamed, sorrowful and rash ... there never was a day that I rebelled against his advice [because] these means ... would be beyond measure, vexatious and embarrassing to him.[10]

At first there seemed little Caroline could do, but once again she returned to the fight, by producing another pamphlet entitled: *A Plain Letter to the Lord Chancellor on the Infant Custody Bill*.[11] It came out in 1839. She adopted a nom-de-plume, presumably because her own name was too notorious to command a readership. Instead, she called herself 'Pearce Stevenson Esq', to suggest that the author was some respectable old lawyer. It was a long and detailed piece of writing in which she reported a series of case histories and threw in her personal opinions. It was not well received. The truth is that she was boring the reading public with these endless repetitions of her case.

By 1839, she was beginning to be invited out rather more, and she became a familiar face once again in a number of Society drawing rooms. Fanny Allen noticed her rather wistful expression and comforted her with the opinion that she had 'the countenance of a Sybil', and went into raptures when Caroline sang songs by herself and Tom Moore.[12] Caroline soon found that melancholy could recruit admirers as well as vivacity. At a reception for her old friend, Babbage, she captivated a young American named John Van Buren. He was the son of the President, and had stayed on for a while after the Coronation. He first came upon Caroline talking to Thomas Talfourd in a doorway, and enthusiastically wrote home to say that, though her figure was rather heavy compared with the 'fragile beauties of New England', there were few women to surpass her in graciousness and spirited conversation.[13] Another American friend was the jurist Sumner, whom she met at a dinner in February 1838, and who admired all the Sheridan women:

> ... [they] were far more remarkable than the men. I unhesitatingly say that they were the four most beautiful, clever and accomplished women I have ever seen together. The beauty of Mrs Norton has never been exaggerated. It is brilliant and refined. Her countenance is lighted by eyes of the intensest brightness, and her features are of the greatest regularity. There is something tropical in her look, it is so intensely bright and burning, with large dark eyes, dark hair, and Italian complexion. And her conversation is so pleasant and powerful, without being masculine; or rather it is masculine without being mannish; there is the grace and ease of the woman, with a strength and skill of which any man might be proud ... I believe her utterly innocent of the grave charges that have been brought against her.[14]

But even at parties, Caroline did not forget her self-appointed task of reforming the law. When Van Buren saw her with Talfourd, they were probably discussing his latest attempt to get an Infant Custody Bill on to the statute book. Talfourd now seemed more hopeful. He thought that, at last, the hard stone of opposition was wearing away. He was right. Caroline's repeated letters to the press, and her pamphlets addressed to politicians, had both had a considerable effect on informed opinion. She had succeeded in communicating to the public just how awful was the situation of innocent women who were separated from their husbands, and thereby deprived of their children. It was also probably true that both public and politicians were a bit sick of the matter, and were willing to let Caroline have her way.

In the summer of 1839, the Infant Custody Bill was passed by both Houses. It allowed regular access to both parents of children of twelve years or under. In this way at least, parents had equal rights. And for the first time since the Middle Ages, a law was passed which acknowledged the existence and rights of married women.

It was Talfourd who moved the Bill but he had no doubt that the triumph was really Caroline's. And she was justified in her pride at the achievement. Even Mary Wollstonecraft had only put the case for women's rights, but Caroline had got an Act on to the statute book. Now, throughout England and Wales, women who were deserted, separated, and divorced might demand to see their children, and the law would support them. It was a practical measure with immediate effect. Caroline herself looked forward to seeing her three sons soon.

But George Norton was a lawyer and fly enough to evade the Act. He sent the boys to Scotland.

XXII

THE COMPANY OF WRITERS

CAROLINE'S PRESENTATION AT COURT gained her only a partial re-acceptance in the London social world of the 1840s, and she continued to spend much of her time among those writers whom she considered her real friends. Chief among these were Tom Moore and Samuel Rogers.

Tom Moore had remained faithful since that first day when he had called at Great George Street to congratulate her on her dancing at Almack's. He had a 'warm and sunshiny nature',[1] which radiated innocent affection and admiration for her. Before her marriage, he used to take her out. One such occasion was their trip to the Summer Fête given by Lord Henry Fitzgerald at Boyle Farm, which he afterwards satirized in a spoof version of *The Rape of the Lock*. In his poem, the debutantes who were there looking for husbands became 'Young nuns whose chief religion lay / In looking most profanely handsome', and most handsome of them all was Caroline, cast as Belinda, receiving the attentions of the young George Norton:

> . . . yon blushing maid,
> Who sits in beauty's light arrayed,
> While o'er leans a tall young Dervise,
> (Who from her eyes, as all observe, is
> Learning by heart the Marriage Service),
> Is the bright heroine of our song, –
> The love-wed Psyche, whom so long, –
> We've missed among this mortal train,
> We thought her winged to heaven again.[2]

It was perceptive of Moore that, even then, he should have detected something of the uncivilized fanatic in the 'Dervish', Norton. He himself was the most civilized and gentle of men, and had supported Caroline with his kindness and sense of fun through many a stiff reception, and used his own popularity to gain acceptance for her. When he was asked to sing in company, he would frequently insist that she should join him in a duet.

Tom Moore was a licensed Irish rebel in the drawing rooms of English Society, where his performances of his own *Irish Melodies* made him a welcome guest. He had gone to the same school as Caroline's grandfather, Sam Whyte's in Dublin, and then come to England to train as a lawyer. He never practised, but chose to make a precarious living as poet and singer, and writer of biographies of his friends Sheridan and Byron. He sang to English lords and ladies of Ireland's wrongs and they clapped him enthusiastically. He was universally loved. Shelley had sought his good opinion; Jeffrey, the editor of *The Edinburgh Review*, took to him at sight; Sydney Smith was a close companion; and Leigh Hunt sang his praises.[3] Moore loved to tell the story of how he had first met Byron, who had indelicately reviewed one of his poems by referring to his [Moore's] 'leadless pistol', in which, 'on examination, the balls . . . were found to have evaporated'.[4] As a result, Moore challenged Byron to a duel but, fortunately, at the last moment, the combatants agreed to meet at a dinner party where they sat down with Samuel Rogers and Thomas Campbell. Byron initially refused all food save mashed potatoes and vinegar, but he found Moore's companionship anything but acidic, and by the end of the night, they were fast friends. Moore would have told Caroline about Byron's little joke, because she liked that sort of thing. Of course, he could tell her only in private.

She liked many other things about Moore, such as his Irishry and his uncompromising loyalty to the values of the Romantics. And she was grateful for his personal kindness. He always seemed to think well of her, and showed great courage in taking her part when she was shunned by Society. Their friendship was above suspicion. She would sing with him the favourites from his *Irish Melodies*, especially: 'Love's Young Dream', 'The Harp that Once through Tara's Halls', 'Believe Me if all those Endearing Young Charms', 'The Last Rose of Summer', and 'The Minstrel Boy', while English aristocrats sat round, deeply moved, as her rich contralto and his high tenor entwined in a passionate Celtic poignancy. And it was these songs of Tom Moore which first suggested to Caroline that she too might write sentimental ballads for young women to sing in Victorian drawing rooms.

Yet it was Samuel Rogers, rather than Moore, who provided Caroline with most of her social life during the early Forties. He was famous for his literary dinner and breakfast parties and, as he was unmarried, frequently asked her to act as his hostess. It was at Rogers's table that she met almost all the important figures in the London literary world at that time. And it was from Rogers that she learned first-hand a great deal more about the lives of the Romantic writers of the previous generation.

Rogers, like Moore, had known Byron and Sheridan, and had attended her grandfather in his last illness. He was an important friend for Caroline. In 1840, he was seventy-seven years old but at the height of his literary influence. His table-talk was 'reported about town', especially by his many American admirers, like Charles Sumner, who found him fascinating company.[5] His literary prestige was so great that, when Wordsworth died in 1850, he was offered the poet laureateship, which he declined with the admirable remark that, at his age, he had little left to say. He was an ugly little man, thin, baldheaded, and usually dressed in an old-fashioned frock coat and waistcoat. Carlyle described him as 'old Rogers, with his pale head, white, bare and cold as snow . . . those large blue eyes, cruel and sorrowful, and that sardonic shelf chin'.[6]

Sometimes, when they were alone, Rogers would tell Caroline about his boyhood. He had been born as long ago as 1763, in Stoke Newington, which was a village two miles from London. He had spent his childhood walking, riding, and bathing in the then unpolluted streams, and reading omnivorously at home. His family were bankers, non-conformists and Whigs. As a boy he had met the famous Dr Price and others of his Stoke Newington circle, including Mary Wollstone-craft. His long life had embraced an astonishing number of changes. He had succeeded as head of the family banking business, and, when he retired, he had moved from Stoke Newington to his present house, St James's Place, opposite Green Park.

He chose St James's Place as an ideal location to help him cut a figure in literary society, and in this he succeeded. He was still writing poetry in his seventies, though his poem *Pleasures of Memory*, published when he was twenty-nine, remained his best-known work. His greatest financial success had been the poetic commentary he wrote to accompany Turner's *Italy*. This book of engravings was an enormous publishing venture. It was completed in 1832 at a cost of £7335 for 6800 copies. Rogers's pace of composition was a joke; he wrote only four verses a day compared to forty by Crabbe. He complained that contemporary writers wrote too fast and that, therefore, their work would not last. Caroline might well have felt uneasy when she heard him say this, for poetry writing came easily to her, and she often dashed off many verses in a day. But, in her defence, she could have pointed out to him that she had to write for money, while he could take his time on a banker's pension.

During the Forties, Rogers frequently invited her to preside at his St James's Place dinners, and it was at these that she learned to admire and imitate his acerbic wit. Such evenings were little holidays for her, because they allowed her to be witty, when that talent was fast falling out of fashion, especially among women. Elsewhere she might have to bite back her tongue, but at Rogers's table she could relax and crack jokes with the men. In such company, she knew that she had little reputation to lose, so she could say almost what she liked.

Rogers was publicly waspish yet privately kind. Lady Donegal said that though he was 'sickly and dissatisfied', he supplied 'a very needful quantity of vinegar' to social life. He certainly had a sharp tongue, and a guest who said something silly soon felt its edge. Rogers was also a famous raconteur. Over the years, Caroline got to know his stories by heart and would listen with affectionate pride as he told once again: how he had visited Paris during the lull in the Revolution, in 1791, and had afterwards been called before the English Privy Council on suspicion of sedition; how he had watched Napoleon Bonaparte receiving petitions from a group of elegant, adoring women; how he himself had founded the 'King of Clubs' which was the nearest thing to an English Academy of Literature; how he had shown Crabbe round London; how Byron had talked; and how Richard Brinsley Sheridan had died. She loved his reminiscences of the Duke of Wellington, who had confided in him that he had met a Spanish woman who had patriotically drowned many French soldiers down a well. And there was his story of Sir Walter Scott's way of disposing of a rival at school. Apparently, this nervous but clever boy had always twiddled a coat button to gain confidence in answering difficult questions. The young Scott noticed this and stole the button; from that time onwards, the boy's performance in class deteriorated, and Scott got the better of him. Sometimes, Rogers would produce a hush round the table as he whispered the story of how he had stayed at Fonthill, the astounding Gothic Abbey rebuilt by the crazed Romantic, William Beckford, and of how his host would creep out at night to pray to a portrait of St Anthony. Then Rogers might end the evening with his conversations with Burke and Talleyrand, and his recollection of the famous dinner when Byron and Moore first became friends.[7]

Caroline was especially interested in his gossip about Holland House. She herself was never invited there, and neither was any other gentlewoman, because Lady Holland had been divorced, and therefore was considered an even more scandalous figure than Caroline. So Holland House had become a kind of club for prominent Whigs, and

Lady Holland presided over evenings where her talk was every bit as coarse as that of some of her guests. Rogers and Moore were regular visitors, and so were Melbourne, Macaulay, Bobus Smith, and his brother, Sydney, who soon became a frank friend of Caroline and described her as 'a superb lump of flesh'. Caroline had already had a taste of Lady Holland's spitefulness, for once in a jealous fit on a public occasion, the lady had snatched a posy from her hair. At another time, while Rogers was in the middle of a speech, she shouted out: 'Your poetry is bad enough, so please be sparing of your prose'.[8] Like Caroline, she loved to queen it in male company, to gossip, to whisper malice and to defy convention. She was a formidable rival, for she welcomed the Whig aristocracy to the magnificence of Holland House, while Caroline could merely act as hostess to Rogers's little supper parties. Yet their salons were complementary. Holland House was chiefly political, whereas St James's Place was artistic, and many guests would go from one to the other. Nevertheless, there was an important difference between them. Lady Holland was socially so powerful that she had no need to court respectability, whereas Caroline was still trying to regain it. When old Rogers told his cronies at Holland House about Richard Brinsley Sheridan's amorous adventures, and how he had pestered Mrs Kemble in a coach, Lady Holland was free to roar with laughter. At St James's Place, Caroline had to be careful not to hear all the jokes.

Sometimes, Rogers might ask Caroline to help him welcome guests to his breakfasts, and she would stand next to his waxen little figure to greet them in the entrance hall. Rogers had an extraordinary collection of paintings and curiosities to show his guests. Hanging in the hall were Georgione's 'Knight in Armour' and a 'Madonna and Child' by Raphael. Providing a commentary on the exhibits enabled Caroline to practise a rich breathlessness, which she knew the men found especially charming, and she also had the opportunity to raise her elegant neck and toss back her raven hair, while she pointed out details in the two Titians, the Guido, and Reynolds's 'Strawberry Girl'. Perhaps Rogers would chime in to tell the tale of how Sir Joshua Reynolds had made his final address to the Royal Academy, which finished with the words: 'Michael Angelo', and how Edmund Burke had then stepped forward to quote Milton:

> The Angel ended, and in Adam's ear
> So charming left his voice, that he a while
> Thought him still speaking, still stood fix'd to hear.[9]

While the old man talked, Caroline would stand smiling and nodding in an affectionate way, and then, in her low melodious tones, would invite guests to examine the chimneypiece by Flaxman, the marvellous collections of drawings by old masters, the miniatures and gold coins, a cabinet decorated by Stothard, and portions of classical statuary. She might let her irony play about the antique female hand which served as a paper-weight, and the antique female foot which was used to stop the door. But she and Rogers were proudest of a simple scrap of paper, framed and glazed, and hanging on a door. It was Milton's receipt to the publisher for the £5 he had been paid for *Paradise Lost*. Milton, she observed, had had three wives, whereas her friend Mr Rogers had to be content with a hostess. They laughed.

Dinner parties at St James's Place provided Caroline with even more dramatic opportunities. Rogers would not allow the candles to be put on the table, but high up on the walls, to show off the pictures, and incidentally, the features of his hostess. Sydney Smith disliked this affectation, and declared that 'above there [was] a blaze of light, and below nothing but darkness and gnashing of teeth'.[10] On the night of 26 January 1845, Caroline was once again to be the only woman present. That night Rogers had invited Moxon the publisher, Henry Crabb Robinson, Spedding, Henry Lushington, James Kenny the dramatist, and, to Caroline's delight, the fashionable poet, Alfred Tennyson, whom she had long wanted to meet. She took care to arrive late, and eventually, swept into the room, where the diners in darkness looked up to see her lovely face on a level with the masterpieces blazing with colour round the walls. As his guests rose awkwardly, Rogers led her to the vacant seat between himself and the *enfant terrible*, Alfred Tennyson. She pretended at first not to notice him specially, and joined in the general conversation 'with an ease and a spirit that showed her quite used to society'. But when she turned to Tennyson, she became aware that this cadaverous, badly dressed man was regarding her with horror. Nothing she could say was right, though she tried all her little ways to captivate him. He answered her remarks only curtly, or not at all. When she left the room, Rogers asked Tennyson what were his impressions of her. Tennyson replied that he 'felt as if a serpent had just dropped off' him, and added that he had 'shuddered sitting by her side'. Afterwards, Caroline complained to Rogers that Tennyson's manner had been offensive, and, when she heard what he had said about her, declared that she would like to see 'all the Tennysons hung up in a row'.[11]

Tennyson was not alone in reacting to Caroline like this. There were always a few men who resented the determination behind her attempts to fascinate them. It must have seemed like a kind of sexual bullying to them, and they would not submit. But Tennyson's dislike was probably initiated as much by prudery as physical revulsion. No doubt he had heard a distorted version of Caroline's story, and to discover her dining alone with seven men merely confirmed his suspicions. He had already concluded that she must be a blatantly immoral woman, before she had addressed one word to him. Every little move she made at the dinner party subsequently seemed to him to be part of her armoury of sensual signals. No wonder she disgusted him.

This incident confirms that Caroline's reputation had not fully recovered from the Melbourne case even nine years later, and that, for many people, her name was still synonymous with scandalous goings-on. Her unfortunate reputation was so widespread, that it had the power to compromise people even at a distance. For example, in the early Forties she had become friends with Charles Dickens and his wife, and in January 1842, they were in Boston, on an American tour. Dickens was an obliging lecturer who was willing to answer questions, and his American hosts were eager for London gossip, and especially news of the famous Mrs Norton and her circle. At dinner at Judge Prescott's house, a fellow guest begged to know whether Caroline, or the Duchess of Sutherland, was the more handsome. Dickens, who was probably in convivial mood at that time, replied: 'Well I don't know, Mrs Norton is perhaps more beautiful, but the Duchess to my mind is a more kissable person'.[12] Unfortunately for him, such talk was considered outrageous in strait-laced Boston, and his hosts were relieved when he left for New York.

It is not known if Caroline heard of the Boston incident, but, if so, it would not have surprised her. That sort of thing was always happening. And it must have seemed so unfair to her, for she was now leading the arduous life of a working writer. Those days were long gone when Disraeli would arrive in 'a coat of black velvet, poppy-coloured trousers broidered with gold, a scarlet waistcoat, [and] sparkling rings worn on top of white kid gloves', to escort her to the theatre.[13] Her mornings were spent mostly at her desk, though occasionally she would make and receive calls. She had to work because Norton made her no allowance. Since she had first gone to live in Mayfair, she had earned her keep, and paid her Uncle Charles regularly.

Her chief source of income was her gift books. She had become a contributor to *The Keepsake*, as long ago as 1836, but, after the

Melbourne trial, she found she was in much more demand with the publishers. People who would not acknowledge her in a drawing room were drawn by her name on a title-page, and publishers knew it. Caroline took on any writing task, however odd. In 1841, for example, she edited *Schloss's Bijou Almanac*, with pages no bigger than postage stamps, on which she printed her own little verses and portraits of her friends. She also edited *The English Annual*, and, from 1846 onwards, *Fisher's Drawing-Room Scrap-Book*, for which she composed poems to set off the exotic scenes printed on adjoining pages. She enjoyed the challenge of this, and prided herself that she was never stumped for a verse, even when the picture was of something as remote from her own experience as a Chinese opium den:

> Life is sad: let us cheat it by dreaming
> Of joys that cannot be real!
> Bring us opium; that one panacea
> A thousand disasters shall heal!
> No lover shall mourn his false mistress, –
> No wronged one deep vengeance recall, –
> No scheme of success mock ambition, –
> No gambler his ruin appal.
>> Bring the drug, – it shall banish our care!
>> Blessed Lethe that save us despair! . . .

Much more important for her reputation, however, was her book, *The Dream and Other Poems*, first published in 1840.[14] In it she included some interesting and thinly disguised portraits of her friends and enemies. For example, a poem about a winter's walk with Samuel Rogers records his kindness to her grandfather, Sheridan, '. . . one whom Heaven endowed with varied powers / . . . one who died, e'er yet my childish heart / Knew what Fame meant, or Slander's fabled dart!' Rogers is glimpsed at his dinner-table:

> Who can forget, who at thy social board
> Hath sat, – and seen the pictures richly stored,
> In all their tints of glory and of gloom,
> Brightening the precincts of thy quiet room;
> With busts and statues full of that deep grace
> Which modern hands have lost the skill to trace . . .
> . . . Th'exact and classic taste by thee displayed;[15]

For those who might recognize it, she also included a bitter sketch of
George Norton:

> Ah! never to the Sensualist appeal,
> Nor deem his frozen bosom ought can feel.
> Affection, root of all fond memories,
> Which bids what once hath charm'd for ever please,
> He knows not: all thy beauty could inspire
> Was but a sentiment of low desire . . .
> . . . And if his cold and selfish thought had power
> T'accelerate the final fatal hour,
> The silent murder were already done,
> And thy white tomb would glitter in the sun . . .
> . . . His palled and wearied senses rove apart,
> And for his heart – thou never hadst his heart.[16]

The greater part of *The Dream*, however, is taken up with a series of
sentimental self-portraits in three long narrative poems. For some
reason, Caroline's literary conception of herself was quite different
from the part she played in social life. In Samuel Rogers's dining room
she was sociable, witty and slightly risqué. As a poet she was solemn
and self-pitying. In the title-poem, 'The Dream', she recounts a long
conversation between a mother and her daughter who is to be married
on the following day. In effect the speakers are Caroline as a schoolgirl
at Wonersh, before Norton had ever set eyes on her, and the
disillusioned Mrs Norton who has suffered brutal treatment and the
loss of her children. The young bride-to-be dreams of a paradisal
world, but her mother warns her of the suffering inevitable to a
woman's lot. The writer's intentions are very clear throughout.
Caroline wants to arouse sympathy for the mother who has known
such suffering, and through her, for herself. A second poem, 'The
Creole Girl', presents Caroline's suffering once again, this time in the
guise of a half-caste girl, whose callous white lover will not acknowledge her. In 'A Destiny', a wife is unable to endure her husband's
crooked gambling, and eventually dies of despair. Caroline Norton
always wanted pity, and, in this book, shamelessly exploits her
opportunities to get it. As a result, *The Dream and Other Poems* is
extremely tedious to the modern reader.

Yet in 1840, the book was a success. This may have been because
the writing exactly suited contemporary taste for moralizing verse,
but that would be only part of the story. What attracted many

purchasers was probably the intriguing combination of aristocratic chic and social notoriety promised by Caroline's name on the cover. Whatever the reason, it brought Caroline literary fame and a small degree of affluence. In *The Quarterly Review* Hartley Coleridge hailed her as 'The Byron of Modern Poetesses' in an appreciation he was writing of the ten best-known contemporary women poets. He ranked Caroline first, just ahead of Elizabeth Barrett Browning.

Shortly after *The Dream and Other Poems* came out, Caroline wrote to Mary Shelley, to say that now she could afford to buy a little one-horse shay for herself, she proposed to go driving round London to see her friends. Since 1836 she had never owned a carriage, and had had to rely on hiring cabs, or being offered a lift whenever she wanted to go out. Then the book went into a second edition, and she became yet more affluent. It was even pirated in its entirety and reprinted in an American newspaper, and there can be no doubt that it was Caroline's scandalous reputation there, which prompted the American interest in her which Dickens had already discovered. Her notoriety was helping to make her a famous writer on two continents. Indeed she had a double advantage, for, though it was her name which initially intrigued the young girls who were the main readers of such poetry, when their mothers inspected the book, they found it reassuringly vapid. And not only did *The Dream* help Caroline's campaign for respectability, it also got her fresh contracts. Requests for more gift-book work rolled in, and the royalties with them, a state of affairs which did not evade George Norton, who could smell money at a distance.

Throughout the Forties Caroline used her literary status to offer help to a number of lesser-known writers. One of these was the Dorset dialect poet, William Barnes. In April 1844, she went down to Dorset to stay with Brinsley and Marcia Sheridan. The house party was worthy but a little dull, and the guest list suggests just how strenuous were Brinsley's efforts to have Caroline accepted back into polite Society again. It included Bishop Denison; Philip Pusey, the editor of the *Royal Agricultural Journal*; Dr Buckland, a future Dean of Westminster; Archdeacon Huxtable; and Fonblanque, the editor of *The Examiner*.

Naturally the Sheridans subscribed to a number of magazines and newspapers, and prominent on the drawing-room table was the local newspaper, *The Dorset County Chronicle*. Turning over the pages, Caroline discovered the queerest little rhymes, which Brinsley told her had been appearing for some time now. They were not printed in the

'Poet's Corner' on page two, with the likes of Lord Byron and Mrs Hemans, but were tucked away among the stock news, alongside advertisements for land or notices of the price of corn. This was, no doubt, because these anonymous verses were not only about the doings of the humble country people, but were actually written in the dialect they spoke. Caroline had always fancied herself as a mimic, and it is likely that she made them all laugh in the drawing room at Frampton, when she read out these poems after dinner. Then she got to wondering about the writer, and asked Brinsley to make some enquiries. He discovered that the poet was a Mr William Barnes, who kept a little school in Dorchester. So, Barnes was invited to join them for the Easter weekend. Caroline probably thought that by introducing him to such company, she might be able to do him some good.

Barnes refused the invitation. He sent a note to say that he was 'unaccustomed to society', but, when Brinsley persisted, he eventually agreed to come. On one fine morning, shortly afterwards, in the drawing room at Frampton, Caroline was surprised to be introduced to a gentle, rather shabby, middle-aged schoolmaster, rather than the bucolic hearty she had half expected. Barnes proved to be a modest, sweet-natured man, with a fund of knowledge about local history and customs. It also turned out that he spoke almost every foreign language that Caroline could name, though he had never been abroad except for a weekend in Normandy. Caroline was flattered and touched by his obvious admiration for her. Barnes warmed himself in the Sheridans' regard and stayed the whole weekend at Frampton, chattering and laughing in his quiet simple way. He even consented to read aloud a selection of his poems 'grave and gay', and the Sheridans and their guests applauded him warmly. Caroline was strongly drawn to him for he was such a nice, unpretentious man, and so respectful of her opinions. She decided to take him in hand, and had to tell him plainly that he would never succeed if he persisted in writing in 'the Dorset', as he called it. If he wanted a wider readership, he must think of 'cocknifying' his poems. At this, he only smiled.

She invited him to visit her at what she called the 'Palazzo Boltoni', for she had recently moved to No. 24 Bolton Street, Mayfair. Rather to her surprise, he accepted, and arrived on Saturday 22 June 1844. At first she had been rather perplexed about how to entertain him, but knowing that he was interested in science, she took him to meet her friend, Professor Wheatstone, who obligingly demonstrated his galvanic telegraph apparatus, which excited Barnes very much. He said it would provide material for the daily lectures on science he gave to his schoolboys. Then she entertained him to dinner among a group of her friends discreetly chosen for their social tact. In the evening, she took him to the opera, but he became rather restive during the last act, and subsequently admitted to her that he was shocked that they had stayed out into the early hours of the Sabbath.[17] Before he left, she told him that she would do her best to champion his work in London Society, and might even be able to arrange a reading of his poems at a fashionable house, such as that of her friend, the Duchess of Sutherland.

A few days after Barnes had left, she opened a letter from him and a sonnet fell out:

TO THE HON. MRS. NORTON

When first I drew, with melting heart, alone
(O gifted vot'ry of the tuneful Nine)
Entrancing melody from songs of thine
Sweet eco'd words of one as yet unknown;
  How much I wondered what might be the tone
Of her true voice, as yet unanswering mine,
And what the hue with which her eyes might shine,
And what the form in which her soul was shown
To sons of men. How busy fancy brought
Before me lineaments of love and grace.
But who can tell what joy was mine at last,
When I beheld the object of my thought
In bright reality before my face,
And found the fairest of my dreams surpassed.

Caroline was amused and touched. She had undoubtedly made a conquest with Barnes. But despite her consortings with deans and bishops, there were still many people in Society who were suspicious of her. Somehow she had to shake off her scandalous reputation.

XXIII

NOT QUITE NICE

SINCE CAROLINE'S SEPARATION FROM NORTON, part of her difficulties in restoring her reputation had been caused by the curious social position in which she found herself. For all practical purposes she was neither married nor single. But she was a mother without children, a Society beauty with little company, and a member of the upper classes with no capital. And, though she had bravely retained her animation in those drawing rooms where she was welcome, and had developed a briskness of manner when dealing with publishers, for most of the time she was deeply lonely. Above all, she missed her boys, and, failing them, someone else to love. But she dare not encourage any man's friendship. She knew that Norton had her watched, and might subsequently use any evidence he could find to prove to a court of law that she was not a fit mother for her own children. So she was obliged to live like a lay nun. In one of her pamphlets, she described the dilemma of such women as herself:

> Alone. Married to a man's name, but never to know the protection of this nominal husband, nor the joys of family, nor the every-day companionship of a real home. Never to feel or show preference for any friend not of her own sex, though tempted, perhaps by a feeling nobler than passion – gratitude for generous pity, that has lightened the dreary days. To be slandered, tormented, insulted; to find the world and the world's law utterly indifferent to her wrongs or her husband's sin; and through all this to lead a chaste, unspotted, patient, cheerful life; without anger, without bitterness, and with meek respect for these edicts which, with a perverse parody of Scripture, pronounce that it 'is not good for a man to be alone, but extremely good for a woman'.[1]

The attitudinizing in this passage may prove irritating to the modern reader, but there can be no doubt that Caroline was describing a situation that brought real suffering to a number of women of her generation.

Another of her difficulties was brought about by the change in public attitudes to morality that was going on all round her. The days of the Regency were long gone, and the amoral licentious cheerfulness of the generation of Melbourne and Moore was being replaced, even among the upper classes, by a new sobriety of conduct. Victoria's accession seemed to have ushered in the age of respectability. Cynicism was now curiously out of date, and earnestness reigned. Gambling and drunkenness were on the decline among the aristocracy. People did not swear so much, at least in public, and nobody admitted to adulterous adventures. There was, therefore, far less tolerance about for Caroline to depend on. As a married woman living on her own in Mayfair, she was an object of suspicion, and probably regarded by many a woman as a threat to a husband or son.

Caroline's own attitudes were not unaffected by this change. At Samuel Rogers's soirées, or in her own intimate little dinner parties at the Palazzo Boltoni, she still played the part of 'old Sherry's' teasing, witty granddaughter. But as a poet and writer of pamphlets she was a very different woman. Somehow she felt it incumbent upon her in her published work to be insistently, deeply moral, as the passage quoted above demonstrates. After 1840, she never wrote a witty verse, except for children, and never in her pamphlets and letters to the press permitted herself to relax her fine moral indignation. Only in her private letters are there glimpses of the spontaneously playful woman, which she still was with her friends.

And it was this playfulness which so often got her into trouble, for, though she dared not become seriously involved, she could not prevent herself from flirting with almost every man she met at a party. The trouble was that she gave out the wrong signals. This had long been the case. Even when she was first married and had spent a few days away from Norton at a house party in Scotland, she had awoken to find the young Lord Tankerville trying to get into bed with her at two o'clock in the morning.[2] Tankerville can hardly be blamed. He was not the first to believe, mistakenly, that the thrilling tremor in Caroline's voice suggested strong emotion, and the hushed breathlessness of her confidences were an invitation to closer acquaintance.

Caroline was not snobbish in her flirtations. At the other end of the social spectrum from Tankerville, was the old boatman on the Isle of Wight, who rowed her round Cowes. She had gone there for a short holiday, and, having little to do but sit in a rowing-boat and take in the view, she turned her mind to charming the old man. She wrote to Abraham Hayward to tell him about it: 'Pray don't think I am in love with my boatman. He is sixty and very weather-beaten.' But she ended the letter with a flirtatious and flattering appeal to Hayward himself: 'I will make my third son "look up to you" when he is at the Bar, as a guiding star. Lest I should be tempted to add to my most lengthy observations something on barristers, I hastily conclude. Do you believe shrimps are happy?' It was this kind of persistent coquetry that continued to feed the gossip about her.

In the winter of 1839–40 Caroline was so depressed at home that her Uncle Charles eventually agreed to go with her on a trip to Italy. They were to accompany Helen, and her husband who had now succeeded to the title of Lord Dufferin. Caroline must have thought that she could forget all about her unfortunate reputation in a foreign country. She was wrong. Italian hotel proprietors and curators of galleries were amazed at what interest there was in Mrs Norton, once that name had been revealed to other English visitors. Caroline wrote to Lord Melbourne: 'my name, my family, & something in myself, makes me an object of attention & curiosity'. But such attention was not welcome, because it was not friendly. Caroline found that, though she was frequently pointed out to her fellow hotel guests, they rarely permitted themselves to speak to her. On the whole it was a gloomy holiday, but she decided to stay on for a while with her uncle after the Dufferins had left for home. Unfortunately, Charles Sheridan hated traipsing round the Colosseum and the Vatican, and preferred to lounge about the hotel lobby most of the day, discussing with perplexed passers-by whether there would be 'Ciniali' [sic – stewed wild boar] for dinner. So there was nothing for it but for Caroline to tour the museums and galleries on her own, pretending not to notice the cold looks of the other English tourists.

This kind of social ostracism went on for many years, and even among her literary friends, Caroline was not always entirely safe from disapproval and unkindness. For example, in the middle of the decade she was friendly with William Makepeace Thackeray, who was then at the height of his career as a novelist. Thackeray had long been in love with Jane Brookfield, the wife of a clergyman who tolerated him as his wife's friend. But when in 1846, it was proposed that Mrs Brookfield should attend a party at which Caroline was to be present, she refused. It seems that, though Jane Brookfield was every bit as great a coquette as Caroline, she was only too aware that she had never lost her reputation, whereas Caroline had. Even Brookfield, her stuffy husband, tried to persuade her that it was 'unfair to punish people simply because they had been accused',[3] but Jane was adamant. She obviously thought that merely being in the same room as Caroline might endanger her own reputation. She was probably right.

Caroline did not hold this rebuff against Thackeray himself, and soon after, tried to help him to a useful social contact. For, though the Mrs Brookfields might think themselves too good for her, Caroline still had friends who were too powerful to care about her past, among them the Duke of Devonshire. It was one of her chief pleasures to introduce fellow writers to her aristocratic friends, and in the summer of 1848, she was able to get such an introduction for Thackeray. She wrote to tell him that she was invited to stay for a weekend at Devonshire House, and that the Duke, 'the kindest hearted of the great', had intimated that if Mr Thackeray wished to accompany her, he would be very welcome. Now Thackeray at that time was professing that he was not impressed by the airs of 'small great' people, and might have been expected to refuse. He had, moreover, agreed to spend that same weekend with Lady Castlereagh. But when he received this invitation, he quickly sent his apologies to Lady Castlereagh, and went off with Caroline to Devonshire House.

What happened next makes a curious connection between Caroline and Thackeray's best-known heroine, Becky Sharp from *Vanity Fair*. This novel had just been published, and the Duke asked Thackeray to tell him what happened to the chief characters after the novel had ended. Thackeray obliged him in a letter written the following week, and his words about Becky Sharp (Mrs Rawdon Crawley), whose story had ended in scandal, seem to bear an extraordinary resemblance to aspects of Caroline's own history:

> Mrs Crawley now lives in a small but very pretty little house in Belgravia, and is conspicuous for her numerous charities, which always get into the newspapers, and her unaffected piety. Many of the most exalted and spotless of her own sex visit her, and are of the opinion that she is a most injured woman. There is no sort of truth in the stories regarding Mrs Crawley and the late Lord Steyne. The licentious character of that nobleman alone gave rise to reports from which, alas! the most spotless life and reputation cannot always defend themselves.[4]

This passage is a private joke between the novelist and the nobleman who, some time during the weekend, must have struck up some sort of banter about Caroline's past. It is true that they both counted themselves as her friends, and, of course, were obliged to her for introducing them. But there is no mistaking the masculine innuendo in this passage, which Thackeray must have been pretty sure that his new friend, the Duke, would appreciate.

Caroline was well used to people whispering and laughing about her behind her back. Even her loyal friend, the Duchess of Sutherland, could not refrain once from observing to an acquaintance: 'She is *so* nice, what a pity she is not *quite* nice: for if she were *quite* nice she would be so *very* nice.'[5]

XXIV

MELBOURNE AGAIN

IT IS NECESSARY TO RETURN NOW to Caroline's holiday in Italy, in the winter of 1839–40. She was still in Rome when, in mid-February, she heard that Queen Victoria had married Prince Albert of Saxe-Coburg on the 10th of that month. The event provoked little interest among the Romans, but to her it was momentous news. She saw at once that Melbourne had inevitably lost that intensive daily companionship with Victoria which he had enjoyed for the past three years. He would soon be wanting other feminine company again. She left for London soon after. When she arrived home at the Palazzo Boltoni, while everybody else was still talking about the Royal Wedding, she quietly let it be known that she had returned. In a few days, sure enough, Melbourne turned up on her doorstep. What else had he to do?

He was, of course, kind and avuncular, called her 'Carrie' again, and told her a fund of indiscreet stories about the Court. Caroline might have congratulated herself that he could be so easy in her little drawing room, in a way not possible among the stuffy draperies of Windsor. And Melbourne certainly must have felt a sense of relief as he sat with his boots once more on the sofa, and retailed anecdotes in his antique drawling manner. He pretended to be indifferent to the loss of the Queen's company, and probably told Caroline about the note Victoria had sent him after her wedding-night with Albert. The Queen had confided to him that she had experienced a 'most gratifying and bewildering' night, and that she was 'very, very happy' with her 'dearest, dearest Albert'. No doubt they laughed at the little Queen's naïveté, but if Melbourne's voice shook while he told the story, it seems likely that Caroline did not want to look into his eyes.

It was especially useful to Caroline to have Melbourne's friendship again at this time, because she needed his help. In her campaign to get her boys back, she had to convince a judge that she had never committed adultery and was, therefore, a fit mother for her children. In such a business she knew that an affidavit sworn by Melbourne, testifying that their relationship had been an innocent one, would be a very considerable piece of evidence. Melbourne was still Prime Minister, and a public testimony such as this would be difficult for the judge to ignore. For him to do so would be like calling the Prime Minister a liar in public. Accordingly, Caroline asked Abraham Hayward, who was acting for her, to go and see Melbourne in South Street to persuade him to sign the paper. Hayward has left a vivid sketch of the visit. The sixty-one-year-old Melbourne had, as usual, got up late:

> Calling between ten and eleven, he found Lord Melbourne in his dressing gown and slippers, in the act of shaving. 'So,' was the abrupt address, 'you are going to revive that business. It is confoundedly disagreeable.'
>
> 'You know, my lord, that Mrs Norton can't live without her children.'
>
> 'Well, well, if it must be done, it must be done effectively. You must have an affidavit from me. The story about me was all a d—d lie as you know. Put that into proper form and I'll swear it.'[1]

So Melbourne became a frequent visitor to the Palazzo Boltoni, but they were never more than old friends now. While he gazed vacantly out of the window, imagining Victoria with her Prince at Windsor, Caroline tried to comfort him with funny stories. She told him about Lord Brudenell, who had kept a mistress in a village on his estate, and regularly visited her pretending he was the doctor. Unfortunately, the village boys had found out who he was, and kept shouting out 'the doctor' whenever he called.[2] And she told him how, when she was in Rome, she had discovered in a shop, 'a small black cabinet inlaid with ivory etchings, of birds'. In the middle, she found, to her astonishment, a picture of Melbourne's 'favourite subject', a 'woman whipping a child (or a nymph whipping Bacchus . . .)'.[3] He was grateful to her. Racy talk was his natural medium, and Caroline knew how to supply him with plenty of it.

Shortly afterwards, Melbourne lost the Queen's company for ever, for in August 1841, his Whig Government failed to get its Corn Law legislation through the House. An election followed and the Tories won. Sir Robert Peel replaced him as Prime Minister.

Caroline was, no doubt, very sorry for him. She could afford to be so. At a stroke, Melbourne had lost his place, his business, and his reason for living. He now spent even more time with her. She tried to cheer him up, and, in return, he told her gossip from the letters he received from the Queen.

Then came a fearful quarrel between them. One day in late November 1841, Melbourne suddenly appeared, white with wrath, and shouting accusations at her. Apparently he had had a letter from Baron Stockmar, Prince Albert's adviser. It was dated the 23rd, just three months after he had lost office. It read:

> Some weeks back I was walking in the streets with Dr Praetorius when finding myself opposite the house of one of my friends, it came across my mind to give him a call . . . For some minutes the conversation turned on insignificant things, when the person talking to me said quite abruptly: 'So I find the Queen is in daily correspondence with Lord Melbourne'. I replied, 'Who told you this?' The answer was, 'Mrs Norton; she told me the other evening. Don't you believe that Lord Melbourne has lost his influence over the Queen's mind; he daily writes to her, and receives as many answers, in which she communicates everything to him.' Without betraying much emotion I said, 'I don't believe a word of it; the Queen may have written once or twice on private matters, but the daily correspondence on all matters is certainly the amplification of a thoughtless and imprudent person, who is not aware of such exaggerated assertions.' My speech was followed by a general silence . . .[4]

Melbourne had every reason to be furious with Caroline. He wanted to know whether it was true that she had told people about his correspondence with the Queen.

She had. If she tried to prevaricate by claiming that she might inadvertently have mentioned the affair at some dinner-table or other, then this was an evasion. She had told Melbourne's secret, though it is doubtful whether he would ever have understood her reasons. For years she had been an outcast, a scandalous woman, whom none but her relatives and a few writers would invite to supper, and she still held Melbourne responsible for this. But since he had come back to her, people had started to ask her out once again, and, of course, they wanted to know all about the ex-Prime Minister. For weeks now, she had been dining-out on the gossip he had been telling her.

It is possible that Caroline did not at first grasp the significance of this betrayal of Melbourne's confidence. Mention of his private correspondence with the Queen was not just a bit of gossip, but the revelation of information with profound constitutional implications. For an outgoing Prime Minister was not supposed to write to the Sovereign, for fear that he might try to exert an undue constitutional influence. Stockmar's letter to Melbourne was an attempt to warn him off before Peel heard about it.

In the event, Melbourne ignored this warning. He had grown so accustomed to talking to Victoria every day that not to have any word at all from her was unendurable to him. Despite this, it was Victoria who raised the matter. When Melbourne had taken his last formal leave of her as Prime Minister, she begged him to write to her, and had subsequently deluged him with letters, so that it would have been impolite – to say the least – for him not to have replied.[5] But his letters went further than he meant. Though at first he confined himself largely to social and domestic matters, he was soon making comments about Peel's nominees for the Royal Household. He told the Queen that Sir Charles Bagot would be 'inadequate and inefficient' as Governor-General of Canada, and that it would be 'unwise' for Lord Haddington to be given the Admiralty. After a while, Melbourne became nervous about the correspondence, and reminded the Queen to keep it secret. He would not even pass a message to Victoria through the Duchess of Bedford, because, though he considered the Duchess to be discreet, 'he did not like to furnish anybody with such ... evidence of communication'. He had never thought to distrust Caroline.

Even after Stockmar's warning, Melbourne was still so smitten with the Queen that he was unable to let the correspondence die a natural death. It was even said that he had written to Victoria to suggest that the time was now ripe to get rid of Sir Robert Peel, and to advise how it might be done. Stockmar became more and more perturbed. His aim was to ensure that the popularity of the monarchy should not be hitched to the fortunes of any one political party, but should be acceptable to all. Consequently, he wished the monarch to adopt a strict constitutional neutrality, so that it could claim never to be at odds with the political will of the people. If the existence of Victoria's correspondence with Melbourne had become generally known, there might have been serious repercussions for the Crown. So Stockmar continued to put pressure on Melbourne to stop writing. Peel had pointedly told Stockmar that he looked for 'honesty in public affairs', and had added: 'on this I must insist, and I do assure you, that the moment I was to learn that the Queen takes advice upon public matters in another place, I shall throw up; for such a thing I conceive the country could not stand, and I would not remain an hour, whatever the consequences of my resignation may be . . ."[6] Melbourne now realized that if he persisted in writing to the Queen, Peel would resign and there would be a constitutional crisis. What is more, Caroline would have caused it.

But Stockmar was able to point out a prospect that was, for Melbourne, infinitely worse. If the Queen were to learn that Caroline had been telling everybody about the contents of her private letters to Melbourne, then she would feel that he had broken faith with her. 'Her pride', said Stockmar, 'would be offended by feeling that her confidence was so betrayed.'[7] This thought was unbearable for Melbourne. He could not stand the thought that Victoria should know he had read her letters to Caroline. So he gave up writing to her, and there was no constitutional crisis. But he blamed Caroline. He may even have suspected that she had chosen this method as a way of paying him back for the trouble and jealousy he had brought her. Of course she would have denied it.

This affair broke Melbourne. On 23 October 1842, he had a stroke and was taken from London to Brocket, his home in Hertfordshire. He was never an effective force in politics again.

XXV

LITTLE BOY LOST

THE AUTUMN OF 1842 was a disastrous one for Caroline as well as for Melbourne. She had suffered misery before, but this year brought her tragedy. And in her opinion, George Norton was to blame for it. Since the passing of the Infant Custody Act in 1839, he had obdurately refused to let her see her boys again. The Act applied only in England and Wales, and he had avoided its effects by keeping his sons in Scotland. They had been sent to Rannoch Lodge in Perthshire, for his sister, Lady Menzies, to look after, and they remained there for nearly six years, save for the few occasions when they had been escorted down to London to see their mother. Caroline herself had experienced Grace Menzies' harshness, and when the boys were first taken from her in 1836, she had feared that they were being ill-treated. At about that time, she had written to a friend to say that:

> The first step she [Lady Menzies] made in their education was to flog this very child (a child of six) for merely receiving and reading a letter from me . . . to impress on his memory that he was not to receive letters from me. Having occasion to correct one still younger, she stripped it naked, tied it to the bedpost, and chastised it with a riding-whip.[1]

Some years later, Caroline discovered that Lady Menzies' treatment of the boys had not been unkind, but the fact remains that she had been made miserable on the matter for many years.

There was, however, a limit to the time Norton could leave the children with their relatives. It is likely that the Menzies themselves were not too happy to look after three boys indefinitely, and Norton knew that he would have to bring them down to England in the end. He probably planned to put them into some sort of preparatory school near his home at Kettlethorpe in Yorkshire, before sending them on to Eton. His problem was that, as soon as the boys were resident in England, he was obliged by the new law to agree terms of access with Caroline. He dare not try to evade the law, first because he was a magistrate himself, and secondly because, if he did so, Caroline was entitled to petition the Lord Chancellor's new court for the right to see her sons. The court, which consisted of the Lord Chancellor, the Master of the Rolls, and other judges, might then bind both parents to *whatever* settlement it thought fair.

Caroline did not petition the court in 1839, as soon as the Act was passed. She still hoped then that Norton would come to his senses and allow her to see the boys. She wrote to him in January 1840, enquiring whether he would consent to access so that she need not petition.[2] His reply, as usual, tried to make access dependent on a financial settlement, in this case a maximum of £400 for her allowance. As usual, she replied that she would not allow money matters to determine her right to see her boys, but added that now she had the law on her side. Norton then offered to send her new portraits of the boys to console her for their absence. Outraged, she replied: 'I, on my part, wonder you can look in the children's faces, or at their pictures either, and not feel ashamed and reproached by the unmanly persecution which has pursued their mother through four dogged, unrelenting years! You always speak as if the refusal of my boys was like a refusal of tickets for Almacks . . .'[3] Her outburst had no effect. Throughout the autumn of 1840, she saw to it that the boys' rooms were regularly aired, and their fires lit, in the hope that they would arrive to stay with her in Bolton Street. They never came.

Yet she had a secret ally in Scotland. It was her old friend, Sir Neil Menzies, who had long acted as her informant, and now let her know that the boys had been taken down to Yorkshire, and that Norton was planning to send them to school in England. At once she began to make preparations for a petition. Her chief task was to persuade the court that she really was a suitable mother to look after her own children. Accordingly, she collected together the many letters that had passed between Norton and herself during the previous five years, and had them printed. She believed that such material placed in the hands of any fair-minded judge would easily prove how reasonable her behaviour had been, and how disgraceful Norton's. Next, she arranged for the swearing of affidavits to use as testimony. Chief among these was one from Melbourne, and that is why Hayward was sent to see him.

Unfortunately for Caroline, Norton was hatching counter-plots. The new law allowed the court to grant access to a mother, provided that she was a woman of spotless reputation. Caroline's petition, therefore, would fail if Norton could prove that she was living an immoral life, and this he tried to do. During the autumn of 1840, Caroline began to sense that she was being followed and watched. Then, quite how she did not know, she became involved in a series of odd and potentially compromising incidents. On one such occasion, she received a mysterious note which advised her to call at a certain house if she wished to hear news of her boys. When she got there, it turned out to be a brothel. Soon after, she was accosted by 'a sort of antiquated old beau, all powder and white waistcoat', a half-pay soldier named Edward Piers,[4] who claimed that he sympathized with the way she had been treated and wished to help her. He then started to follow her about and, one afternoon, when she opened the door to let her mother in, Piers pushed past Mrs Sheridan into the hall and would not leave the house. Fortunately, Caroline had alerted the police a week before. When they arrived, they found Piers sitting in one of the ground-floor rooms, looking up at a portrait of Richard Brinsley Sheridan, who he said had once been his patron. Piers was brought before the magistrates at Marlborough Street Police Court, on 23 December, and Caroline was summoned to attend. In the upshot, she agreed not to prosecute him if he promised not to pester her.

Caroline was convinced that Piers was an agent employed by Grantley and Norton to try to gain evidence to damage her reputation. When she said as much to the press, Norton, as a magistrate, was terribly embarrassed, and begged one of his fellow magistrates to assure her that he was not involved. But his position was untenable, because people were at last becoming aware that, though he was a magistrate himself, he was trying to blacken his wife's name, to prevent her seeing her own children. Accordingly, he gave in. Caroline never had to present her petition, because, with as much bad grace as he could muster, he finally agreed to let her see the boys again.

They were sent down to London during Christmas 1841. It seems to have been the same arrangement as before, with the boys visiting their mother daily, but sleeping at their father's house at night. The reunion was bitter-sweet for reasons Caroline explained later:

> He yielded simply so far as the law would have compelled him, and was necessary to save himself from the threatened and certain exposure which my appeal under the new law would have entailed. I saw my children in the most formal and comfortless manner. There was no mercy or generosity. I expected none. He

even made it a personal quarrel with his colleague and fellow magistrate, Mr Hardwicke, because Mr Hardwicke had permitted me one evening to be in his box at the play with my children. He locked the children themselves up for a whole day, to punish them, and impress upon their memories that they were not to be seen with me in any public place. Their interviews with me were to be in private, that no one might know or guess he had been obliged to yield.[5]

After Christmas, the boys went back to Yorkshire, and Caroline did not see them again until Easter 1842. Brinsley's birthday fell during this holiday, and Caroline roasted a whole pig to celebrate not only that day, but his five previous birthdays when she had not been with him.

In 1842, Fletcher was thirteen years old, Brinsley ten, and William eight, and they had spent only a few weeks in Caroline's company during the previous seven years. By now, Fletcher and Brinsley both attended Eton, though Caroline had warned Norton of the bullyings and beatings they would have to endure there. In the holidays, the boys were still regularly sent to Rannoch Lodge, or allowed to knock about their father's estate at Kettlethorpe. Caroline was always worried about them. She was afraid that, because they were left so long in the care of servants, they would be both coarsened and neglected. It was only natural that they were spoiled on their rare visits to her. The boys' lives alternated between 'boozings and snoozings' in Yorkshire, and 'playgoing and pleasurings' in Bolton Street.

In September 1842, Caroline suddenly received a message to go to Kettlethorpe urgently, because William was ill. The note said he had fallen off his pony. So she had to take the train up to Yorkshire on her own, not knowing all the while how William was getting on. It is no wonder that she was distraught when she stepped out at the bleak little station. She was met, not by Norton, but by a hard-faced woman she had never seen before. The stranger introduced herself as Lady Kelly, the wife of Norton's lawyer. The woman was exceptionally blunt. When Caroline said: 'I am here. Is my boy better?' Lady Kelly replied: 'No, he is not better, he is dead.'

She was taken to Norton's house, where she was permitted to gaze upon the features of her son, cold in his coffin. Norton told her that he had been riding alone on his pony and had come off. He was not very much hurt but had received a scratch, which had turned poisonous. He had died of lockjaw. Caroline knew what that meant.

He had died for lack of a mother's care. She wrote to Samuel Rogers from Chapel Thorpe on 13 September:

> He died conscious; he prayed and asked Norton to pray; he asked for me twice. He did not fear to die, and he bore the dreadful spasms of pain with a degree of courage which the doctor says he has rarely seen in so young a child. He had every attention and kindness that could be shown, and every comfort which was needed. He was kept here, not at first from any apprehension of danger, but because in his father's house there is no attendance – nothing but an old woman who opens the gate. It may be sinful to think bitterly at such a time; and at least I have not uttered the thoughts of my heart . . . But it is not in the strength of human nature not to think, 'This might not have happened had I watched over them! . . . Half what is now so lavishly expended in ceremony on decoration of the coffin which contains the senseless clay of my little lost one would have paid some steady man-servant to be in constant attendance in their hours of recreation. My poor little spirited creature was too young to rough it alone as he was left to do.'[6]

Her anger had increased by the time she wrote to her sister, Georgiana, on 20 September:

> The accident would not have happened if they had the commonest attendance granted to gentleman's sons. It is as easy to say (as Grantley did) that there was no help for it, and it was God's will he should die. On that ground we might never call in a doctor, or take any other precaution. He died because he was too young to rough it alone, as he was obliged to do; and it is in vain to say that he did not. He lies now in a decorated coffin of purple and silver and enclosing one of lead, that when Norton is Lord Grantley he may 'remove him if he pleases to the family vault'.[7]

The funeral was a ghastly occasion for Caroline. Her Uncle Charles came up to Yorkshire to give her some moral support, but apart from that, she was surrounded by grim-faced, crêpe-swathed Nortons and Grantleys. Though she would probably have preferred to remain impassive before these enemies of hers, when it came to it, she could not restrain her grief and sobbed during the ceremony. What surprised her was that Norton stood next to her and cried too, which made Brinsley think that his mother and father were reconciled. The boy had a sort of fit when he saw his brother in his coffin, and, after the ceremony, he busied himself writing notes to Caroline's friends who could not be there. Rather pathetically, he wanted the sad event to bring all their friends together in one loving company.

Soon after the funeral, Caroline got Norton to discuss with her the future of their two surviving boys. But when it came to practical problems, the mellow mood induced by his son's death soon disappeared, and he became his sulky self again. Caroline tried to persuade him that Eton was not a suitable school for their two remaining sons, because they were too gentle for such a rough place. She suggested that they should go to school elsewhere. Her choice, now as always, was Harrow, her grandfather's school. But Norton would not hear of the boys going anywhere other than to Dr Hawtrey, at Eton, and that was that. Caroline had to console herself by thinking how pleasant were 'the green play fields' by the Thames, and how much 'free exercise and fresh air the young creatures' got there.[8] She did, however, succeed in getting two concessions from Norton. Up to that time, the headmaster of Eton College had been forbidden to allow her contact with her sons without Norton's written permission. She had only recently been turned away at the gate. Now Norton agreed to inform the school that, from that time onwards, it was to recognize her parental authority over the boys. He also agreed that she should have the custody of the boys for half the year, though he tried to make it dependent upon her supervising them at Kettlethorpe. In the end, and much to her relief, he consented that she should have the boys with her in London. Bitterly she reflected that, though she had at last obtained the custody of her children, it was only at the cost of the death of one of them.

During the early Forties, Caroline seems often to have been suffering from depression induced both by bereavements and fears about her own health. She regularly complained of feeling unwell. Her doctor usually diagnosed influenza, which was serious enough in the mid-nineteenth century, but she always dreaded she might have inherited consumption from her Linley grandmother.

William's death was not the only one to contribute to her gloom. In July 1841, Helen's husband, Lord Dufferin, died from an overdose of morphine, taken while crossing over to Ireland. Then, in 1843, the dreaded family disease made its reappearance, when her brother Frank died of consumption while serving as treasurer to the British colony at Mauritius. Her younger brother Charles also succumbed to the disease in 1847, in Paris, where he was serving at the Embassy. One of his nephews left a memorial of him in his last days; he was: 'perhaps the most charming of all the Sheridan men, and an enchanting companion. Even when enfeebled by the fell disease which destroyed his father and beautiful grandmother ... [he sat] ... in one of the drawing rooms of the Embassy [in Paris] when a ball was going on, surrounded by a circle of men and ladies, kept away from the dancing by his sallies.'[9] But the loss that most affected Caroline was that of her Uncle Charles, in November 1843. This quiet scholar had given her a home since her marital troubles began in 1836 and had made her new life possible. He had reunited her with Lord Melbourne, accompanied her to Rome, and even stood with her at her son's graveside.

Some years later, Caroline composed what is possibly the most famous of all Victorian ballads about death. It was recited in later years in thousands of parlours. If it is too stagy and rhetorical for modern tastes, it is certain that its solemn religiosity suited the temper of the time, and helped to comfort many grieving people:

NOT LOST BUT GONE BEFORE
How mournful seems, in broken dreams,
    The memory of the day,
When icy Death has sealed the breath
    Of some dear form of clay.

When pale, unmoved, the face we loved,
    The face we thought so fair,
And the hand lies cold, whose fervent hold
    Once charmed away despair.

Oh, what could heal the grief we feel
    For hopes that come no more,
Had we ne'er heard the Scripture word,
    'Not lost but gone before'?
. . .

Oh, sadly, yet with vain regret,
    The widowed heart must yearn,
And mothers weep their babes asleep
    In the sunlight's vain return.

The brother's heart shall rue to part
From the one through childhood known;
And the orphan's tears lament for years
A friend and father gone.

For death and life, with ceaseless strife,
Beat wild on this world's shore;
And all our calm is in that balm, –
'Not lost but gone before' . . .

XXVI

My Secretary

AFTER SHE HAD ACHIEVED SOME CUSTODY of her two surviving sons, Caroline seems to have felt that she could relax the severe standards of conduct she had set herself. Norton no longer had her watched, and she was free at last to seek affection from other men, provided she did it discreetly. But she never did things by halves. Having for some years been a rival to the most famous woman in the world, Queen Victoria, she now started an affair which not only set her against the most famous heroine of the century, Florence Nightingale, but also, for the third time, provoked a scandal which threatened the existence of a British government.

When her Uncle Charles died in 1843, Caroline was left quite alone. It is true that the boys now came home regularly for their holidays but, between times, the Bolton Street house was empty and too big for her. In the autumn of 1843, she went for a holiday at St Leonards-on-Sea to think things over, and when she returned, moved out of Bolton Street into temporary lodgings while she looked round for a smaller house. In March 1845, she moved to 3 Chesterfield Street, Mayfair, where she lived for over thirty years.

It was a small terraced house, pleasantly shaded at the back by plane trees. In later years Caroline kept a large aviary of singing birds in a back room, and especially loved to show it off to children. Her widowed sister, Helen Dufferin, had recently moved to Lower Brook Street, close by, and Mrs Sheridan, now nearly blind from cataracts, had joined her. During the parliamentary terms, Caroline was always welcome at Brinsley and Marcia Sheridan's house in Grosvenor Square, or the Seymours' place in Spring Gardens, and in holiday time, she would visit them at Frampton or Maiden Bradley, where a growing band of nephews and nieces partly consoled her for the loss of her own sons' childhood.

Many old friends visited her in Chesterfield Street, including Edward Bulwer, now Lord Lytton. And in the mid-Forties, she began to acquire a new set of friends. These included John Gibson Lockhart, the biographer of Burns and Scott, and Sir Alexander and Lady Lucy Duff

Gordon, who lived in Queen's Square. Lucy Duff Gordon soon became Caroline's closest friend. She was one of the few women whom Caroline had ever met who was both warm-hearted and intelligent. As an intellectual, she cared nothing for Caroline's scandalous reputation. Lucy was the daughter of John Austin, a neighbour and friend of the great Utilitarians, Bentham and James Mill. She had been brought up in the company of highly intelligent men, and was still deeply interested in ideas, the arts, and social welfare.

Another new friend was Alexander William Kinglake, the author of *Eothen*, who one day in 1840 or '41 invited her to join a party of friends going to Greenwich to eat whitebait with him, and it was there that she was introduced to Sidney Herbert. Of course, she had heard of him before that. He was thirtyish, and a rising politician. He was very good looking, indeed one commentator described him as 'beautiful as an angel'. He and Caroline were immediately attracted to each other.

In the early 1840s, Sidney Herbert was already becoming famous as one of the most brilliant and ambitious politicians in the country. He was the second son of the Earl of Pembroke and of Countess Woronzoff, who was of Russian descent. Herbert was, therefore, a direct descendant of the saint-like Sir Philip Sidney, the sixteenth-century soldier and poet. The family home was Wilton, near Salisbury, which house he loved so much that he spoke of it as if it had been a person. He was a Conservative with a social conscience, and the MP for Wiltshire South. The Prime Minister, Sir Robert Peel, regarded him as a friend and confidant.

After they had got to know one another, Herbert must have told Caroline more about his personal life. At Harrow School he had preserved a morally impeccable character in what seems to have been a sink of iniquity. When he left the school, his housemaster wrote to his parents to say that he had 'the unspeakable satisfaction of restoring him [Herbert] from the dangers of [such] a place ... not only untainted, but ... confirmed and strengthened in principle'.[1] His master's verdict seems to have been correct, for even in public life, Herbert was regarded as a perfect Christian gentleman. He was upright, kindly, hard-working, and generous. He combined Puritanism and nobility to the extent of self-sacrifice. At Wilton, not only his family, but the tenants and estate workers adored him. He was the hope not only of the House of Pembroke, but also of the Conservative Party and, in the view of some, the country.

Herbert's life contrasted greatly with that of his own dissolute

father. The twelfth Earl of Pembroke kept two mistresses simultaneously. They were the ballet dancers, Elisa Scheffer and Adeline Plunkett,
who at one time had created uproar in a theatre by fighting on stage
during a performance of *Ondine*. Each wanted to secure the Earl's
favours for herself. Scheffer won, perhaps because she had previously
served the Earl a love philtre. It must have been a powerful one, for
he soon took her off to Paris to live with him. Herbert was disgusted
by his brother's behaviour. He could not understand how anyone of
Christian principles, and with a high public position, could become
ensnared in sensuality. He probably told Caroline this, and no doubt
she said she agreed with him. Herbert was, of course, deeply naïve,
whereas Caroline had become a sophisticated woman of the world.
And, without meaning to do so, she corrupted him.

She was certainly indiscreet. From the first, she passed on most of
what Herbert told her to her old friend, Lord Melbourne. After all,
she probably thought she was only being kind in this. Melbourne did
not have much to make him laugh shut up alone at Brocket:

> My Secretary wrote me word that Pembroke had 'discovered'
> Scheffer's depravity [in using a love philtre]. The Secretary is so
> extremely shocked, that it is difficult to gather any connected
> history from his broken ejaculations of sorrow & shame . . . [and]
> . . . it seems there has been a row. My Secretary is too intellectual
> to get into those sort of scrapes. Love be damned, as an idle
> vagabond boy, is our motto, and that is a great satisfaction.[2]

Herbert did not understand that he was falling in love with Caroline.
At first he liked to think of their friendship as merely an amusing
diversion. He would have reminded himself that, as a rising star of
the Conservative Party, he could not afford to compromise himself
with a married woman, despite her sympathetic intelligence and the
obvious pathos of her situation. He probably explained very earnestly
to Caroline that, as heir to Wilton (his elder brother being childless),
he had to make a good marriage. In fact, he already had someone in
mind. It had been long understood that he would eventually marry
Elizabeth, the daughter of General A'Court, who had been his
childhood sweetheart, and had been in love with him all her life. So
he made it plain to Caroline that they were to be no more than good
friends and jolly companions. They would enjoy their parties and
theatres together without the need for emotion to come into it. He also
got used to sharing his political confidences with her, for theirs was

a friendship of head as well as the heart, and Caroline had a considerable knowledge of politics. No doubt Caroline reflected wryly that, as far as his career went, her advice was of much more use to him than any he could get from Elizabeth A'Court. Nevertheless, she and Herbert were soon so much together, and so engrossed in each other's talk, that she knew people would say they were lovers, but she did not care. She began to take a proprietory manner with him and call him 'My Secretary' to his face, but when she did so, he just smiled his charming smile.

Then there came a change. Herbert found that he needed to see Caroline regularly and there were simply not enough receptions and dinner parties to satisfy this need. Little by little, they began to make covert arrangements so that they might meet, talk, and touch each other. Caroline soon became an adept in conducting this discreet affair among the fashionable salons, shops, parks and hotels of London. She was careful chiefly for Sidney's sake. She had little to lose herself. Norton was no longer interested in her comings and goings. For many years she had acted innocently but had been treated as if she were an immoral woman. Now she wanted to keep her new-found respectability, while taking a lover. And she did. Their affair lasted some five years.

At last Caroline had learned discretion, and neither she nor Herbert ever acknowledged their affair. But contemporary London opinion was convinced that they were lovers, and it was surely right.[3] It is inconceivable that such a close relationship, over such a long period, should not have been consummated. Caroline's friendship with Melbourne was not comparable; she and Herbert were about the same age, whereas Melbourne was nearly thirty years older than her. Besides, she was now a separated woman. There are also clues in Caroline's writing which indicate that Herbert was her lover. For example, in her novel *Lost and Saved*, which came out in 1863, she describes a character named Milly Nesdale conducting just such an affair in fashionable London. These passages are so knowing on how to go about it, that it is a reasonable assumption that the writer herself had some experience of such doings. The novel also includes the following passage:

Reader, have you ever loved – untowardly, rashly, it may be wrongfully? Have you ever sat listening – no, not listening, but conscious of words; conscious of advice, or scorn, or scolding, or imploring, of some flow of sentences from human lips, addressed to you, intended to save you, and alter the course and current of love; and have you, through all that louder sounding of syllables, heard as it were an undertone (like the chorded accompaniment in music) of some dearer voice; felt the warm flickering over your soul of a smile for whose sake you would die . . . and felt the pressure of that hand which is the link between you and happiness – which to surrender, never to clasp again, would be simply the blank and bitterness of death?[4]

Meanwhile Herbert's political career flourished, and in May 1845, he was made a real secretary – Secretary at War in Peel's Cabinet. Peel had been returned in 1841 with a pledge to preserve the Corn Laws, for his Conservative Party drew its strength from the agricultural interest, and was committed to protecting domestic farm prices by maintaining heavy duties on cheap foreign corn. Opposed to him were the Radicals who wanted the Corn Laws abolished, so that bread would be cheaper for working people, and the Whigs who represented the manufacturers, who also wanted bread prices to fall, but in their case, so that they could pay their workers lower wages.

Then came the Irish potato famine. In 1845, the news from that country told of the spread of potato blight, and a land full of starving people. There is no doubt that, as a person of Irish descent, Caroline would have supported the Whig view that the Corn Laws should be repealed to allow the people to buy cheap bread, and she would have told Herbert as much. For a short while in September, things looked rather better in Ireland; the new crop was good, and promised well for the late digging. But signs of blight appeared in November and, within a month, the whole crop had rotted. Those large parts of the country where people were almost totally dependent on the potato were now threatened with mass famine. Something had to be done about it. Herbert was a humane man and must have been distressed by the situation. No doubt he told his worries to Caroline.

Peel could not now avoid a decision. He had to respond to the outcry for cheaper bread. For some time he had been facing up to the necessity of repealing the Corn Laws, because it was clear that the only way to relieve mass starvation was to allow cheap corn into both England and Ireland. But he dare not single-handedly reverse the policy of his Party overnight. He needed time to negotiate and talk his colleagues round. Yet even while he was trying to manoeuvre, he was required to answer a parliamentary question on the effect of repeal on the landed interest. He dodged it, by asking Herbert to reply for him.

Some of Caroline's old friends were amused both by Peel's discomfiture and Sidney's performance. Disraeli, who was now a power in the Conservative Party, commented that Peel had 'sent down his valet, a well-behaved person, to make it known that we are to have no whining here'.[5] Melbourne was most amused when he heard this remark, and recollected that Disraeli had declared long ago in Caroline's drawing room that he wished to become Prime Minister. Melbourne now ventured the opinion that he would do it yet.

Meanwhile, in early December, with the dreadful news coming in from Ireland, Peel was faced with the task of persuading and uniting his Cabinet behind a policy of repeal. It had to be done with tact and in secrecy, and the country had to be prepared for the change of policy. If he muffed it, the Party would split; if he did nothing, the Irish would starve. Then, just as he was beginning to get discussions going in the Cabinet, *The Times* came out on 4 December 1845 with a confident report that the Cabinet was about to repeal the Corn Laws. This premature announcement was inaccurate, because the Cabinet had only just begun to discuss the matter, but it was enough to finish Peel. Conservatives in the country were outraged; support collapsed, and, within months, the Government fell. So severe was the split created among Conservatives, that they were in office for only a total of five out of the next twenty years.

In those months, Sidney was almost ill from worry, and it was plain that his health could barely take the strain of public life. Meanwhile, a major talking point in the world of politics was the question of how Delane, the editor of *The Times*, had learned of Peel's change of heart. That newspaper had often been used as a mouthpiece by governments, and it is true that the Foreign Secretary, Lord Aberdeen, had had consultations on the matter with Delane, with the intention of slowly 'softening up' public opinion. But *The Times* was usually entirely reliable in obeying official instructions when leaking news for the Government. There must have been another source, an informant less reliable than Aberdeen, but who had placed no embargo on the information. People wondered who the mole might be. Apart from Aberdeen, only Sidney Herbert knew Peel's full opinions on the matter. Then there went round a rumour that Sidney Herbert had told the secret to his mistress, Mrs Norton, and she had sold it to *The Times*.[6]

There may have been some truth in this, though it is doubtful whether Caroline actually sold the information. She was quite capable of blurting it out, however, if only to boost her reputation as someone with an inner knowledge of the political world. If so, she betrayed Herbert, and he must have felt as Lord Melbourne did on a previous occasion when Caroline told his secret. Herbert now knew that he could never trust Caroline again. It is likely they had a tremendous row after this incident. It certainly seems to have ended their affair, though not their affection for each other.

In August 1846, a month after the fall of Peel's Government, Sidney Herbert married Elizabeth A'Court. Shortly before the wedding took place, Caroline went to Ireland. She had previously promised Herbert that she would make no trouble for him.[7] Years later, she described the end of the affair in *Lost and Saved*:

> If Traherne married one of the Wollingham girls, they knew beforehand, with what tact she [Milly] would fade into being Traherne's 'friend'. None of your vulgar regrets and sadnesses, and calling the world's attention to the past, but a proper fashionable carelessness; a carelessness calculated to make all but the initiated really feel puzzled and doubtful whether they had not all along been mistaken as to the degree of intimacy which had subsisted between the parties . . . she vaguely anticipated that their union must end 'some day or other, as these things always did . . .'[8]

Their friends thought she had behaved very well in the whole business.

Fortunately, or unfortunately for Herbert, his political career was not finished. He went on to further success as Caroline had assured him he would. In 1852, he took office again, as Secretary at War, in Aberdeen's Government, and, during the Crimean War, was responsible for sending Florence Nightingale out to open the hospital at Scutari. His work-load was enormous. Caroline's friend Monckton Milnes, afterwards Lord Houghton, said that he wished that 'some of the thousand who justly [celebrated] Miss Nightingale, would say a single word for the man of "routine", who devised and projected her going'.

But Herbert was unfairly blamed for many of the errors made in the conduct of the Crimean War in 1854, so that when he came back to office in Lord Palmerston's Cabinet in 1859, he was obsessed with the desire to redeem his name. Now he worked harder than ever, in devising reforms for the Army. He also devoted much of his time to good works. He spent hours designing model lodging houses at Wilton for his farm labourers, and in rebuilding Wilton Church. Even when he went to bed his labours did not cease, for Elizabeth bore him seven children in the next few years.

It was as if he were trying to exorcize some demon by sacrificing himself to duty. His life now left little time for pleasure, and less for romance. And his character changed. He lost that charming boyish openness which people had loved him for, and now became calculating and wary. It was his 'strength of principle' that his Harrow house-master had praised, but at his death, Lord Houghton wrote that: 'He was just the man to rule England, birth, wealth, grace, tact, *and not too much principle.*'[9] Caroline was partly to blame for this change.

Curiously, Herbert's wife Elizabeth bore no resentment towards Florence Nightingale, who had helped to undermine his health when her peremptory demands had overworked him during the Crimean War. Indeed, Elizabeth's obsessive jealousy over Sidney did not extend to Florence at all. After the war, the two women met in Rome, and became very good friends. After Sidney's death, Elizabeth wrote to Florence to say: 'You know all I have to bear more than anyone else . . . It is strange that his whole family believe that he did not love me.'[10] So the weak and grieving wife clung to the powerful woman as if for support from a mutual rival. Between them, they represented family honour and public duty, Wilton and the Crimea. And between them they ground Sidney Herbert to death.

What had these women to fear? The answer was Caroline Norton and romance. Long after Herbert had ceased to be 'her' secretary, guest lists at various country-house weekends occasionally included the names of Mrs Caroline Norton and Mr Sidney Herbert.

But towards the end of his life, Caroline saw Herbert very rarely. Then she heard that he was to be created Baron Herbert of Lea. It was a bad sign, because it meant that the Government had recognized at last that he could not support the extra strain of contesting a seat in the Commons. Even then, Herbert refused to give up his post at the War Office and went on working at his desk. In the event, the ennoblement came too late, and his health broke down.

By the summer of 1861 he was very ill indeed, and Bright's Disease was diagnosed. Somehow or other, Caroline contrived a meeting with him, but it was to prove their last. Later, she recorded in a poem the moment when she had her final glimpse of him:

> Even as I write, before me seems to rise,
> Like stars in darkness, well remembered eyes
> Whose light but lately shone on earth's endeavour,

Now vanished from this troubled world for ever.
Oh! missed and mourned by many, – I being one, –
HERBERT not vainly thy career was run.
. . . Oh! eyes I first knew in our mutual youth.
So full of light and earnestness and truth;
Eyes I saw fading still, as day by day
The body, not the spirit's strength gave way;
Eyes that I last saw lifting their farewell
To the now darkened windows where I dwell, –
And wondered, as I stood there sadly gazing,
If Death were brooding in their first upraising.[11]

It was a discreet memorial. Sidney Herbert died at Wilton, on 2 August 1861.

In 1867, a statue of Herbert by J. H. Foley was erected in front of the old War Office in Pall Mall, where Caroline would have seen it frequently. It has been moved a little since then, and stands now next to one of Florence Nightingale. They are not looking at each other.

XXVII

CHANGING ROLES

CAROLINE NORTON WAS A CONSUMMATE ACTRESS. Her behaviour was always intensely dramatic. She loved playing roles, telling stories, creating mysteries, spreading gossip, and provoking incidents. Her behaviour was by turns tragic, comic, melancholy, witty, puzzling and teasing. But because she was disqualified by her social position from appearing on a stage, she became a writer instead. As a result, she regarded her poems and novels as opportunities to justify herself, and to tell her life story over and over again, which accounts for their wearying and persistent egoism.

To say that Caroline was always playing a part does not mean she was insincere. As she grew older, her earnestness became increasingly evident. But she would dramatize incidents, and like all actresses, she was constantly calculating the effect she was creating on people. Her extraordinary range of acquaintance and activities meant that she had the opportunity to play many parts, especially during her middle years in the 1840s. In her letters, stories and poems of the period, she may be glimpsed trying out new attitudes, or adopting new roles to demonstrate aspects of her own personality.

In 1843, for example, she had an opportunity to play the parts of virago and victim simultaneously. It happened when the Poet Laureate, Southey, died, and her old friend Rogers refused the post. Caroline seems suddenly to have realized that here was a public appointment which was not necessarily restricted to men. It was merely a matter of tradition that only men had ever been considered. So she applied for the job. She simply wrote to the Prime Minister, Peel, and asked for it.[1] She employed two arguments to support her case, the first that it was time for a woman to be appointed, and the second that she had been hard done by, and society should make it up to her. She told Peel in her letter: 'I do not know if there be any precedent for appointing a female poet laureate even in a Queen's reign . . . [but] . . . this seems an easy thing to grant if there be any disposition to befriend me and would be of very great service.' She reminded him that she was a successful writer, and hinted that the appointment would be some recompense for all her sufferings. When at last she received a reply, Peel merely informed her that he did not personally appoint the Poet Laureate, and that anyway the Lord Chancellor had already offered it to Wordsworth.

Her application may be regarded as comic, or arrogant, or both, but it must be remembered that she was a popular poet whose work had been compared to that of Byron by Hartley Coleridge, though no doubt she had been encouraged to think that she was rather better than she was. In addition, she may have been egged on in her application by Rogers, or even Sidney Herbert, who seems always to have encouraged Caroline to take herself more seriously, and who also had great influence on the Prime Minister, though in this case not enough. At any rate, Caroline must be awarded full marks for cheek, and some for courage, in trying for a prize which to this day no woman has ever won.

A more attractive side of Caroline is demonstrated by her treatment of Lord Melbourne. After his fall from government, he had remained for a short time in fashionable and political life, but this ended in 1842 when, at the age of sixty-three, he had a stroke. He retired to Brocket and soon became a pathetic, almost forgotten man. Augustus had died, and he lived alone apart from servants. Soon his health began to deteriorate. Caroline still did not dare go and see him, because of the risk to her fragile reputation, but she wrote to him, probably quite regularly, though only three letters from this period have survived.[2] They are, in effect, love letters, in which she still played the flirt and the tease, in order to recreate their old, light-hearted intimacy. Sometimes, however, her remarks are shot through with poignancy and sadness.

They had changed roles. Whereas Caroline had regained her self-confidence and was, even then, deeply involved with Sidney Herbert's, Melbourne's power and vitality had ebbed away. So Caroline used every possible means in these letters to cheer him up. She told him little stories, flattered him, scolded him playfully, and pretended to believe that he was still a ladies' man. Sometimes she gave him advice, as when she wrote to urge him to pay some attention to an old supporter fallen on hard times. By this method she subtly achieved two ends. First she encouraged Melbourne to believe that he still had some influence in the world, and secondly she signalled that she herself would never desert him:

How can you turn such a deaf ear, and such a turned up nose,

– to the claims of old Jack Morris? Why don't you help the man that helped your brother at Westminster? in the good old days, when you wasn't weak and sick, & he wasn't faint and starving? Do you think that the God that made Jack Morris & you, does not judge it as selfishness? Something also perhaps of ingratitude? for no doubt when he had his riches, and his 20 stall stable, & his Westminster votes, very civil words you all said to him! O! rouse your sluggish old heart to write to someone for him. (November 1844)[3]

And she still pretended to be jealous of his lady guests at Brocket, if only to make him laugh and stir his vanity:

Why don't you write? Who have you got at Brocket? Does Emily hang her long gowns up, like banners of Victory, in the cupboards? Does Sow's Body sit there, talking ill of you to Pig's face? Does Lady Holland cut herself into four, to help and serve you? Are Fanny Jocelyn's soft purple eyes at your table under the lamp? or does the 'Minny' who rivals our 'Georgy' rouse you to any love & admiration of your own relations?
Send us a line, oh! Hoy.[4]

She knew perfectly well, of course, that there were no women in his house, but guessed it would please him to dream, if only for a moment, that he was still an attractive man, and that she was only one of his many jealous women. And though she could do little by letter to stir the life in him, she tried to persuade a number of his old friends to go down to see him at Brocket.

Even when she was ill herself, in December 1843, at St Leonards-on-Sea, a month after the death of Uncle Charles, she still found the strength to write to her old admirer:

Dearest Old Boy, pray do write. I am ill in bed myself and if you don't write, I shall think you are ill in bed too . . . I did imagine I had coaxed you into scribbling by asking you that information for my poem. You always say you are glad to teach me things and supply me with scraps of knowledge. How shall I get on if I am so neglected by my Tutor? . . . Do write to me! I do not ask it altogether out of selfishness. I am sure if you don't write to me – you do nothing: and that is very bad for you. See now, I have written to you, tho' I am in bed, with leeches for my Pillow-

Fellows. (I call them Pillow-Fellows because Bedfellows take up more room.)

God Bless you,
Ever Yrs
Caroline[5]

Perhaps her letters helped Melbourne a little, but his life was progressively lonely and depressed. He dined alone, drank too much, and went to bed at nine o'clock. His doctor and nurse had little influence on him, and he began to imagine that he was on the point of bankruptcy. His worries included the fact that he had to keep up both Brocket and his house in South Street, and pay an annuity of £1000 to Lady Branden. To cap it all, his own servants were stealing the wine from his cellars. He was so distressed by his imagined financial problems, that he actually wrote to another of his old loves, the Queen, to ask her for a loan. Out of pity, Victoria let him have £10,000 at 3%, simply to relieve his anxiety.[6] Then, in April 1848, Melbourne had a second stroke. He sank rapidly during the summer and, on one dark November day, Caroline heard that he had died. There were no jealousies or disputes between them in his final days, and it must have been some consolation to her that, at the last, she was able to prove to him she was indeed his loving, loyal friend.

Loyalty was one of Caroline's significant virtues, especially when it applied to her men friends. She had an opportunity to demonstrate it again, in her response to Sidney Herbert after the end of their affair in 1845 and his subsequent marriage to Elizabeth A'Court. As has been seen, Caroline had agreed to fade from his life, but she still wanted his attention and admiration if only from afar.

She used her writing for this purpose. She could no longer send letters to Sidney Herbert, but she could refer to him, however obliquely, in her published work, and she knew that he would be bound to read her. So she wrote a poem, and later a series of letters to the press, which gave him ample proof that she was still loyal to him and his ideas. Her long poem was called *The Child of the Islands*, and it came out in 1845. A brief glance at the pages reveals that Caroline could not get Sidney Herbert out of her mind, for every sentiment in it echoes his view of society and politics. She quotes him in the epigraph: 'There is too little communication between the classes of this country. We want, if not the feeling, at least the expression of more sympathy on the part of the rich towards the poor; and a more personal intercourse between them.'[7] The poetry itself reads like Herbert's political opinions versified:

> A Life of self-indulgence is for Us,
>   A Life of self-denial is for them;
> For us the streets broad-built and populous,
>   For them, unhealthy corners, garrets dim,
>   And cellars where the water-rat may swim?
> For us, green paths refreshed by frequent rain,
>   For them, dark allies where the dust lies grim!
> Not doomed by us to this appointed pain –
>   God made us Rich & Poor – of what do these complain?[8]

By means of this poem, Caroline was able to let Herbert know that she had not forgotten all those talks they had about politics, and that she was still his partner in the great causes he supported. Though they might meet only rarely, she was a valuable ally in that she could publicize his ideas through her writing.

Another opportunity for her to advertise Herbert's views came in 1848, 'the year of revolutions'. In that year, radical and nationalist forces were gathering throughout Europe. In February, Louis Philippe abdicated in Paris after riots in favour of democracy; reform was also advocated by many German newspapers; in Prague, a provisional Czech government was set up; Hungary gained its independence; and the Austrian army was driven out of Italy. Soon it was feared that the Chartists would encourage riots in England. At this critical moment, Caroline decided to give British working men the benefit of her thoughts by writing to *The Morning Chronicle*.[9] In her letter she explained to them that the working classes were best served not by revolution, but by a benevolent aristocracy (she had Sidney Herbert in mind but did not say so). She pointed out that, though the French revolutionaries had banished the Royal Family and seized their property, there were now some 800,000 starving people in Paris.

The Chartists seem to have been unimpressed by her argument for, shortly after her letter appeared, their leaders in London met at Kennington Common, and tried unsuccessfully to lead a crowd across the river to Westminster, to present a petition to Parliament. Again, Caroline wrote to the paper. 'Rioting', she said, was 'the one employment for which no wages can be had'. Though she herself was 'heart and soul' with the people, and dreaded their failure, they should realize that there would always be a need for different classes, social superiority, and leaders. The people were not 'unlinked from, or oppressed by [the] aristocracy', and there was already a group of MPs to represent them. The people should not riot to get better conditions, they should place their complaints before their natural rulers, and ask for them to be put right.

Her letter includes a disguised portrait of Sidney Herbert, whom she imagines toiling away for the good of others. Indeed, she points out that aristocrats work just as hard at their trade of governing, as the button-maker does at his. Democracy will not work in her view, because most people are incapable of grasping the issues: 'A man knows that he cannot make buttons, but will not believe that he cannot make laws.' The sub-text of these letters is, of course, that people should leave it all to Sidney. If only those rioting Chartists could comprehend the nobility of a nature like his, then they too would be content to let him govern them. Curiously, her ideas do not seem to have convinced anybody.

Like her letters to Melbourne, these also are love letters, but this time dressed up as political theory and published in the press. Caroline would have been very happy herself to be ruled by Sidney Herbert, and thought that everybody else should take the same attitude. The 1848 riots were useful to her, for they provided her with an excuse to enter a public arena, from which she could display to the whole world her reverence for his ideals. It may also have just crossed her mind that, when Herbert read her words, he was bound to contrast her blazing political loyalty with the feeble support he could expect from his insipid wife.

In 1848, Caroline was forty, and had long been a regular visitor at Frampton Court. By that time, Brinsley and Marcia had two little children, to whom she had become 'Aunt Carry'. When Caroline went down to Frampton, she spent hours playing with them and telling them stories. She even published a little book of tales for them, *Aunt Carry's Ballads for Children*.[10] Yet even when she made up stories for children, she could not resist retelling her own, and presenting herself as a victim. One of the 'ballads' in this book is called 'The Story of Blanche and Brutikin', and the domestic scenes it describes are very like those Caroline played out with George Norton years before:

> But fiercely Brutikin struck down
> The Palings where she stood,
> Till in his sister's face he sent
> The splints of rotten wood;

'And do you dare to lecture me?'
He passionately said:
'Get in! Or I will make you hide
Your bold presumptuous head'.

Because it is a fairy story, Caroline gave it a happy ending. Brutikin's anger melts when Blanche rescues him with her tracker dogs from a death in the snow. Norton's malevolence had never thawed like that.

A more ambitious version of her story became the novel *Stuart of Dunleath*.[11] In the book, her heroine, Eleanor Raymond, after a disappointment in love, marries the brutal Sir Stephen Penrhyn who out-Nortons Norton by breaking her arm, and taking his mistress to live in the gate house. After both her boys have been drowned, and the man she loves marries another woman, Eleanor dies of a broken heart. Caroline put a lot of her own life into the book, including her recollection of her first visit to Rannoch Lodge, when as a young bride she was greeted by the vixenish Lady Menzies:

'Well, you seem tired enough and pale enough', said she gruffly, making a sort of gesture as if motioning her to stand nearer the warm blaze.
'I am not much tired' said Eleanor, 'and I am always pale.'
'Humph! my brother wrote us word that you were a great beauty, that's all. I suppose London hours and fine lady ways –'
'I have been very little in London.'
'Humph! how old are you?'
'I am seventeen.'
'You look much older; I should think, now you're safely married, you could have no objection to tell your real age.'[12]

Eleanor, like Blanche in her children's story, is a victim, and this is the part in which Caroline increasingly cast herself in later years. As she grew older, she liked to represent herself both in her writings and her social life as a woman of sorrows, and one with a tragic and mysterious past. Such a role had dramatic possibilities for her. Nevertheless, in company with her family or her male admirers, her naturally comic wit would keep breaking in and spoiling the effect.

Stuart of Dunleath took her four years to write because she had had so many problems with her sons. And though Brinsley had been lazy and rebellious at Eton, it was Fletcher who worried her more. After school he had gone into the diplomatic service, at the British

Legation in Lisbon under Sir Hamilton Seymour, but Caroline knew his health was delicate, and she dreaded that, when he was posted to a hot country, he would contract the family disease of tuberculosis. She realized that, should he become ill in a foreign country, she would have to go out and nurse him. To do that, she needed money, and as fiction could earn more money than poetry in the late Forties, she had started on her novel.

In autumn 1847, she learned that Fletcher was ill in Lisbon. Without a moment's hesitation, she took the fifteen-year-old Brinsley away from school, and sailed for Portugal to nurse her elder son. She spent the winter sitting in the sick-room, scribbling her novel, entertaining the Pope's nuncio, visiting among the 'stiff and disjointed' Portuguese Society, and riding about the Lisbon area on a donkey. When Fletcher was a little better, she sat talking to him for hours, telling him stories of her life, and making up verses for Brinsley to strum on the guitar. One song, especially, appealed to her younger son. It told of a beautiful, dark-eyed young woman, with a mysterious past which drives her to forsake her lover:

JUANITA

Soft o'er the fountain,
Ling'ring falls the southern moon,
Far o'er the mountain
Breaks the day too soon;

In thy dark eyes splendour,
Where the warm light loves to dwell,
Weary looks, yet tender,
Speak their fond farewell.

Nita! Juanita!
Ask thy soul if we should part!
Nita! Juanita!
Lean thou on my heart.

When in thy dreaming,
Moons like these shall shine again,
And daylight beaming
Prove thy dreams are vain;
Wilt thou not, relenting,
For thine absent lover sigh,
In thy heart consenting,
To a prayer gone by?

Nita! Juanita!
Let me linger by thy side!
Nita! Juanita!
Be my own fair bride.

Caroline was aware that, with her black hair and dark eyes, she had frequently been thought of as a Mediterranean beauty in her younger days, and the mysterious Juanita was in some ways a revival of one of her most successful roles. The song itself became very popular, and even a century later, was a standard piece in the repertoire of certain dance bands.

Fletcher recovered slowly, and Caroline was at last able to return to England. But she had created trouble for herself by taking Brinsley out of school to go with her to Lisbon. For he had not merely studied the art of indolence there, he had been captivated by the sight of Portuguese girls. Now he wanted to find a Juanita for himself.

XXVIII

NORTON VERSUS NORTON

THEN CAME CAROLINE'S FINAL STRUGGLE WITH NORTON, and the only occasion they came face to face in a court of law.

In 1848, Caroline received a letter from his solicitors, asking her to sign a separation agreement. Norton claimed to be short of money because the rents from his Yorkshire estates were dropping in value, and he proposed a solution which, he argued, was in the interest of them both. If she would agree to his mortgaging a trust fund that had been settled on her, he would make her an allowance of £400 to £500 a year, until he inherited the estate of Lord Grantley and could afford to be more generous. He also promised never again to interfere in her affairs, provided that she promised not to charge her debts to him. Her trustee, Sir John Campbell, refused to sign the agreement on her behalf, because he said it was against her interests for him to do so. Caroline would probably have gone no further in the matter, had not Norton got Fletcher to persuade her. Fletcher was still convalescing at home, after his illness in Lisbon during the previous year. Caroline was so concerned about his health at that time, that it was difficult for her to deny him anything, so when he took his father's side about the agreement, it was a powerful inducement for her to sign it herself. Norton was taking advantage of her fears in this, because he knew she wanted to have enough money to go back to Portugal at any time, so that she could be with Fletcher if he needed her. Despite Sir John's continued objections, therefore, Caroline agreed.

Autumn 1848 was a time of grief and anxiety for Caroline. Her mother was now old, ill and nearly blind; it was then that she heard of Lord Melbourne's death; and Brinsley, who was back at Eton, seemed determined to be as indolent as ever. But her greatest concern was still for Fletcher. By November his sick leave was up, and though he was still far from well, he was obliged to sail for Lisbon. Meanwhile, she went to Scotland to make arrangements to follow him, and while there received the news of Melbourne's death. Then she heard that Fletcher had arrived in Lisbon, but was thought by his Portuguese doctors to be dying. She was frantic with worry, but could not follow him immediately because she had not got enough money for the passage. So when the separation agreement arrived from London signed by Norton and his solicitor, Mr Leman, Caroline lost no time in signing it and sending it off at once. Soon she received the cash and, by mid-December, she and Brinsley had embarked on a boat for Portugal. Throughout the winter and the spring of 1849, she was in Lisbon nursing Fletcher. Against all predictions, he recovered once more.

It was not until the following summer, when she returned to Chesterfield Street, that she received news from her solicitors that Lady Palmerston had made her an allowance, probably of £200 a year, from the estate of her brother, Lord Melbourne, in accordance with his dying wishes. This was, no doubt, the fulfilment of the promise he had made her at their reunion in Green Street in 1837. In the autumn, she received her first cheque from this legacy. She told nobody about it because she probably thought that it was no one else's business. All she cared about was that, if Fletcher's health failed once again, she would have sufficient money to take him to the Cape of Good Hope, just as Mrs Sheridan had taken her husband many years before. But Fletcher's health continued to improve.

During the next few years, Caroline lived abroad as much as possible. This enabled her to live cheaply, write her novels in peace, and keep an eye on Fletcher. Holidays were spent with both her sons, wandering the Continent, searching for the healthiest locations. But neither George Norton, nor Brinsley's Eton schoolmaster, Mr Coleridge, approved of the boy leading a sort of Gypsy life, dragging about Europe with Caroline. But the lively and skittish Brinsley was his mother's darling, and she persisted in taking him with her during the school holidays. Then in 1851, this 'kindly, clever, handsome and wild' young man was sent to University College, Oxford, where he proceeded to go through his allowance as fast as possible, and amass a pile of debts. When he was told of Brinsley's bills, Norton flatly refused to pay them. Unfortunately, Caroline did not have the money to do so either.

What was worse, Brinsley was now starting to cough in a horribly familiar way, and Caroline knew he must be taken to a warmer climate. So when Fletcher, now in better health, told her that he was to be Secretary at the British Embassy at Naples, her way was clear. She removed Brinsley from University College after only one year, and took him to live cheerfully and cheaply with her and Fletcher in the Neapolitan sun. Norton did not object, provided that he did not have to meet their expenses. He said he had paid for the boys' upkeep at school and college, but he declined further to maintain grown-up young men. Caroline, however, was convinced that Brinsley's life was at risk, and that it was essential for him to live in the south. She proposed to work at her new novel, *Lost and Saved*, in Naples, both to help to pay off his creditors, and also to purchase his entry into some respectable profession or other when he was better. Even so, she could not do it all out of her own income, and she wrote to remind Norton of his obligations to his sons, and to ask him for more money.

On 9 June 1851, Mrs Sheridan died at Helen Dufferin's house in London. Naturally, her estate was divided among her children, and Caroline's portion consisted of two quite separate bequests. One of them, her life-interest in her father's estate, had not been secured to her in law, and therefore was payable to Norton. But Mrs Sheridan had had money in her own right, and had always mistrusted Norton since the time he had cheated her over Caroline's marriage agreement. She had therefore been determined that none of her own money should get into his hands. Consequently, the £480 a year she bequeathed to Caroline was secured to her under the laws of Equity, so that Norton could not touch the money. It was a great help, for Caroline's expenses had increased as her sons had grown older and her husband meaner. Her total annual income now consisted chiefly of her literary earnings, her £500 from Norton arising from the marriage agreement of 1848, her legacy from Lord Melbourne, and now her mother's bequest of £480.

When he learned of it, Norton was stung by the ingenuity of his mother-in-law's will, and determined to have his own back on Caroline. His income was much greater than hers. He had well over £3000 a year coming in, from his salaries as magistrate and recorder, his estates, his life interest in Tom Sheridan's pension, and his life mortgage on Caroline's trust fund. Legally, he also had the right under Common Law to appropriate her earnings as a writer, though he did not go that far in 1851. But, despite the fact that he was well off, he still could not bear to be done out of a penny. So he wrote to her, to remind her of the depressed state of agriculture in Yorkshire, and the diminishing income from his rents, and to enquire, in the light of her mother's recent bequest, what sum she would agree to his deducting from her allowance.

Even after all their years of struggle, Caroline was aghast at this new exhibition of meanness. She replied that she would not consent to any deduction from the £500 he had agreed to pay her; that her mother's bequest was intended to eke out this meagre sum; that years of litigation, dispute, debt, their son's illness, and consequent journeyings and residences abroad had impoverished her; and that her mother's assistance was intended for her and her sons, and not for the husband who had wronged her. Norton replied that she would either agree to accept a deduction of £200 per annum or get nothing. As for the agreement drawn up by Mr Leman, he informed her that 'as, by law, Man and Wife were one, and could not contract with each other . . . the deed was therefore good for nothing'. When she reminded him that he had signed the deed in order to mortgage her trust fund, and that he, a magistrate, had already had the advantage of it, Norton merely laughed at her. When she took legal advice, Norton's view was confirmed. Of course *in honour* he was obliged to keep his word, but legally the deed had no force.

In March 1852, Caroline was in Italy with both her sons when her cheques bounced for the first time. It was a great shock. Norton had decided not to pay his allowance into her account, even though he knew it was to be another six months before she was to receive anything from her mother's will. It is likely that her brother, Richard Brinsley, helped her out at that time, but it was clear to her that she was in grave financial trouble. When she returned to England in 1853, she realized that she would have to do something, for she was unable to pay her debts. Again she appealed to Norton to behave properly, but he refused to discuss the matter, and when she persuaded two of his relatives, Mr Norton of Elton, and Sir Frederick Thesiger, to talk to him about it, he declined to do so.

There was only one way for her to fight back. Since the agreement of 1848, she had faithfully kept her side of the bargain, and had paid her own debts. At times she had been obliged to borrow further to pay her creditors, but she had never referred an account to Norton. Now her solicitors persuaded her that she would have to do so. If she allowed only one of her creditors to bring an action against her husband, the mere threat of court action might bring him to heel. If not, the resultant trial would be a kind of test case of his position. Reluctantly, she accepted the advice, and referred to Norton the bill of a carriage builder, Mr Thrupps, for repairs to the little vehicle she had bought so long ago from the proceeds of *The Dream*. Norton, of course, refused to pay it, and the resultant action of Thrupps versus Norton took place in the Westminster Court on 18 August 1853. Caroline must have known what was involved in such an action. The

British public would regard it as a kind of re-run of the famous Melbourne trial of seventeen years before, and her scandalous story would be dragged out again. But she probably felt that she had no choice.

The courtroom was packed for the case. There were many curious spectators, and also a number of reluctant witnesses whom Norton, in an excess of malevolent energy, had sub-poenaed to be present. These included one of Caroline's own maids, from whom he hoped to extract evidence of her extravagance; and her bankers and publishers, whose testimony about her financial position he hoped to use to prove that she was well able to earn her own living. What was more, Caroline learned that Norton had sub-poenaed herself to appear, presumably because he hoped to elicit some sort of admission from her. This no doubt gave her some trepidation, but also the thrill an actress enjoys when she learns she has been picked to appear in her favourite part at last.

After the presentation of the case for Thrupps, which was purely a matter of fact about repairs and the unpaid bill, Norton's counsel proceeded to launch the defence by questioning some of the many sub-poenaed witnesses. Norton himself sat with his lawyers, muttering instructions about the questions they were to ask. Much time was taken in the examination of Caroline's bankers, for in order to sustain his case, Norton had taken away all the documents concerning her accounts, which as her husband he was entitled to do. By revealing the contents of these bank-books in court, his lawyers hoped to prove that Caroline was much better off than she had claimed, and that consequently Norton was justified in withdrawing his allowance.

After the servants and the bankers, Caroline herself was called to the stand. So, for the first and last time in a court of law, she and Norton confronted each other. This was the climax of the case, and for many spectators it was a fascinating sequel to the sensational quarrel that had started when they themselves were only children. For them the real contest was not Thrupps versus Norton, but Norton versus Norton. Caroline afterwards recorded her experiences in the courtroom:

> When I first saw my husband my courage sank; the horrible strangeness of my position oppressed me with anger and shame; my heart beat; the crowd of people swam before my eyes; and the answers I had begun to make, and declarations I had intended

to struggle through, choked in my throat, which felt as if it were full of dust. Mr Norton rose, gathered up his papers, and saying with a sneer, 'What does the witness say? Let her speak up; I cannot hear her!' he came and seated himself close to me – there was only the skirting-board that divided the court between us. I saw the glare of the angry eyes I remembered long ago in my home, the sneer of triumph and determination to crush me at all hazards. I felt as I looked for an instant towards him, that he saw in me neither a woman to be spared public insult nor a mother to be spared painful sorrow, but simply a claimant to be non-suited, a creditor to be evaded, a pecuniary incumbence he was determined to be rid of. More than one of the professional gentlemen present appealed to the Judge whether he should be permitted to sit where he had placed himself; but there he continued to sit, instructing his counsel in an undertone what questions to put to me, making notes of the case, and occasionally peremptorily addressing me himself.[1]

Norton's threatening behaviour at first made her senses swim, and as a result, her answers were feeble. Then he made his mistake.

He had always misjudged her, and now he forgot the great lesson that she had been trying to teach him all their married life: that she could be bullied too much. His attempt to intimidate her came in his final statement through his counsel. He began rather disingenuously by admitting that in not paying Mr Thrupps, he was knowingly breaking the separation greement he had made with his wife in 1848. But he insisted that, even though he had no legal obligation to keep this agreement, he would have honoured it, had not his wife misled him. Then he produced his dramatic flourish. He had broken the agreement he said, because, when his lawyers had examined his wife's bank-books, they had discovered that, contrary to her solemn assurances in 1848, *she was receiving payments under the will of the late Lord Melbourne*. At the name of Melbourne, there was uproar in the court, and no doubt Norton was secretly delighted at the effect he had created.

Caroline must have seen at once the significance of what Norton was at. He was once again smearing her reputation by reviving the ancient scandal. He suggested to the court that in 1848, as part of their agreement, she had promised never to receive money from Melbourne, and that he regarded that promise as proof of her innocence. But now he announced that he had found the proof of just such a legacy, and implied that, because it proved she had been guilty of adultery with Melbourne all those years ago, the jury should sympathize with him.

But he had forgotten that Caroline was a much greater exponent of the dramatic effect than ever he could be. When she heard his allegations on the lips of his smooth-tongued attorneys, her blood rose in her face and she was almost overcome with indignation. Once he mentioned the old smears about her friendship with Melbourne, *which he had several times since declared that he had never believed*, her mood turned from helpless timidity to burning indignation. She rose to confront the court:

From the moment the questioning began about Lord Melbourne I lost all self-possession. Not because I was ashamed of having accepted his bequest; if I had thought that there was shame in it I should not have taken it; but because I then saw all the cruel baseness of Mr Norton's intention. All flashed upon me at once. I felt that I no longer stood in that court to struggle for an income, but to struggle against infamy. I knew by sudden instinct that the husband who had so often, to me and to others, asserted that the trial was the work of advisers, was now about to pretend he believed the charge brought against Lord Melbourne in 1836. The wild exasperation came over me, which seemed so inexplicable to those who did not know our real story. He who had falsely accused me long ago, he who had taken my young children, and let one of them die without even sending for me till too late, he who had embittered and clouded my whole existence, who was now in my presence only to cheat me – was once more going to brand me before the world.

I felt giddy, the faces of the people grew indistinct; my sentences became a confused alternation of angry loudness and husky attempts to speak. I saw nothing but the husband whose mercenary nature Lord Melbourne himself had warned me I judged too leniently; nothing but the gnome, proceeding again to dig away, for the sake of money, what remnant of peace, happiness and reputation might have rested in the future years of my life; turning up, as he dug, dead sorrows and buried shames, and miserable recollections, and careless who was hurt by them, so long as he evaded payment of a disputed annuity, and stamped his own signature, worthless.

I tried at first confusedly enough, as the broken sentences in the report showed, but afterwards as connectedly as I could, to explain that Lord Melbourne had left me nothing in his will; that I believed that he could not, his property being strictly entailed. But that I had never been his mistress; that I was young enough, and more than young enough, to be his daughter, and that he had never treated me otherwise than as a friend; that dying he had left nothing but a letter solemnly repeating his assurance of my innocence, recommending me to the generosity of his brother, and stating the amount of provision he wished made for me; that his brother and sister had abided by, and fulfilled his intentions, because his memory was dear to them; and none but my husband had ever accused him of baseness.[2]

The crowded courtroom was as quiet as death while she spoke. For the first time, she was pleading her own case before a public audience, and, as she went on, she gained in confidence and eloquence. She was a re-embodiment of her grandfather, Richard Brinsley Sheridan, the greatest orator of his day, enthralling a court with his famous speech on the Begums of Oude. When she finished there was a silence, and then a 'burst of applause from some two or three hundred people in the body of the court, which was at once properly suppressed by order of the judge'.

It was now plain to everyone present that in the case of Norton versus Norton, Caroline had won the argument hands down. Even Norton's solicitor, Mr Leman, felt impelled to jump to his feet to deny his client's statement that there had been a clause or understanding referring to Lord Melbourne in the 1848 agreement, though this, of course, had little to do with the case in hand.

But the action of Thrupps versus Norton went on, and Caroline was questioned about her household expenses and even her charities. Now, however, she was supremely confident. She knew that Norton had lost the sympathy of the court by his innuendo about her relationship with Melbourne, and the feeling in the room was all against him. It therefore came as a terrible shock to her when Thrupps lost his action on a legal technicality. Apparently, he had presented his bill before Norton had withdrawn his allowance to Caroline, and therefore, under the terms of the 1848 agreement, she should have paid it.

When the verdict was announced Caroline rose to her feet magisterially, and the court hushed to hear her. She declared:

I do not ask for my rights. I have no rights; I have only wrongs.

I have no doubt I have a very ample income, upon average for some years £1,500; and now that I know my husband can defraud me, I will not live abroad with my son.

Again the court burst into applause. Then Norton rose purple-faced, and started to shout that she had been telling lies. He fought his way towards her, ranting and waving his fists, while the people in the courtroom hooted and groaned their disapproval. Abraham Hayward helped her out through the tumultuous crowd. The usher found it difficult to clear the excited courtroom.

Soon afterwards Caroline made a decision. She now considered it to be unacceptable for the law to transfer a woman's property to her husband from the moment she married him. The law would have to be changed. So she decided to change it.

XXIX

PROPERTY

IT WAS NOT THE PROPERTY QUESTION which first concerned Caroline after the Thrupps trial, but the need to put right newspaper reports of what had been said there. A number of newspapers printed very prominently all Norton's slanders about her relationship with Lord Melbourne but ignored her own refutations. So, despite the pleadings of her family, she insisted on writing to *The Times*, to give a detailed account of her answers in court. For example, she explained to readers how Norton had stopped her allowance *even before* he had examined her bankbook and found evidence of Melbourne's bequest.

Unfortunately, just as her family predicted, her letter provoked a long reply from Norton. He set out his side of the story in an enormous letter which filled over eight columns of print. In it he claimed to have been suspicious of Caroline's conduct with Lord Melbourne from the first, and he even cast doubts on the paternity of Brinsley and William. He also accused her of burdening him with her private debts.

Then other people joined in. Mr Leman, Norton's solicitor, verified Caroline's claim that the 1848 agreement, between herself and Norton, had never mentioned Lord Melbourne; Sir John Bayley wrote to remind readers that he had initially represented Norton, but was so shocked by his client's unreasonable conduct to his wife, that he refused to act for him further; and Messrs Currie & Woodgate, on behalf of the late Sir William Follett, pointed out that it was untrue that he had advised Norton to bring an action against Lord Melbourne in 1836, and, indeed, until the day before the trial, he had not known on what evidence it would rest. Norton replied to all these charges, even accusing Campbell of changing sides because he had fallen in love with Caroline. Naturally, she could not resist writing again to reply to it. So the public correspondence went on.

But Caroline's friends became increasingly impatient with her, and her sister, Helen Dufferin, and Abraham Hayward tackled her together about her letter-writing. Hayward was usually brutally frank, and he almost certainly told her straight. Her endless self-justification in the press was making her into both a bore and a laughing-stock. It would have been far better had she let the whole thing drop so that the Melbourne business could be forgotten. Hayward may have added that, whereas once she had been a noted wit in the literary salons of London, she was now generally regarded as a wearisome woman, with neither the style to conduct a love affair with discretion, nor the good taste to keep her personal problems to herself. He asked her for an assurance that she would write no more letters to the press, and it seems that she refused. She took the view that if Norton printed lies about her in public, she must answer them. At this point, Hayward declined to act any further for her as her solicitor. He afterwards wrote: 'No-one can be Mrs Norton's adviser, for she never follows advice. I ended by telling her in Lady Seymour's presence, that she ought to be interdicted to use of pen and paper.'[1]

But, by this time, Caroline was far from caring what Hayward or anybody else thought about her conduct; she was obsessed with her need to put the record straight about her and Melbourne. So, when even the newspapers were reluctant to print any more of her lengthy letters, she started work on a pamphlet intended to tell her version of her friendship with Melbourne and her marriage to Norton. Later she had it printed at her own expense, and distributed to her more influential, but not always grateful, friends. It was called: *English Laws for Women in the Nineteenth Century*, and it came out in May 1854.[2] The pamphlet embarrassed her friends, and tried the patience of her readers because it exhibited no sense of reticence, and was tediously long. The enterprise probably lost rather than gained her sympathy, both personal and public. But, buried among all the recriminations, there are some shrewd pieces of argument, and even one or two passages which still have the power to resonate in the mind.

She took as her motto the epigraph Dickens had given to his recent novel, *Bleak House*: 'it won't do to have TRUTH AND JUSTICE on our side; we must have LAW AND LAWYERS'. In the pamphlet, she goes over her life with Norton, describes his brutalities, and itemizes their quarrels over many years. Of course, she was aware by now that many people such as Harriet Martineau would say that she was once again telling her story merely to have the law changed to benefit herself personally, but Caroline now claimed that her ordeal as a wife was of general significance. Many men, especially better educated ones, still thought of women of their own class as Romantic ethereal creatures. What she wanted to do was to show people how degrading were the experiences of women parted from their husbands, and to explain why the laws had to be changed to protect them:

> . . . it is of more importance that the law should be altered, than that I should be approved. Many a woman may live to thank Heaven that I had the courage and energy left, to attempt the task; and, since no one can foretell the future, even men may pause e'er they fling my pamphlet down with masculine scorn; for a day may come – however improbable – to some of my readers, when he would give his right hand, for the sake of sister, daughter, or friend, that the law were in such a condition as to afford the chance of justice; without the pain of a protracted struggle, or the disgrace of a public brawl.[3]

Her purpose, she told readers, was to disturb the 'duckweed on the still pond' of Society, to reveal the vibrant life beneath. In doing this, she showed with some success how the laws of the day were anomalous or even self-contradictory.

Her examples of legal confusions are taken from British, French and American case histories. She notes that the laws of these countries generally uphold the right to self-defence, but also require women to respond to violent husbands with humility and passive endurance. She refers to the case of the Duchesse de Praslin, who had recently been brutally murdered by her husband, and demands to know what the poor woman should have done. Should she have obediently allowed her husband to kill her, or was there a point at which the right to self-defence came into play, so that she might lawfully defend herself? How far might any battered wife legally resist her husband?

Another anomaly was highlighted by a court case from Kentucky, which had featured recently in the English press, and which Caroline thought had implications for English law. Sam Norris was a negro slave who had paid over his earnings for many years to his master, in return for his ultimate freedom. At the last moment, however, his owner, Mr Patten, had changed his mind, pocketed the cash, and kept a hold on Sam. On appeal, a Kentucky court had found in favour of Patten on the ground that 'a slave cannot make a contract, nor can he have monies of his own'. But as Caroline points out, Sam's situation was precisely the same as that of married women in England, for they were not allowed to own property either. Therefore, she concludes triumphantly that, though it was generally thought that Wilberforce and the anti-slavery campaign had brought the end of slavery throughout the British Empire in 1833, this was not true. Married women were still slaves. For the law to be consistent, it must free married women to own property, just as it had freed the slaves.

Her pamphlet was chiefly addressed to men, and especially parliamentarians who had some influence in changing the law:

> How often in the course of this session will the same men who read this appeal with a strong adverse prejudice be roused by some thought in a favourite author, touched by some beautiful pageant of human feeling . . . yet I have an advantage over these, for my history is real. I know there is no poetry in it to attract you. In the last act of this weary life of defamation I went down in a hack-cab, to take part in an ignoble struggle, in a dingy little court of justice, where I was insulted by a vulgar lawyer, with questions framed to imply every species of degradation. There was none of the pomp and circumstance of those woes that affect you, when some faultless and impossible heroine makes you dream of righting all the wrongs in the world. But faulty as I may be, it was unjust; and unjust because your laws prevent justice. Let that thought haunt you through the music of your Somnambulas and Desdemonas, and be with you in your histories and romance . . . I really wept and suffered in my early youth for wrong done, not by me, but to me, and the ghost of whose scandal is raised against me this day . . . I really lost my young children, craved for them, struggled for them, was barred from them, and came too late to see one who had died a painful and convulsive death, except in his coffin . . .
>
> . . . Will none of you heed the cause I advocate, and forget that it was advocated by me? Think what it must be to spend all one's youth, as I have spent mine, in a vain series of struggles to obtain legal justice. Or do not think at all about me; forget by whose story this appeal was illustrated. I can bring you others, from your own English law-books; and let my part be in this only as a voice borne by the wind, as a cry coming over the waves from a shipwreck, to where you stand safe on the shore, and which you turn and listen to, not for the sake of those who call – you do not know them – but because it is a cry for help.[4]

It is the unfairness of the property laws that is the most significant new emphasis in this latest pamphlet. Of course Caroline had long been aware of the anomaly that, whereas in Scotland a wife kept all her property, in England everything a woman owned was legally transferred to her husband from the moment she married him. Indeed, a passage from her novel *Stuart of Dunleath*, published in 1851, probably echoed many rows she had had with Norton on this very subject as far back as the 1830s. In the book, the heroine, Eleanor, has a conversation with her brutal husband, Sir Steven:

'D—n it, how stupid women are, in all matters of business. Your fortune's mine: do you understand that?'
'The fortune father left me!'
'The fortune your father left you. No married woman has a fortune of her own, as you call it, that isn't specially settled upon her. There's no such settlement in your case, the money has fallen in, and been replaced, that's all, I'm your husband, and it's mine.'
'I do not understand.'[5]

But it was Caroline's recent personal experience which sharply brought home to her the need for property reform. For, in order to get his evidence for the Thrupps trial, George Norton had removed all her bank-books and her contracts with her publishers. He was now in effective charge of her financial affairs. What was more, Caroline now realized with horror that the law would support him if he withdrew all her money from the bank. As the cheques from the publishers came in, he could take the money out. She could not protect her own income. Her only hope was a change in the law.

She was quite right in her assessment of the gravity of the problem, for the reform of property laws as they affected married women was soon generally recognized as the most important of all feminist issues. It was, for example, far more urgent than gaining the vote for women. But when Caroline began to look into the matter to write her pamphlet, reforming the law must have seemed an impossibility, because the legal machinery of England in the mid-nineteenth century was in a state of utter confusion. There were four legal systems operating, some deriving from mediaeval times, and each with its own courts, concerns and procedures. No fewer than three sets of courts had some authority in matters of marriage, divorce and women's property rights, and they had sometimes been known to arrive at conflicting verdicts. Ecclesiastical Law held that marriage was a sacrament, that a husband and wife were one person in imitation of Christ and his Church, and that, therefore, the wife had no legal existence. Common Law agreed that husband and wife were one person, and therefore did not recognize the separate existence of the wife. Only the law of Equity allowed property to be secured to a woman before she got married. Equity law was the response to a situation which had arisen in the eighteenth and nineteenth centuries. In the Middle Ages, when Ecclesiastical Laws and Common Laws were codified, the only significant property was land. As land brought with it the owner's legal responsibility to support the king in war, and as a woman could not do this, the land became accredited to her husband who could. But since the Industrial Revolution, new commerce had produced much personal property in the form of money and bonds. Many people, like Mrs Sheridan, who had had such property, were determined to secure it to their daughters so that unscrupulous husbands should not simply abscond after the wedding ceremony with the hard-earned family money. Equity Law enabled people to do this but its procedures were tedious and quite beyond the pockets of most people. There was literally one law for the rich and another for the poor.[6] As humble people said on so many issues: 'it may be law but it isn't justice'.

What was needed was a new law to give women the same property rights as men. What is more, it was essential that only one kind of court should have the power to rule in such matters, and its procedures needed to offer speedy decisions at a cost people could afford. Therefore a change in women's property rights necessitated reforms in the entire legal system. Caroline must have realized that the task was enormous.

Fortunately, there was help at hand.

CHAPTER

XXX

A RACE TO REFORM

THEN BEGAN A CURIOUS CONTEST in which Caroline Norton, for the only time in her life, found herself in rivalry with other women to bring about legal reform. It was a rivalry both of personalities and methods. Discreet charm was pitted against committee work, poetry against petitions, aristocratic influence against democracy, and the upper against the middle classes. The contest soon turned out to be a race over the hurdles of the mid-Victorian political agenda, and it was one with a close finish.

In 1850 a Royal Commission had recommended that the legal system should be tidied up, including the workings of divorce law. By the middle of the decade, Lord Chancellor Cranworth was at work upon his plans for a Divorce Bill. Caroline welcomed this news, for it simplified her task. All she had to do was to persuade Cranworth to include in his Bill clauses which would ensure that wives could retain their own property after marriage, and she was confident that she could do this by her usual methods of lobbying and pamphleteering.

It must have come as rather a shock to her to discover that she had a rival. In 1854, the same year in which she published her *English Laws for Women in the Nineteenth Century*, there appeared another pamphlet entitled *A Brief Summary, in Plain Language, of the Most Important Laws Concerning Women, Together with a few Observations Thereon*,[1] written by a certain Barbara Leigh Smith. Just like Caroline's pamphlets, it furnished details of case histories crying out for reform. Barbara Leigh Smith had dreadful tales to tell. There were cases of husbands absconding with their mistresses, taking with them the life savings of women they had just married. Then there was the poor woman who had set up as a laundress to provide for herself after being deserted by her husband, only for him to return some years later and take all her money away. Another appalling story told of the woman whose husband had been sent to prison for assaulting her, and who had later inherited a little money from her father, only to have the Crown authorities seize the whole of it on the grounds that her property was legally her husband's, and the Crown was entitled to the property of convicted felons. Yet another woman lost all her hard-earned savings when her husband died and willed them to his illegitimate children.

But Barbara Leigh Smith was not merely an author. She was a political organizer, and the head of a 'Women's Committee', which met regularly at her home, at 5 Blandford Square, off Lisson Grove. To this unmistakably middle-class address, the Committee came once a week, to discuss the need for reform of laws affecting women. Barbara herself was a very attractive personality. She was plump (though her friends described her as 'junoesque' and Dante Gabriel Rossetti 'fat') with healthy colouring, golden hair, and an abundance of energy and good spirits. Both her father and grandfather had been Unitarians and Radical MPs. She claimed to have been inspired to take up women's causes by reading the works of Caroline Norton.

Caroline had never met Barbara, and was, no doubt, flattered to hear of her admiration. In 1854 it must have seemed that she had nothing to fear from such an obscure person. This matter-of-fact woman was so different from herself that it was difficult to see how she could hope to have any influence in persuading Members of Parliament to change the law. Lisson Grove was a long way from Westminster, both geographically and socially, and it was most unlikely that she would have personal access to members of either House. Besides, Caroline could not have imagined Lord Melbourne agreeing to receive a deputation of women in the old days, and it was unlikely that the new Prime Minister, Lord Aberdeen, would do so now. Caroline might have been permitted the thought that changes in the law came about by methods more subtle than the 'Women's Committee' understood. She probably decided that when she received an invitation to join their committee – perhaps as President or Chairwoman or the like – she would decline their invitation, for she knew her light would not shine among their agendas and minute-takings. Yet she would be friendly. Such women really ought to be encouraged.

In fact the 'Women's Committee' needed little encouragement from her because it included some very formidable middle-class women, a type of whom Caroline had little experience. Bessie Rayner Parkes was from a Radical, Unitarian background, and descended from the chemist, Joseph Priestley. She had published several volumes of poems and her book: *Remarks on the Education of Girls* came out in 1852. Another member, Mrs Howitt, had written a good many popular handbooks with her husband, and together they had edited *Howitt's Journal of Popular Progress*. Other Committee members included the artist, Eliza Fox; Mrs Anna Murphy Jameson, a battered wife who had made herself an authority on Shakespeare; and Elizabeth Sturch Reid, a philanthropist, who had founded Bedford College for Women in 1849.[2] These women had two influential supporters in Parliament: Lord Brougham, who was all for reform, so long as it did not derive from Caroline Norton; and Matthew Davenport Hill, MP for Hull, who was highly respected for his campaigns defending civil rights.

It was Hill who brought Barbara Leigh Smith's pamphlet to the attention of the Law Amendment Society, who passed it to Sir Erskine Perry MP, chairman of their Civil Laws Committee. In 1856 Perry's Committee reported. Members could not condone the continued existence of both Common Law and Equity: 'two different sets of courts [which] dispense diametrically opposite rules [and which was] most discreditable to our system of laws'. The Committee observed that 'the rich are enabled, in many cases, to avoid the harshnesses of the common law, from which the middle classes, and those too poor to encounter the expenses of the courts of equity, are unable to escape.'[3] The remedy was simple. The protection that the code of Equity afforded to some few wealthy women, should be extended to all women at a reasonable cost. This conclusion was anticipated by the Women's Committee which had already begun a campaign for reform. Its strategy was: to publish evidence of how badly the current laws served society; to recruit legal expertise; to advise on how the laws should be changed; and to petition Parliament for those changes. In 1854, Barbara Leigh Smith and her friends had begun the task of collecting signatures. Within months there were about 70 petitions in circulation and 26,000 signatories. Mrs Howitt told how one old lady asked to be allowed to sign the petition on her deathbed 'and thus wrote her signature for the last time'.[4]

Caroline must have observed all this activity with mixed feelings. The aims of the Women's Committee were nearly the same as her own but they had never asked her to join them. No doubt, as the leading campaigner in the country, she expected to be asked, and may even have thought that the Committee hesitated to invite her because they thought her too grand for them. Whatever the reason, they did not ask her. Then came the matter of signing the petition. Naturally the Women's Committee wanted it to be headed by the names of the most prestigious women of the day. With the exception of the Queen and the aristocracy, the only well-known women in the country were writers. So the Committee began to canvas for signatures. Top of the list was the name of Mrs Elizabeth Barrett Browning who had signed while home on holiday from Italy with her husband. Mrs Gaskell was rather more reluctant, for reasons she explained to Eliza Fox:

> I don't think it [the petition] is very definite and pointed; or that it will do much good . . . a husband can coax, wheedle, beat or tyrannize his wife out of something and no law whatever will help that I see . . . However our sex is badly used enough and legislated against, there's no doubt of that – so though I don't see the definite end proposed by these petitions I'll sign.[5]

Other famous signatories included the writers: Mrs Harriet Martineau, Mary Cowden Clarke, Jane Webb Loudon, and Geraldine Jewsbury. Mrs Jane Carlyle added her name, as did Barbara Leigh Smith's personal friend Mary Ann Evans, soon to be famous as George Eliot. Meanwhile, Caroline waited with growing impatience for an invitation to sign. No doubt she expected her signature to head the list, because she was not only the most successful women's rights reformer in the country, but also a poet at least as well known as Mrs Browning. She waited and waited. But the invitation never came.

Why did the Women's Committee so pointedly fail to invite Caroline to join them and to sign their petition? They cannot have forgotten her, so it must have been a deliberate decision. The only conceivable answer is that they thought her name was still too scandalous, and that association with her would do their cause no good. Opponents of women's rights persistently argued that, if wives retained their own property, they would be much more likely to take lovers and leave their husbands. The Women's Committee, therefore, chose only the most respectable sort of married women, such as Mrs Browning or Mrs Carlyle, to head their petition. It is significant that George Eliot's real name, Mary Ann Evans, was placed low down in the list, presumably because she was living openly with a married man, George Henry Lewes.

Some time about 1855, Caroline seems to have decided that, if the Women's Committee could do without her, then she would go ahead with her own project in spite of them. There was a potential conflict here, for, whereas the Women's Committee were concerned to reform the property laws relating to all women, Caroline's campaign was directed only to Cranworth's Divorce Bill and the property of separated women. Nevertheless, she went ahead with her usual methods. She charmed Lord Lyndhurst, and made a point of captivating as many liberally minded MPs as she could find in Society drawing rooms. She acted as if the Women's Committee and their petition did not exist. By 1856, it was clear there would be a race to reform.

The 'Petition for Reform of the Married Women's Property Law' was presented to Parliament on 14 March 1856. Lord Brougham laid it before the Lords and Sir Erskine Perry the Commons. The petition stated:

> That the manifold evils occasioned by the present law, by which the property and earnings of the wife are thrown into the absolute power of the husband, become daily more apparent. That the sufferings thereupon ensuing, extend over all classes of society. That it might once have been deemed for the middle and upper ranks, a comparatively theoretical question, but is no longer, since married women of education are entering on every side the fields of literature and art, in order to increase the family income by such exertions.[6]

The formal document which petitioners had signed stated that, though among the upper classes, some cumbrous machinery of trusteeship, or the operation of the Courts of Equity might once have protected a woman's property after marriage, these means were often inadequate and beyond the pockets of many women. Poorer women such as 'sempstresses, laundresses and charwomen' had no redress against the theft of their earnings by a husband, who might spend them in a gin palace rather than upon their children's education. As the petition was to be presented to an all-male jury, its supporters also rather cunningly pointed out that a husband had little protection against the debts contracted before and during marriage by a profligate wife. They concluded:

> That since modern civilisation, in indefinitely extending the sphere of occupation for women, has in some measure broken down their pecuniary dependence upon men, it is time that legal protection be thrown over the produce of their labour, and that in entering the state of marriage, they no longer pass from freedom into the condition of a slave, all whose earnings belong to a master and not himself.[7]

Meanwhile, Caroline had concentrated her efforts upon Lord Cranworth's Bill to reform the English Marriage and Divorce Laws. It had been introduced to the House in June 1854, but because the Crimean War had broken out, subsequently languished in Parliamentary Committee. Caroline soon feared that it would lapse entirely, or worse, turn out to be inadequate. For Cranworth had been instructed only to tidy up the law by transferring all matrimonial cases from the Ecclesiastical Courts (or Doctors' Commons) to a new court. Here the Chancellor would have the authority to grant divorces or not, as he thought fit, and to consider all matters relating to the separation of husbands and wives. But the Bill did not help in such cases as her own, where women were still married, but separated from their husbands. Accordingly, she decided to give Cranworth a shove by circulating her objections to his proposals, and in 1855 she published *A Letter to the Queen on Lord Chancellor Cranworth's Marriage & Divorce Bill*.[8]

The idea of presenting a pamphlet as an open letter to the Queen was a rather ingenious one. After all, as Caroline pointed out, the Queen was 'the one woman in England who cannot suffer wrong; and whose royal assent will be formally necessary to any Marriage Reform Bill'.[9] Like herself, the Queen was no feminist, but it was known that she had expressed support for justice for all her subjects. Caroline did not get a reply to her 'letter', nor is it sure that the Queen ever read it, but in adopting this format Caroline could keep the tone intimate, as if one woman were talking to another in a world run by men.

Unlike Caroline's previous pamphlet, the *Letter to the Queen* is an effective combination of clear argument, flattery and ridicule. She begins by complaining to the Queen that divorce reform was being delayed. In this she was right, for Cranworth had introduced his Bill in June 1854, and subsequently withdrawn it; then he had announced in March 1855 that, though a Bill was 'nearly prepared', it must take its turn after other legislation. Caroline's second complaint was that Cranworth's proposed reforms were inadequate, because he intended 'simply to take away power from the Ecclesiastical Courts, and to transfer it to the Court of Chancery'.[10] But the chief argument in this and all her other pamphlets is that husbands and wives are treated differently by the law, and that this is not fair:

As the husband, he has a right to all that is hers: as his wife, she has no right to anything that is his. As her husband, he may divorce her . . . as his wife, the utmost 'divorce' she could obtain, is permission to reside alone, – married to his name. The marriage ceremony is a civil band for him, – and an indissoluble sacrament for her; and the rights of mutual property which that ceremony is ignorantly supposed to confer, are made absolute for him, and null for her.[11]

Caroline took care never to forget that she was supposed to be writing to the Queen, and she laced her letter with flattering references to Victoria's favourites. For example, she points out that those who first attacked her own reputation were the very people who abused the Queen's chief Minister, Lord Melbourne. Then, even more craftily, she links that line of argument with references to the Queen's special favourite. Lord Melbourne was the Minister who staunchly defended Prince Albert's taking an interest in public affairs. And Prince Albert, a prince renowned for his respect for justice, had recently been elected a barrister in those very Inns of Court in which the Divorce Bill was being prepared. Furthermore, Caroline asked the Queen whether or not Miss Nightingale, when she returned (God willing!) from the Crimea, would expect to see women treated with greater respect than hitherto.

Caroline's opponent was Lord Cranworth himself. Not only was he procrastinating about the Divorce Bill, but he had recently made a speech in Parliament which infuriated her. In answer to the charge that a woman paid dearly in law for a single infidelity, whereas it was treated as a minor matter in regard to her husband, Cranworth had replied that a woman should not look to dispose of her husband because he had been 'a little profligate'. Caroline leapt on the phrase. A little profligate indeed! What kind of morality was that? Later, she so hounded Cranworth about this indiscretion, that he was forced to deny that he had ever used it, though it was recorded in *Hansard*.

Though Caroline was rarely a poet, she was always a mistress of rhetoric, and in the *Letter to the Queen* she creates a dramatic effect by taking a public oath. Though women, she informs us, are often dismissed as the mere 'tapestry-working sex', some like Florence Nightingale dedicate themselves to great causes. She is willing to do the same:

I believe God gave me the power of writing. To this [cause] I devote that power. I abjure all other writing till I see the laws altered. I care not what ridicule or abuse may be the result of that declaration. They who cannot bear ridicule and abuse are unfit and unable to advance any cause; and once more I deny that this is my personal cause – it is the cause of all the women of England. If I could be justified and happy tomorrow, I would still strive and labour in it; and if I were to die tomorrow, it would still be a satisfaction to me that I had so striven. Meanwhile, my husband has a legal copy-right of my works. Let him claim this![12]

This pamphlet was a great success. People had nothing but praise for it. Even Lord Brougham said that it was: 'as clever a thing as ever was written, and it [had] produced great good'. He declared that he was certain that the Law of Divorce would be 'much amended', and that Caroline had greatly contributed to it.

Meanwhile, even before her pamphlet came out, Cranworth's Bill had run into trouble. Lord Aberdeen's coalition government was accused of incompetence in its handling of the Crimean War, and was dismissed in January 1855. When the Government fell, Cranworth fell, and the Divorce Bill fell with him. Fortunately, he was reappointed Lord Chancellor in Palmerston's Whig administration formed in February. In 1856, he reintroduced his Divorce Bill, which was then sent into committee by Lords Lyndhurst and Brougham. The amended Bill was then brought before the Lords, passed, and sent back to the Commons, but it was too late in the session for the House to deal with, and the Bill had to be reintroduced into the Lords in 1857.

Because of all these delays, Caroline seized the opportunity of the Christmas recess of 1855–6 to publish yet another pamphlet, A Review of the Divorce Bill of 1856,[13] in which she advanced twenty 'Propositions' for the consideration of Parliament. She proposed, among other things, the payment of alimony, desertion as a ground for divorce, the abolition of 'criminal conversation', and the restoration to a divorced or separated wife of all powers over her own property. The eighth proposition read:

That, on a decree of divorce a vinculo matrimonii, on the petition of a wife, the Court shall be empowered to order that the whole, or any part of her fortune, or property, surrendered to her husband on their marriage, or then, at any subsequent period received or taken possession of by him, shall be restored to the wife, or settled on her and the children of the marriage as the Court may direct.

By now she had published nearly 500 pages about divorce, in three lengthy pamphlets.

The parliamentary battle was joined again in 1856. Her chief supporter was Lord Lyndhurst, and her opponents were the High Anglican party, which regarded marriage as a sacrament, and thought divorce should be discouraged as far as possible. In the Lords, all the Bishops voted against reform, and they were led by 'Soapy Sam', the Bishop of Oxford, who later debated so disastrously against Thomas Huxley at Oxford after the publication of the *Origin of Species*. He argued that Parliament should not 'encourage' divorce by making it easier to obtain. If the Bill were passed, it would open the floodgates of licence, and introduce a 'universal laxity'. Her friend, Lord Lynd- hurst, now in his eighties, spoke from a wheelchair. He launched his argument that women should receive equal treatment in matters of divorce, by reminding their lordships of certain well-known cases of 'criminal conversation', in which women were unable to answer attacks on their own reputation made in open court. He also proposed a series of amendments which addressed many omissions of the Bill relating to the property of married women separated from their husbands. In so doing he took out a copy of Caroline's latest pamphlet and read long extracts to the House. These were subsequently embodied in his amendments, and the Lords passed the Bill and sent it to the Commons.

The race to reform was running very close now, for Perry's Married Woman's Property Act, promoted by the Women's Committee, had its second reading on 15 July 1857, and Caroline's own Divorce Bill on 24 July 1857. The High Anglican party, led by Mr Gladstone, set its face against both Bills, but more moderate opinion in the House tended to regard her Divorce Bill as a kind of half-way measure, righting wrongs of separated wives, but not undermining stable marriages by making husband and wife financial rivals. Of course she encouraged this view, and her friends impressed it on the Prime Minister. In the end, Palmerston placed his full support behind the Divorce rather than the Property Bill. Even so, Gladstone, who had just resigned as his Chancellor of the Exchequer, seemed determined to be difficult, and the House was exasperated by the length and complexity of a measure which kept it sitting through hot days of July. But Palmerston himself advised members that they should not be 'frightened by the names of July and August', and informed them that they would 'sit here day by day and night by night until this Bill be concluded'. On 21 July, the House had done with it, and sent it back to the Lords. Again their lordships amended it, and sent it back. On the following day, 23 August 1857, the House of Commons passed it, only three days before the session ended. Caroline and Lyndhurst had won the race both against the parliamentary time-table and Sir Erskine Perry and his Property Act.

She had triumphed again. It was true that the principle change in the divorce laws, which allowed for the setting up of a special court to consider all cases, was not Caroline's doing, nor was she responsible for the abolition of the old 'Doctors' Commons' courts. Both these measures were part of Cranworth's original tidying-up job. But it was in the crucial amendments to the Bill that she had been successful, for a number of them were taken word for word from her *Review of the Divorce Bill*. Lord Cranworth had complained that these were outside the original scope of his Bill, but other members had considered them to be 'a sort of Bill of Rights for married women', and Lyndhurst had argued that they were essential. Four clauses especially were reproduced almost word for word from her writings:

By Clause 21, for instance, a wife deserted by her husband may be protected in the possession of her earnings from any claim of her husband upon them.

By Clause 24 the new Court may direct payment of separate maintenance to a wife or her trustee.

By Clause 25 a (married) woman may inherit and bequeath property like a single woman.

By Clause 26 the wife separated from her husband is given the power of contract and suing, and being sued in a civil proceeding.

One anonymous commentator wrote that from henceforth an English matron might 'stand erect as a citizen' and that 'to Mrs Norton as a writer, and to Lord Lyndhurst as a statesman, will be due and will be paid all the glory and the gratitude'.

Lord Palmerston now clearly felt that he had done enough by women for a bit, and turned his attention to the Crimea, rumours of a mutiny in India, and a war in America. Sir Erskine Perry agreed. He said that Lord Lyndhurst's success with the Divorce Act had taken the 'wind out of the sails' of his efforts with the Property Bill, and decided not to go on with it.

The Women's Committee were upset but could do very little about it. They were right, however, in maintaining that their Bill, which would have defended the property rights for all women, had been sabotaged by Caroline's Divorce Act, which merely established such rights for the comparatively few women who, like herself, were separated from their husbands.

There is no record that Caroline and Barbara Leigh Smith ever met. After the failure of the Property Bill, Barbara gave up the fight. She married a French surgeon named M. Bodichon, and went to live in Algeria where she spent much of her time painting.

The Divorce Act had now ensured that Caroline's income was safe from George Norton, and she was never troubled again by his haggling over money. Of course he was never reconciled to such a measure. It was contrary to his whole notion of the right relationship between men and women. But then, as Caroline may have reflected, there are some members of the race who simply cannot be reformed.

XXXI

DANGEROUS, TERRIBLE, BEAUTIFUL

IN 1858 CAROLINE WAS FIFTY. In middle age, her beauty was still powerful, and she knew it. She was stouter, but her swan-like neck rose just as elegantly, if from a fuller bust. Her eyes were still splendid and her shining black hair untouched by a hint of grey. Once, when an admirer complimented her on her looks, she replied: 'Yes, I shall be handsome, even in my coffin'.

Her behaviour was full of paradox. She was fiercely tender, discreetly scandalous, sweetly malicious, and sentimentally witty. Her long years of reticence were over, and she seems no longer to have cared what people thought of her reputation. She was very knowing, and there was a pride and authority in the way she carried herself through the drawing rooms of High Society. After all, her poetry had been ranked above Mrs Browning's, she had been the friend of statesmen, and she had twice reformed the law. Her temper had become shorter, and her tongue sharper. She was a formidable presence.

Despite this, she still had many men friends, though none who admired her more than William Stirling. She seems to have met him as far back as 1850, perhaps at Abraham Hayward's, or perhaps at the house of Helen's friend, Lord Gifford. Caroline probably paid little attention to him then, because she was still getting over her affair with Sidney Herbert, and also because William was ten years younger than herself, and older men were far more interesting to her. He was an eccentric, diffident person, tall and bony, with a scholar's stoop, and very Scots. He was a farmer, he said, from Keir in Stirlingshire. He kept shorthorns and Clydesdale horses. When he was at home, he wore a suit of black wool, clipped from his own ewes. Caroline found all this very amusing, but she could not help being touched by his evident high regard for her.

On enquiry, she discovered that there was far more to William Keir than he had told her at first. He was an historian of Spanish art, and had published a highly regarded three-volume history entitled: *Annals of the Artists in Spain*. He kept a splendid library at his fine town house, 128 Park Street, Grosvenor Square. What was more, he was a considerable landowner, having succeeded to the family estates of Archibald Stirling of Keir, where he had remodelled the family mansion.

Caroline was never quite sure whether William Stirling intended his remarks to be amusing, or whether they merely were so. If he provoked a laugh among her sophisticated London friends, he was never abashed but would merely smile at the mirth he had caused. He told her dryly that he had written his own epitaph:

> Here lies Stirling of Keir,
> A very good man, but queer,
> If you want to find a queerer,
> You must dig up Stirling of Keirer.[1]

And it turned out that he knew a lot about many interesting subjects that Caroline had never considered. He was an expert on engraving, cartography, photography and cattle-breeding as well as art. These matters were not the usual topics of conversation among Caroline's Society friends but somehow, when William explained them to her, even she became interested in livestock or lenses, at least for a short time. And it made no difference that Stirling hoped to become Conservative MP for Perth, while she still professed to be a Radical. It was only the old-fashioned Tories of the Norton type that she detested, and her friendship with Sidney Herbert had long accustomed her to the company of 'moderate' Conservatives. Stirling was a kind, intelligent, cultivated man; that was more than enough to secure her regard. So she was pleased when he was subsequently returned unopposed at Perth. In 1851, he invited her to pay a visit to his home at Keir, and she accepted without a second thought. There would be no talk in the neighbourhood about Mr Stirling and the married English lady, for he was known to be an upright man, even a religious one in a quiet sort of way. In his youth, he had explored Mount Lebanon, lived on Mount Carmel with the monks, studied the Bible while exploring Palestine, and even published a volume of his own, *Songs of the Holy Land*.

What flattered her most about this quizzical young Scot, however, was his obviously deep respect for her. Despite his piety, and his sober prosaic manner, he did not seem to consider her to be shallow and immoral, as such people generally did. And he ignored her scandalous reputation. He merely smiled when she told him that, only if Norton survived his brother, and she became Lady Grantley, would her good name be at last restored. He seemed not to doubt her for a moment, and though she could see that he was often ridiculous, she was touched by his regard. Unfortunately, there was a great barrier between them. It was not the difference in their ages, but the inescapable fact that she was still married to Norton. William was far too pious to accept any arrangement other than marriage, so they had no future but friendship.

This friendship had continued throughout the Fifties. Caroline's annual round of visits to Frampton Court, Maiden Bradley, and her aunt, Lady Graham's at Netherby, now included an additional autumn holiday at Keir. She needed her family and friends in these years, for though she was engaged on the national stage in the struggle over the Divorce Bill, privately she was very lonely. She had her two grown-up sons, it is true, but they were no substitute for mature male affection. Shortly after the passing of the Divorce Bill in 1857, her friend and solicitor, Edward Ellice, brought her a present of a beautifully bound copy of all her pamphlets on marriage and divorce. He meant well but the book depressed her. It seemed to her that here were all her wasted years bound up in covers. She might have spent them happily with her children, but all she had to show for them were these records of old quarrels. She told Ellice: 'I look, believe me, with more sadness & regret than the world would think possible, at this heavy volume, – I know my cause was just, – I am conscious I have written with great intelligence, – I believed it a necessity to write, – as it was, God knows, the greatest possible temptation, – for I desired to justify myself . . . But, all being done and over, I would give my right hand never to have lived to have done it at all.'[2]

Masculine company was still a necessity to her. She saw Sidney Herbert only occasionally now, when he was allowed to take a weekend off from the War Office, and his wife and seven children. But when she wished, she could still sumon the energy to trawl men behind her in an expedition to the opera, or a play. And though her old friend, Rogers, died in 1855, there were still dinner parties where she might be glimpsed as the only woman at the table, still flirting as she did when she was twenty-five. She cared little what she said at such occasions, but, though she was rarely proper, she was always 'nice'. In May 1857, her brother Brinsley, sensing she needed a bit of male company, brought Stirling, Hayward and Gifford to help her choose a new horse at the livery stables in Green Street, and afterwards they all went on to an exhibition of French pictures and finally to supper.[3]

Her temptation to entice men was still strong. The American diplomat and historian, John Lothrop Motley, met her in 1858, at one of Thackeray's lectures. Lady Airlie came up to him to say that Mrs Norton would like to be introduced to the eminent author of *The Rise of the Dutch Republic*:

I turned and bowed, and there she was, looking today almost as handsome as she has always been. She is rather above the middle height. In her shawl and crinoline of course I could not pronounce upon her figure. Her face is almost certainly beautiful. The hair is raven-black – violet black, without a thread of silver; the eyes very large with dark lashes, and black as death; the nose straight; the mouth flexible and changing, with teeth which in themselves would make a fortune of an ordinary face. Such is her physiognomy; and when you add to this extraordinary poetic genius, descent from the famous Sheridan who has made talent hereditary in the family, a low sweet voice and flattering manner, you can understand how she twisted men's heads off and hearts out; we will not be particular how many years ago.

She said, 'Your name is upon every lip.' I blushed and looked a donkey. She added, 'It is agreeable is it not?' I had grace enough to add, 'You ought to know if anyone' . . .

She told me that she would be happy to see more of me. A day or two afterwards, accordingly, I went to call on her. She received me with great kindness and was very agreeable. She has a ready, rapid way of talking, alludes with perfect aplomb to her interminable quarrel with Mr Norton . . . She is also intimate with the Queen of Holland . . . she was always animating and interesting. My impressions of what she must have been were confirmed; certainly it was a most dangerous, terrible beautiful face in its prime, and is very handsome still.[4]

Motley was clearly susceptible, but protected by Yankee puritanism and a fond wife, Lily, who trailed round Europe with him. As for Caroline, she seems to have liked Americans a lot, perhaps because their manners were more open and straightforward than those of most of her English acquaintances, and they knew and cared less about her scandalous past. So she decided that the Motleys would be family friends, and made a point of inviting both Mr and Mrs Motley along to her dinner parties and receptions.

Another friend was Richard Monckton Milnes, later Lord

Houghton, the author of the *Life & Letters of John Keats*, which had first come out in 1848. Caroline liked to think of herself as the successor to the Romantic poets of the previous generation, and still remembered that she had once been hailed as the 'Byron of poetesses'. Before they died, she had pestered Rogers to tell her his stories about Wordsworth, and Melbourne for his memories of Lord Byron and Caroline Lamb. She had also persuaded Mary Shelley to tell how, during that magic Swiss summer in 1816, she and Shelley, her sister Claire and Lord Byron, had sailed their boat on Lac Leman, and spent the evenings discussing poetry and telling ghost stories, and how she had first thought of her story of *Frankenstein*. Now here was Monckton Milnes to tell her tales of the luminous John Keats.

Most of her political friends were out of office by the Sixties, but she proudly showed off to Motley her ageing collection of former statesmen. One evening, she presented him to a 'plain, quiet, smallish individual in a green cutaway coat, large yellow waistcoat and plaid trousers', who turned out to be the one-time Prime Minister, Lord John Russell. On another occasion she called out in front of him, 'Oh there is my lover, I must go and speak to him', and a 'plain-looking benignant little old gentleman in a white hat and [with] a kind of old-world look about him that seemed to require a pig-tail and top boots' came forward to meet him. It was Lord Lansdowne, sometime President of the Council:

> Old Lord Lansdowne sat beaming and genial in the centre of his system, and had evidently acquired a good deal of fresh warmth and radiance from Mrs Norton, who sat next to him, and had been looking handsomer than I had ever seen her before. She was dressed in white, and from where I sat it would have required a very powerful telescope to discover that she had passed thirty . . .[5]

Caroline liked to play the Châtelaine of Chesterfield Street by giving little dinner parties herself. In the early Sixties, she welcomed to her home such men as Monckton Milnes, Macaulay, and Motley. Lord Lansdowne was also a regular guest, but Delane, the editor of *The Times*, ignored her letters to his paper, and even refused her invitations to dine. Clearly, he thought her no longer influential. It was true that she was obliged to play lesser fish nowadays, but she still enjoyed conquest for its own sake. During a trip to Ireland, her sister Helen wrote home:

We had two professors from the 'Godless College' at Belfast staying with us [at Clandeboye] last night. One had a wife with him to take care of him, but the other, being defenceless, was instantly spiflicated by Caroline, whom we set at him, having no other way of amusing him, with permission to do her worst. The poor man was bowled over like a rabbit before he knew where he was, and is gone home in a frenzy of admiration 'of that remarkable woman'.[6]

Women, especially those plainer than Caroline, were less easily charmed by her. Her blatant pleasure in captivating men often aroused their animosity. As far back as 1851, Lady Eastlake had met her at a dinner and recorded in her diary:

January 28 – At the Bunsen's yesterday I saw Mrs Norton, and looked at her well. Her beauty is, perhaps, of too high an order to strike at first, especially as she is now above forty. It did not give me much artistic pleasure, but I could see that I should probably think her more and more beautiful. Also I did not see her speak or smile as she was listening to music. Lady Lyell was in great beauty; to my mind she has far more beauty of a legitimate kind than Mrs Norton, though she does not use her eyes so ably and wickedly.[7]

But Caroline in middle age was easily fatigued by social life, and found late hours exhausting. Her new friend, Motley, was concerned for her:

Mrs Norton, however, was a good deal indisposed, so much as to be obliged to leave the table. She recovered however, and remained till 12.30 in her salon, at which time Hayward and myself retired. The descriptions of Mrs Norton have not been exaggerated. In the noon of her beauty she must have been something wondrous.[8]

In the 1860s, Caroline lost the two men she cared most about. In 1861 she learned of the death of Sidney Herbert and had to bear it without showing her distress. Four years later, in April 1865, William Stirling came to her with important news. He had recently inherited a baronetcy and estates from his maternal uncle, and had become Sir William Stirling-Maxwell. Now he told her that he had decided to marry because the estate required heirs.

It was the same problem that she had encountered with Sidney Herbert.

Stirling had proposed to, and been accepted by, Anna, the daughter of Lord Leven, and they were married in Paris at the end of the month. Caroline had met this gentle young woman at Stirling, and must have acknowledged to herself that she would make William a good wife. But, though Stirling assured her that their friendship would in no way be diminished by his marriage, and that Anna had sent a message to tell her that she would still be welcome to visit Keir each autumn, Caroline must have been depressed by the news. No doubt she told herself that she must not be surprised. After all she was fifty-seven in that year, and William was noticeably younger. But she probably suspected that, had she not already been married herself, he would not have looked elsewhere.

It seemed that Caroline's beauty had lost its terrible power to hold men to her, and that her romantic life was over. So, being a born actress, she began to meditate a new role for herself. Sadly, fate was already preparing her one.

XXXII

SHAME AND GRIEF

WHILE CAROLINE WAS BUSY promoting the Divorce Bill, and charming Stirling, Motley and other admirers, her family life was going to pieces. For in the 1850s, her younger son went into voluntary exile, and the older succumbed to the family disease, so that, by the end of the decade, she was left to live alone. To explain how these disasters happened it is necessary to return to 1852, when Caroline's preoccupation with Fletcher's health began to be tempered by the realization that her younger son had hardly any prospects in life.

In that year, Brinsley was twenty, with no obvious advantages save his charm and social position. Caroline used to explain quite openly to her new friends that she had two sons, of whom Fletcher was the 'heir to a peerage', and Brinsley 'the heir to a beggary'. Brinsley had no expectations, no degree, no profession, and no obvious talents, save that of strumming on the guitar to please young women. She was partly to blame herself. She had taken him away from Eton prematurely to go with her to Lisbon, and later she had removed him from Oxford to trail round Europe with her. In neither case did she have to do so; she could have nursed Fletcher alone. But she wanted Brinsley's company, and to get it she sacrificed his interests. Brinsley did not complain. He was naturally lazy and never resentful at being compelled to do nothing for long periods. He was an excellent travelling companion, and very gentle and patient with his sick brother.

It is difficult not to have some sympathy with Brinsley. It is not surprising that he was unambitious and unenterprising, for there was little for him to do on sultry afternoons in hotel bedrooms in Lisbon, while his mother sat by Fletcher's sick-bed. Perhaps he might pick out a tune on his guitar to amuse his brother, or perhaps his mother might send him for a bottle of pills to ease the headache she had started by sitting up half the night writing her novel in the hope of making a little money for them all. That was his only work. Caroline's irritation grew with Brinsley's indolence. It was a situation which bred resentment all round.

Then came an event which shocked her profoundly. She had already noticed, while in Naples in 1852, that he had an eye for working girls. Two years later, she took him to Capri, and one day they went to see a local pageant in which a group of young peasant girls danced in their local costumes. During the performance she became aware that Brinsley was intensely excited by the dancing of one of these girls who, unusually in Capri, was fair-haired. Brinsley must have contacted the girl after the pageant for some days later he brought her home. Her name was Maria Federigo. She had no English, so it was Brinsley who explained proudly that, on the island, she was regarded as a great beauty, because of her blonde hair. He told Caroline that he was in love with the girl and was going to marry her.

There are no records of Caroline's response, but it is not difficult to imagine. She was horrified. For Brinsley was throwing away his future. Marriage to Maria would mean that he would never be acceptable in polite Society in England, and therefore he could not return and enter a profession. If he had few prospects before, he would have none now. What was more, he had no private income with which to keep a wife and family. She must have repeated these arguments to him over and over, coupled with the observation that she had very little money to give him and it was almost certain that his father would cut him off. Any mention of his father must have sent a chill through Caroline. For how would the snobbish Nortons react to the news that a possible heir to the title had married a foreigner and, what was worse, a peasant? Brinsley was entirely unmoved by her arguments. He had absolutely no sense of class, at least as far as young women were concerned, and as he had no ambitions he did not care what the Nortons thought of him. He was besotted with Maria. So, late in 1854, the third in line to Lord Grantley married an Italian peasant girl.

When the Sheridans got to know her, Maria soon dispelled any suspicions they might have had, that she was a conniving lower-class woman using an innocent English boy to promote her social ambitions. She was, in fact, a very ordinary, well-meaning, unintelligent girl. Percy Fitzgerald, a distant relation of Caroline's, described her as a 'quiet, harmless, fair-haired and very un-Italian looking young woman'. And Brinsley made it plain to his mother that he did not care that Maria was not his intellectual equal. One of the ironies of the situation was that he was sufficiently a Norton to dislike clever, argumentative women. His mother's struggles for her rights had alienated him. He wanted an uncomplicated sort of woman as his wife, and one that would do as she was told.

As for the Nortons, they behaved predictably. Brinsley's action even seemed to give his father some sort of grim satisfaction. George Norton let it be known among his friends that he had expected nothing better from Brinsley, and the boy's behaviour proved that he was not his son at all. The Norton logic was simple. No Norton had ever married a peasant, therefore Brinsley's behaviour proved that he was no Norton. Therefore his father must have been Lord Melbourne. With this dubious argument, Lord Grantley instructed his solicitors to work out whether or not he could legally prevent Brinsley from inheriting the title.

Of course Caroline knew that the tale of Brinsley's marriage would become yet another Sheridan scandal for London Society to enjoy. After the wedding, she would be obliged to go home and brave the questions and knowing looks of people whenever Brinsley's name was mentioned. So she decided not to go back to London at once, but to maunder about Italy a little, avoiding as many English ladies as she could. But one day in Venice, she discovered a middle-aged English-woman staring at her, and it was difficult to avoid her indefinitely. It was Lady Eastlake, just the kind of censorious, malicious English-woman she detested. But Lady Eastlake was very affable, probably because she was curious to know more about Caroline. They struck up an acquaintance, and Caroline started to unwind and to talk freely. Meanwhile, Lady Eastlake was writing critical comments about Caroline in her diary:

Several evenings we went to the Piazza to listen to the band and gaze at the moonlight on St Mark's, which looks as if made of silver and gold. Mrs Norton generally joined us there, and I studied her. She is a beautiful and gifted woman; her talents are of the highest order, and she has carefully cultivated them, has read deeply, has a fine memory, and wit only to be found in a Sheridan. No one can compare with her in telling a story, so pointedly, so happy, and so easy, but she is rather a professed story-teller, and brings them in, both in and out of season, and generally egotistically. She still has only talents; genius she has nothing of, or of the genius nature; nothing of the simplicity, the pathos, the rapid changes from mirth to emotion.

No, she is a perpetual actress, consummately studying and playing her part, and always the attempt to fascinate – she cares not whom . . . Occasionally, I got her to talk thinkingly, and then she said things which showed great height of thought and

observation quite oracular and not to be forgotten. I felt at first
that she could captivate me, but then the glamour wore off. If
intellect and perfect self-possession and great affected deference
for me could have subjected me, I should have been her devoted
admirer.[1]

It was the enforced company of women like Lady Eastlake that decided
Caroline to return to England, for her experiences as a tourist proved
to her that the English were even more censorious abroad than at
home. Brinsley did not follow her, because there was no place for him
and his wife in English Society. He announced that he had decided to
make his life on Capri. Caroline still tried to persuade him to apply
for a post in the Consul's office, but it seems that this only made him
angry. He intended to live cheaply and do no work. Sadly, they both
recognized the truth, that his marriage had cut him off from polite
Society for life. Who could imagine his peasant wife at diplomatic
dining tables or in the salons of Mayfair? So Caroline made him what
little allowance she could, and left him on his island, lazing and
sunning himself, playing the guitar and occasionally scribbling little
poems he called the '*Pinocchi*'. He was twenty-two years old, and she
felt that his life was squandered already. He was lost to her. Only
Fletcher was left.

In the years that followed, the news from Capri was as good as
could be expected. Maria, they said, was proving to be loyal, loving
and practical, but more of a servant than a wife. Then, in quick
succession, she bore Brinsley two children, Richard Norton, in 1855,
and Carlotta in 1856. It seemed so sudden to Caroline. Within a few
weeks she found herself the mother-in-law of an Italian peasant girl,
and now she was grandmother to two dark-eyed little children she
had never seen.

Her comfort now was entirely in Fletcher, whom everyone loved
because he was 'very handsome, clever, and one of the sweetest and
gentlest creatures'.[2] But even Fletcher made his gesture to shock the
Nortons; he became a Catholic. There was something in his solemn,
deeply artistic nature which craved symbol and ceremony. Despite his
ill-health, his sweet reasonableness and willingness to work hard had
helped him to rise in the Diplomatic Corps, and Caroline had
accompanied him successively to Lisbon, Naples and Paris, where he
was attaché to the British Embassy in the years of the Great Exhibition,
1854–5. She spent her winters with him, living quietly and as cheaply
as possible, looking after him and writing her novels. But his health

continued to be a worry to her. He coughed continuously, and never seemed any better for the various 'cures' she made him take. In September 1854 his doctors told him that he would never get rid of his cough.

But there were times when he felt better, and she could leave him to his work. In January 1859, she was easier in her mind about Fletcher than she had been for some time, and felt that she was able to go off on a literary jaunt with William Stirling. They went to Edinburgh, where the centenary of the birth of Robert Burns was about to be celebrated in an atmosphere of teetotal solemnity which would have puzzled the poet. Of course, Caroline had always admired Burns, and when asked by *The Daily Scotsman* to provide a brief tribute, she was only too willing to offer one to 'The Master of Sweet Song', as she called him, though the result reads like a collection of clichés:

> How many hearts have read with honest pride,
> That 'man's a man' with wealth & rank denied?
> How many woo'ed through him, their Bonnie Jean?
> How many mourned their 'Mary' in his strain?
> How many lingered, o'er the Arcadian light
> That made the 'Cotter's Saturday' seem bright?
> How many tears have dipped like ocean brine,
> When clasping hands have hallowed 'Auld Lang Syne'?
> We know not.[3]

One of the festival events was a vast open-air 'tea', but Caroline did not go because she had caught a chill, as she told Abraham Hayward:

> I missed the Ayr dinner, which I intended to have contemplated, by catching a cold walking in the wind and rain, in petticoats as short as Tam o' Shanter's Witch's sark . . .
> . . . Edinburgh was very quiet on the 'Centenary' day. Even the enthusiasm of the Scotch is frappé à la glace. It is a new acquaintance, and they don't feel familiar enough with it to be jolly – and think of three thousand sitting down to Temperance tea-trays! I'd as lief be a duck and sit in a pond with my chin upon duckweed. As it is, my chin is obliged to rest on the edge of a warm gruel-bowl, where with disconsolate snufflings I consider whether a hundred years hence (when it can do me no

good) people will be reading 'Hayward's biography of that remarkable woman', and going to look at the turnpike gate on the road from Guildford to Shalford on the scene of inspiration for the story of Rosalie . . .[4]

The Festival organizers had offered a 'Crystal Prize' for a poem on Burns but, after reflection, Caroline did not go in for it. She probably thought that it would be too risky to compete against amateurs. The prize was won by a Miss Isobel Craig, a woman of Scottish birth and impeccably humble origins. Caroline told everybody how glad she was that a woman had triumphed.

She spent the summer holidays of 1859 at home in Chesterfield Street with Fletcher. He seemed better. In the autumn he was to take up his new post as Secretary to the Legation at Athens. When the time came, they arranged that they would not say 'Goodbye' in London, but would rendezvous in Paris. Then he would take the train for Athens, and she would take another to Capri, where she was to visit Brinsley and his family. But when she got to the Paris hotel in early September, she was greeted with the news that M. Norton, who had recently arrived, was very ill. She found him in bed, coughing blood, and looking for all the world like the portraits of those frail Linley children who had ravished Bath with their singing in her grandfather's day. She could see that her arrival had cheered him up, and for a time she thought that her usual care would soon see him out of bed. But as the September weeks wore on, he seemed more and more feeble, and she became alarmed. At last, she decided to send for Brinsley, and then, reluctantly, for George Norton. While she waited, she spent her days in the darkened bedroom holding his hand and talking gently, while he attempted to disguise his coughing and spitting as best he could. He loved music, and one day she hired a Tyrolese band to play to him in an outer room; but when he heard their plaintive melody, which reproduced the sound of bells dying away, he burst into tears and she had to dismiss them. When Brinsley arrived, he too sat in the outer room, singing and playing his guitar, but soon Fletcher found even this experience too exhausting.

To the last, Caroline was not sure just how ill Fletcher was. She had nursed him through many such crises before:

The morning of the day he died he said, 'I feel very strange.' I said, 'Worse dear?'

He said, 'No dear. Don't look at me with such kingdom-come eyes. I only feel strange. There is no other way of expressing it.'

I said to Dr Chepmell (who stayed with him most anxiously and kindly), 'If he does not rally today, he will never rally at all.'

Dr Chepmell said, 'It is a critical day.'

I afterwards learned that he had said that Fletcher would not live forty-eight hours.[5]

Then George Norton arrived. Caroline had not seen him for six years, since that day in the County Court when he was dragged away from her shouting abuse and waving his fists. Now he was pathetic and frightened. On the last day of Fletcher's life, 13 October 1859, she sat on one side of the bed with his head on her shoulder, while George sat on the other, leaning low to catch his son's words. Fletcher addressed him in a whisper as 'Dear Father'.

Towards evening he said, 'Quelle étrange nuit!'

Then after a silence, 'I do not see you – any of you – dear ones. But I see, oh! what is it I see? So many – so many – so beautiful. Beautiful.' It is impossible for words to describe, or for those who saw it ever to forget, the wonderful radiance of his face while he said this, or the expression of earnest ecstasy in the beautiful eyes that no longer saw the things of earth. No picture of saints or martyrs that I ever beheld equalled the intense beauty or rapt look of his countenance. He said in a soft, sad tone, 'Mother'. That was the last word he ever spoke.

We could scarcely tell when he died, but the restlessness, the sadness, and the ecstasy all passed out of his face, and there was nothing but peace; and we had only to close his beautiful, soft eyes, that from the hour they opened on the world had never looked hardly, or scornfully, or unkindly on any human being. I am thankful, when so many women have soldier sons dying away from them, that I was permitted to witness this blessed gentle creature go from us in such peace.[6]

Fletcher had asked that he should be buried next to William at Kettlethorpe, so Caroline was once again required to take the dreary railway ride to Yorkshire. But this time she had to take the body with her, and all the way from Paris. First the coffin rested overnight in the Madeleine, and then the following day she saw it on to the train for the long journey north. Meanwhile, Norton had gone ahead to make preparations for the funeral, and the result was a masterpiece of Victorian obsequies. At Kettlethorpe station, Caroline was greeted coldly and formally by the Grantleys and Nortons, each one in strict mourning. Fletcher's body did not lie in state in the parish church, presumably because he was a Catholic. Instead, Norton had had the boathouse decked out like a chapel. Its walls were hung with black and the coffin was set on high in the middle, surrounded by great bunches of everlasting flowers. Candles were set burning along either side and three mutes stood with candles at the head of the coffin.

On the morning of the funeral, a priest from Wakefield conducted the service in a small chapel, originally erected at Wakefield Bridge to commemorate the death of the Duke of York in 1460, but which Norton had had removed to Kettlethorpe. Then, Caroline and George Norton followed their son's coffin round 'the little lake over the green sward without the sound of a footfall, or any sound but the singing of the birds on the tiny island in the lake, opposite the door to the chapel'. Here Fletcher was buried next to William, who had died seventeen years before. The grave was covered with a stone inscribed 'Parva Domus, Magna Quies'.

Throughout the time at Kettlethorpe Caroline was too drained of emotion to care about the hostility of the Nortons. Her husband, though, had seemed to her a bewildered creature, overawed by the solemnity of an occasion which was too great for his small soul to comprehend. He even tried to be kind. Each day he took her to dine, away from the Nortons, at the Pledwick Well Inn. The local newspaper remarked wonderingly that he had paid her every attention. After the ceremony, she took an awkward, emotional leave of him.

But Caroline could not bear the thought of Fletcher left alone among the Nortons, and wanted some other memorial to him. Her chance came when her brother, Richard Brinsley, began the restoration of Frampton Church. It was here that he placed a memorial to their father, Tom Sheridan, whose body had been brought home from the Cape by their mother over forty years previously. Richard Brinsley now agreed that Caroline might place a memorial to Fletcher in the same church. It was a stained glass window with two panes. One commemorates Fletcher's love of music, and shows the young David playing the lyre to King Saul, to rid him of evil spirits; the other symbolizes Caroline's feelings for her son, by depicting King David grieving for Absalom. Beneath the window she placed a tablet which read:

This window was offered towards the restoration of
Frampton Church by,
CAROLINE NORTON
The distinguished Authoress;
In sacred remembrance of her eldest son,
FLETCHER CAVENDISH CHARLES NORTON;
who died at Paris, AD 1859, aged 30

Lent – only lent! From his first hour of birth,
A ray of sunshine on my life on earth:
Death came and all my path grew dark as night;
But he passed on – into a better light:
HIS gentle spirit there found full release,
Eternal brightness and Eternal peace.

XXXIII

LOST AND SAVED

AFTER FLETCHER'S FUNERAL, Caroline's only thought was to get away from
England, so she arranged to join Brinsley, Maria and their children at
Dinan, in Brittany, where she spent the winter of 1859–60 with them.
Brinsley was depressed and coughing a good deal, and 'Mariuccia'
was alarmed by his bouts of weakness and short temper. They had
intense conversations in their mixture of Italian and English which
made Caroline feel like an intruder in their company.

It was then that the children discovered her. In her grief about
Fletcher, Caroline had hardly noticed them, but they insisted on her
attention. Richard was now almost five, and Carlotta, nearly three,
and the two grave, dark-eyed children turned to her instinctively. She
felt awkward, at first, with these small strangers. Time and distance
had little prepared her for the role of grandmother. But each morning,
when she had resigned herself to being 'more dead than alive', they
came romping to her pension just outside the town, to remind her that
she was still more alive than dead, and that though she had cause for
grief, she still had reason for joy. In her misery, Caroline had written
to Georgiana to say that, now Fletcher was dead, she had no comfort
and that the world had ended for her. But even while she was writing,
the children were insinuating themselves into her affections, and
providing her with new objects of love and more useful work to do.

Eventually she seems to have taken sole charge of them while Maria
nursed Brinsley. They went to stay with her in her own pension and
in the early mornings they would come creeping into her bed, and she
would have to get up, get their breakfast, and take them for walks
round the town. Together they would gaze down from the old ram-
parts of the Promenade Duchesse Anne, while she would point out to
Richard how, far below, the road from the Mont St Michel to St
Brieuc, crossed the River Rance and the valley to the coast. Then she
might take them past the mediaeval gables of the Place des Merciers,
to hobble hand in hand down the cobblestones of the rue de Jerzual,
with its weaving and glass-blowing shops. In their company, she began
again to notice the beauty of the world, and the charm of the little

town: 'built on a height with a bastion all round, and immense towers and gateways, the most lovely valley, "la vallée des Noyers" ... outside'.[1] She took the children everywhere with her on sketching expeditions. One day she came across an ivy-covered gateway which she was told had once been the entrance of an old Hospital for Incurables founded by the late Comte de La Garaye and his wife. They had been local benefactors who had shared a great sorrow, and had died within two years of each other. Later Caroline sketched a portrait of the Comtesse from a likeness she was shown in a local convent.

She dreaded the coming of the New Year when they were to part and go home. It seemed to Caroline that, having lost her own children, these newly discovered grandchildren had been sent to console her. They had saved her from giving way to grief. But when January came, the children took the train south to Capri and the sunshine; while she boarded the steam packet for England and grimy London.

In February, she was back in Chesterfield Street, lonely and sad. She missed the children terribly, and every piece of news seemed to be of old friends ill or dying. The loss of Fletcher was still a great ache she carried about with her; Sidney Herbert died in August; and her sister Helen was seriously ill. And if she had not griefs enough, there came within the next two years a piece of news that set the whole country mourning. On 14 December 1861, without warning, Prince Albert died of typhoid fever. Somehow Caroline felt that her own recent bereavements especially qualified her to speak for the nation about this event. Though Lord Tennyson was the official Poet Laureate, and had set the elegiac fashion with his *Ode on the Death of Wellington* she believed that it was she, who recently suffered the loss of a son and a lover, who was the true laureate of grief. In February 1862, readers of *Macmillan's Magazine* opened its pages to find:

GONE!

By the Hon. Mrs Norton

Gone! gone! the bells toll on,
But still the death news seems to stun:
The sudden loss, the warning brief,
Bids wonder mingle with our grief!
Like fearful heralds sent to know
If life's defeat were true or no,
Our startled thoughts went forth to meet
Dark rumour in the busy street,
And less lamenting, than dismayed,

Our frozen tears were strangely stayed.
What – he whose busy brain had planned
So much for his adopted land –
He, who had scarce yet turned the page
Dating past youth to middle age,
The counsellor of wisdom proved,
The chosen of a Queen beloved,
In prime of life & princely rank –
Gone? – gone! fill up the blank . . .[2]

In the early 1860s Caroline was in an autumnal mood. It was time to assess her life and write her account. She had found a new role for herself, that of a woman with a tragic past, dignified and serene, like the Comtesse de La Garaye. Her poem *The Lady of La Garaye* came out in 1862. It told of the young Count and Countess, lately married, who enjoy all the advantages of birth, rank, beauty and happiness, but whose lives are brought to disaster by a riding accident to the Countess, which crippled her for life. After a period of despair, however, the Countess is shamed by a holy man, who reminds her of the sufferings of others. She and her husband resolve to live to help the poor and sick, and, after their deaths, are remembered as benefactors. Caroline found many parallels between this story and her own. And like the Countess, she wished to be remembered as a woman whose early married life had been ruined by misfortune, but who lived to be wise and beloved.

She dedicated *The Lady of La Garaye* to her old friend, Lord Lansdowne, and in her dedication, reminded him of the transience of human achievement:

Yet, friend, I feel not that all power is fled,
    While offering to thee, for the kindly years,
The intangible gift of thought, whose silver thread
    Heaven keeps untarnished by our bitterest tears.

So, in the brooding calm that follows woe,
    This Tale of LA GARAYE I fain would tell, –
As, when some earthly storm hath ceased to blow,
    And the huge mounting sea hath ceased to swell;

After the maddening wrecking and the roar,
    The wild high dash, the moaning sad retreat,
Some cold slow wave creeps faintly to the shore,
    And leaves a white shell at the gazer's feet.[3]

She probably had less faith now in the permanent value of her writing, but she could not afford to give it up, and besides, work was her salvation. Her life in the mid-Sixties was taken up with her family and friends, visits by or to her grandchildren, and continuous writing, especially in the late hours, of literary works which still provided her main income. She composed poetry, articles and reviews, many of them anonymous. But her main hope was now pinned on the novel she had been writing for nearly ten years, *Lost and Saved*, which was eventually published in 1863.

Her story was based on the old Sheridan theme of elopement. Seventeen-year-old Beatrice Brooke is tricked by Montague Treherne into accompanying him on a day's trip from Venice to Trieste, but after they have set sail he reveals that the boat is actually bound for Alexandria. She understands at once that she is irredeemably compromised. In Egypt she develops a fever and on her 'deathbed' she is married to Treherne by an English clergyman. When she recovers, Treherne tells her that it had all been a pretence to comfort her during her last moments, and that they are not really married at all. He promises to marry her in two years' time, when he is free to inherit the family property. Beatrice then lives with him for a while in London, but he deserts her and her child, and she learns to scrimp a living by lace-repairing. In the end, her family find her and take her back, while Montague, who likes to sail the seas in his yacht, dies of poison in the Bay of Biscay.

The story is in essence Caroline's own. Like the young Caroline, Beatrice is a girl both married and not married, living alone in London, obliged to provide for herself, yet disqualified by her class and sex from any trade or profession. She is passionate by nature, and feels 'more than a great proportion of her fellow-creatures'; her heart aches and her eyes water at a touching sight or song. Beatrice's epileptic son, Frank, dies young like Lord Melbourne's Augustus in 1836, and in describing Beatrice's grief at that moment, Caroline was remembering the death of William. Throughout the story, Beatrice walks the London Caroline knew, Spring Gardens to Grosvenor Square, and across St James's Park. Beatrice's snobbish treatment at the hands of the English in Italy was taken from her own painful memories. Treherne is her Norton figure, a selfish sensualist, all lust and no affection, who has scant respect for the truth, and never keeps his promises. Beatrice's faithful young brother, Owen, is as loyal as Richard Brinsley had been to Caroline, and like her he writes a letter to the Queen. Caroline also put in other signs to be read by those who could. The discreet affair between Treherne and Milly Nesdale is carried out among the fashionable salons, shops, parks and hotels of London, just as hers had been with Sidney Herbert.

Lost and Saved is a fine achievement, and Caroline's best novel. It contains many good things but the most memorable of all is the monstrous character of the Marchioness of Updown, an amalgam of all those cold Society women who had sneered at and libelled Caroline over the years. Here were the embittered spinsters and awful old dowagers who had tried to destroy her reputation, such as Augusta Norton, Margaret Vaughan, Lady Menzies and Lady Jersey; and here were Mrs Brookfield and Lady Eastlake, who had snubbed and patronized her as a scandalous woman:

Her sisters called her The Marchioness, as the servants did. Her husband called her The Marchioness. It seemed as if there was no other Marchioness in the world. As there is a Whale among fishes, so was this Marchioness among her peers, and among the minnows of less aristocratic society. That great Leviathan of the deep was not a whit more remarkable or superior in the water than our Marchioness on dry land. If there was a ball, party, or soirée to be given, her absence was as bitter as that of the hero of the old-fashioned song 'Robin Adair'. If there was a procession, coronation, or festive ceremony of any kind, the world stood still on its axis till the Marchioness had a place assigned to her. She went to Court not spangled with scattered diamonds, like the sky on a fine night, but crusted over with them, like barnacles on a ship's hull. Diamonds, rubies, emeralds, turquoises, and pearls were spread over her as the farmer spreads lumps of fertilizing lime over his land. And like the land she appeared to thrive under them. Every year, her arms were rounder, her bracelets larger, her figure more corpulent. Every year the sweep of her full drapery encroached more and more on the ground occupied by her scantier-skirted neighbours. Every year her step became more flat-footed and imperious.[4]

This character is Caroline's revenge upon Society which had rejected her for so many years. For the Marchioness is social snobbery made flesh; she is absurd and disgusting.

To Caroline's delight, the novel was an initial success. In its first year, it went into four editions. But the reviews came only slowly, and when they did, they were not complimentary. The book was pronounced to be immoral. Especially hostile was the influential *Illustrated London News* which remarked upon the 'painful and repulsive picture' it presented of a heartless fashionable society, and added that it was a good thing that 'she who has had the boldness to describe them in all their naked deformity is one so elevated both by social position and literary reputation as the Hon. Mrs Norton'. But more serious for sales was the frequently repeated assertion that Caroline had dared to publish a novel in which the heroine 'lived by consent with her lover after she became aware that she was not married to him'. From the moment of the publication of this review, sales began to drop off. Caroline's publishers probably explained to her that the greater part of the novel-reading public tended to be young girls, and that any adverse publicity would persuade their parents to ban the book from the home.

The damage done to the book's sales was serious but not yet fatal, until Caroline, despite the pleadings of her publishers to keep quiet for a bit, decided to write to the press to defend her book. It seemed obvious to her that the reviewer of *The Illustrated London News* had not understood that the novel was written for adults rather than young girls, and this needed to be explained. In her rambling letter she hit out at a number of targets. She argued that her book may not have been suitable for the young but that was because she was not writing for them. And she loftily dismissed the complaint that her story dealt with a young woman who was living with a man not her husband. Such themes, she announced, were common in the librettos of Grand Opera 'unquestionably the favourite amusement of the English aristocracy'. Then she traced the 'immoral' themes of half a dozen operas, involving seduction, the corruption of nuns, love affairs in monasteries, elopement, and incest. These topics, she informed the no doubt aghast *Times* readers, were 'the subjects which twice or three times a week recreate the understandings of the higher classes of Great Britain'.[5] Unfortunately, many parents understood her better than she intended. They forbade their daughters to read the book. Sales dropped. *Lost and Saved* was lost.

Luckily, she still had her grandchildren to comfort her, and she visited them in Capri as often as she could afford. Brinsley may have given up all ambition for himself, as he declined into bad health and Italian ways, but she was anxious that his children might still enjoy the advantages of their English connections, and be brought up as gentle people. So, throughout the Sixties, they returned with her to spend their summers in Chesterfield Street, where they would stand with their black eyes wide with wonder, while she gently stroked the plumage of her parakeets, who seemed to know more English than they did. Afterwards, the children were allowed to romp and shriek, until she pretended to be cross with them and sent them out of the room. At night they slept in her bedroom, and while they were falling asleep she told them stories of elves and sprites, and a mermaid from Capri washed up on English shores. Then she would tip-toe to her dressing room, where in the custom of many years, she would sit up late writing.

There is no record that George Norton ever agreed to see Brinsley's children when they were in London, though Caroline certainly would have wished to establish their link with the Nortons. Lord Grantley had not succeeded in barring Brinsley from the inheritance and, therefore, after the death of his Uncle Fletcher, Richard was third in line to Grantley himself. The awareness of this seems to have made Caroline even more determined that Richard and Carlotta should not be allowed to grow up like Italian peasants.

As the children grew older, it seemed that they would never be especially gifted people, and it might be supposed that this would have lessened Caroline's interest in them. All her life she had striven to be remarkable herself, and was committed to the idea of an inherited Sheridan genius. But it was the very limitations of these grandchildren which increased her affection for them. She wrote to a friend: 'The girl is short in stature, rather clumsy in figure, – and with those peculiar black Italian eyes which seem rather to look at you than allow you to look at them . . . the boy . . . is very intelligent, but not industrious, rather grave, reticent, and fonder of a sort of shallow cursory studiousness, than of real hard work . . .'[6]

She liked to encourage in her grandchildren the idea that, though they were Nortons, they were also part of the Sheridan family. In doing so, she introduced them to their Sheridan cousins at Frampton Court, and tried to keep the two sets of children in touch by giving them news of each other in the letters she wrote to Dorset and Capri. A typical letter is one written to Richard and Carlotta who were staying in London, while she was unwell at Frampton. She covered her letter with little drawings, to please them:

This picture is cousin Nelly, that is Frampton Church in the distance. She has a little bird on her finger. Very small – but you can see it, if you look close. Mamma was much pleased at getting to the warm sunny country. She ended in a letter – 'it is like

summer dearest madre! Viva l'Italia!' – not meaning that Gibral-
ter [*sic*] is in Spain; but that she was glad to be in sunshine like
her own country's sunshine – poor little brown Jenny Wren!

I have made a song about the snow – which I wrote in my bed
when I saw the snow. That is me reading what I have written.

God Bless my Darlings
Now as always amen

I'm very sick still

THE SONG

Sing hi-ho! The feathery snow!!
It covers the road, & the fields below.
We saw it lie thick in the morning light
As though, while we slept thro' the cozy night
Those fleecy clouds that in Heaven have birth
Sank softly down to rest on the Earth.
The little red robin, – in search of crumbs, –
Slants his brown eye as he fluttering comes;
From the nursery window he gets his store
So he hops about and he looks for more!
He cannot beg – for he cannot speak –
But he twitters and pecks with his smooth small beak
And he says, – as plain as it can be said, –
Twit-too-wee! Richard fling me some bread!
Sing hi-ho – the feathery snow!
Sweep it out of the path where we want to go.[7]

She had always insisted that Richard should go to school in England,
to be brought up as an English gentleman, and Brinsley agreed.
Naturally she chose Harrow, the school which Richard Brinsley
Sheridan had attended. In November 1866, she accompanied the
eleven year-old boy to the school where he took the entrance examination, which was chiefly a paper in Latin. She was so nervous for him
that, for the whole time, she 'forgot there was anything in the world
that signified except the slight difference between "ob" and "nam" in
addressing the Gods'.[8] Richard was much less anxious for himself than
she was, and to her delight, he gained an entrance to his great-great-
grandfather's old school. His surname might have been 'Norton', but it
seemed to her that Sheridan intelligence would shine out. He was
saved.

A VISITOR TO CHESTERFIELD STREET

THE ELDERLY WOMAN STILL SAT DOZING in her wheelchair on a dark February day in 1877. Occasionally, the peace of Chesterfield Street was broken by the sound of a hansom, and Caroline Norton would lift her head anxiously to hear the scrape of its wheels as they approached her door. But time after time, the horse went on and out of earshot. It was the late lunch hour. She had been sitting there daydreaming of the times when the children used to arrive from Italy for the summer holidays, and would stand on tip-toe in that very room, while she, with a canary on her finger, would coax the bird to sing for them. But that was years before. She was sixty-nine years old now, stiff with rheumatism and subject to giddy fits. Richard and Carlotta were grown-up young people living far away with their parents in Capri. With a sigh she realized that she had been sitting for hours in that room, throughout most of the short day, lost in a reverie of children, campaigns, literary life and lost lovers.

But something had happened to destroy her tranquillity. William Stirling had written to say that he was coming down from Scotland that day and he wanted to see her at once. Such a very unexpected message from her friend agitated her, and it may be that, for a moment, she guessed his errand. If so, she would have dismissed the thought quickly, perceiving that she was too old for that sort of thing, and that there was no reason why any man, even William, should wish to visit a sick woman like herself. She had been ill on and off for years; if it was not a cold, it was influenza, and if it was not influenza, it was her faintings and the rheumatism which the doctor said he could do nothing about. She strained in her chair to look in the mirror above the mantelshelf. She could see only her neck and face. She could still be proud of them. She was right when she had said that she would be handsome in her coffin. But her body was old and heavy, and it seemed a good thing that she could not see it.

Caroline's temper had suffered even more than her figure in the fifteen or so years since Fletcher had died. Now she always seemed to be quarrelling with somebody or other, like Delane, the editor of *The*

Times, who refused to publish her letters, and advised her to be silent 'for good and all'.[1] Then there was Mrs Henry Wood whom she had accused of stealing one of her own stories, which appeared years before in *The English Annual*. According to Caroline, this woman had republished the story under the title of *East Lynne*, and, when she was con- fronted with it, had denied it was the same story at all.[2] George Meredith annoyed her just as much. Lucy Duff Gordon had introduced them, in the naïve belief that writers would naturally like each other. Caroline had not liked him. He had refused to be charmed by her, and showed no respect for her literary achievements. All he wanted to do was to ask her questions about her past, about Lord Melbourne, Sir Robert Peel and Sidney Herbert. Their conversation had become a 'sparring bout'.[3] Caroline later felt that she had been tricked into saying too much about her past. She acknowledged that Meredith was an interesting man, but suspected that he had not sufficient breeding to be trusted.

She quarrelled with her servants too, and complained about their tantrums and 'notices to go'. She was less trusting with servants after the Melbourne trial, when so many had given evidence against her. But some of her domestic disputes had their funny side. On one occasion, when Richard was an adolescent, Caroline challenged her housemaid to explain why 'every chemise and handkerchief of linen or cambric' in the house had disappeared, and she also wanted to know the whereabouts of 'Master Richard's warm winter cricket shirts'. The girl was saucy, and said that the clothes were 'lost in the wash'. Unfortunately for her, Caroline had caught a glimpse of colour beneath her cuffs, and discovered that 'she was wearing Richard's winter comforts'. At that, the girl burst out laughing and shouted: 'Taking is not stealing you know'. She had to go.[4] Careless servants annoyed Caroline even more than dishonest ones. When she was becoming frail, a nursemaid ran a perambulator over her foot, and she had had to threaten to sue the girl's employers to get them to take the matter seriously. Worst of all were disloyal servants, like the Italian maid Lina, who accompanied Caroline and Carlotta to Italy in 1876. Lina had had no references, but claimed that she had been employed by a Mr and Mrs Robert Browning. Caroline had met the Brownings briefly, and now wrote to enquire about Lina.[5] Browning vouched for her, but when they had gone to Italy she became fierce and impertinent. It was not just that she showed no kindness when both Caroline and Carlotta were prostrate with fever, she simply deserted them. Afterwards, Caroline came to the conclusion that the girl had simply used her to get a free ticket home. Her visits to Keir were a great comfort to Caroline in her later years. At Keir she could get away from sulky servants and the struggle to balance her household accounts. Anna Stirling-Maxwell was always kind and, when Richard and Carlotta were young, Sir William would take them all round the farm to admire the animals. In return, Caroline taught the two little Stirling-Maxwell boys to draw and paint, and built them models of houses and castles which were lit up from within by candles. Most spectacular of all was a castle with a moat and four fountains which played real water. The children loved it.[6]

But even Keir was not proof against suffering and tragedy, and Sir William's marriage lasted only nine years. In November 1874, just after Caroline had arrived for her annual holiday, Anna Stirling-Maxwell suffered a dreadful accident. One night, when she got up from her bed to make her husband a hot drink, she suffered a fit of giddiness while near the fire, and fell and seized the hot bars. She burned herself terribly, and also scalded herself with water from the kettle. The injury to one arm was so bad that it had to be amputated. Caroline wrote to Lily Motley on 27 November to report on Anna:

> Matters here are progressing favourably – and every day is a day gained: but it is sad to see Sir Wm. so broken! He cannot lift from the depression: & evidently doubts all he longs to believe of the Doctor's reassurances. The amputation does so fearfully complicate matters! . . . The dressing on the back slipped last night, and she suffered much & the nurse not being enough to lift her, they sent for Sir Wm. . . . Oh poor soul, I thought I could scarcely feel more affection for him than I felt already, after twenty-five years close friendship – but I assure you my heart seems to go out of me with a strange and pitiful yearning, as I see him coming down the road to this door – and as to the boys – when she sends to me with little merry messages of her being 'in a cozy nest' etc. – it is all I can do not to frighten them by bursting out crying . . .[7]

A few days later, Anna Stirling-Maxwell died, and Sir William was left heartbroken.

By the 1870s, many of Caroline's friends were long dead or close to dying. Lord Melbourne and Caroline Lamb now lay together beneath the aisle of St Etheldreda's at Bishop's Hatfield, while the statue of Sidney Herbert stood looking down at her in Pall Mall. Her old friends of the dinner-table, Samuel Rogers, Sydney Smith and Lord Lansdowne, and her faithful confidante, the Duchess of Sutherland, were all dead. Her sister, Helen Dufferin, had died in 1867, and Lady Palmerston, sister of Lord Melbourne, in 1869. In that year she also learned of the death of Lady Duff Gordon from consumption, at Geneva. Lucy Duff Gordon had been her closest friend for many years, had shared her enthusiasms and experiences as no one else had done, and always accorded her unstinting admiration.

Caroline continued to write until the early 1870s. Her last success was a serial story, *Old Sir Douglas*, which contained an acidic sketch of Margaret Vaughan, who had made so much trouble between Norton and herself. The book came out in 1867, and paid well, because it was serialized both in *Macmillan's Magazine*, and in the American journal, *Littell's Living Age*. After that, what with her giddi- ness and rheumatism, and the effects of a recent fall, she just could not go on writing. Even if she had been able to hold the pen, the work was too exhausting for her. Besides she had no more stories left in her.

Curiously, no loss affected her more than the one she suffered in the spring of 1875. She was on holiday in Capri when she received a letter to say that George Norton had died at Wonersh Park on 20 March. Brinsley and Maria were amazed at how hard-hit she was by the news. So was she. She had spent most of her life fighting this man through the courts and newspapers, but his death undermined her as no other had done. When she came home to Chesterfield Street, she was ill and depressed, and spent some weeks in bed. Then she heard that Lord Grantley had died, which news must have seemed ironic to her. For if George had made the effort to live a little longer, or Grantley to have died a little sooner, she would then have been Lady Grantley. The Nortons cheated her to the end. Perhaps the only amusement she got out of all this news was to hear that Lady Grantley had declared that, contrary to her husband's last wish, she was not prepared to be buried with him when her time came. She said that she had had to live with the Nortons all her life, and would not be buried with them.[8]

With such memories, Caroline had passed the hours in Chesterfield Street. Now there was a sharp rap at the door, and she heard at last the familiar Scots tones of Sir William in the hall. She felt her heart race as it had done when, as a young woman, she first heard Lord Melbourne coming up the stairs. She recollected herself. She was determined not to appear agitated. There was barely time to pat her hair and smooth her shawl before Sir William was in the room, but it was done. She had composed herself.

There was no witness to their conversation, but what William Stirling-Maxwell said may be deduced from subsequent events. At first she could hardly take it in. She replied to his kind enquiries but it was the tone of his voice that held her attention. Yes, she was still expecting him; yes, she was pleased to see him; no, he had not disturbed her rest; yes, her health was improving. He stood looking at her intently as her sentences tailed off. There was a pause. Then, in his slow Scots way, he came forward and took both her hands. He said he had something to say to her. He had come down from Scotland that day, to ask her to be his wife. They had been friends, he said, for so long, so very long, that they ought to spend the rest of their lives together. He hoped she could not doubt his affection. Would she accept?

Of course, she refused, though all along her senses were singing. There were so many reasons against such a marriage. She was so much older than he, ten years. People would remark on that. Then again, she was a sick woman, a cripple, with little life left in her, and people would pity him. What was more, she had battled against her first husband, and marriage itself, for over thirty years, and the public would find it ridiculous for her to marry again. Had she not dedicated her life to showing that a woman could live alone, free and independent? Above all, she was still a scandalous woman, unacceptable even now to so many people. Was she the sort of creature for the Rector of Edinburgh University, and the Chancellor of Glasgow University, to get mixed up with? They would say she would corrupt their students.

He smiled. As for their relative ages, he said, these were advantages. There would be no dispute or opposition from their families caused by the complexities of inheritance. As for her health, she had just told him it was improving. And who could tell? She might even enjoy being married a second time round. As for the public's opinion of her campaign on marriage rights, well she had proved her point, and had her victories. Was it not time now for some comfort? He could put up with a little gossip if she could. Then he produced his most telling point. Caroline had always said that it would take a new name to stop the last malicious comments about her. Well, she could have a title. He had heard that he was soon to be offered a peerage, and would become the Earl of Keir. If she wanted to, she might put away her old reputation as a scandalous woman for ever, and become the Countess of Keir. He very much wanted her with him in Scotland. Would she come?

With some such persuasive arguments, Sir William Stirling-Maxwell proposed to Caroline Norton on a February day in 1877. Then he stood waiting for her reply.

XXXV

LADY STIRLING-MAXWELL

CAROLINE NORTON COULD NOT BE MARRIED IN CHURCH, because she was unable to get out of her chair, so the ceremony was performed in the little sitting room at Chesterfield Street on 1 March 1877. *The Pictorial World* reported on 10 March:

NOTES FROM THE NORTH

And so Sir William Stirling Maxwell, Bart, MP and KT, is married. This interesting event came off in London on Thursday last; the distinguished and hon. bridegroom being 59 and the bride 69. *sic*. And thus a long-standing attachment has been celebrated and confirmed in matrimony . . .

Wiseacres in Perthshire (the county which Sir William represents in Parliament) profess to see in this alliance the first step towards the baronet's elevation to the peerage, the marriage having taken place in order that the honour to be conferred upon the one may be shared by both. So, if my friends in Perthshire should hear that Sir William has gone to the Upper House as The Earl of Keir, let them not wonder thereat . . . By the way, your veracious contemporary, 'The World', announced the marriage as having come off on Tuesday. This was premature; but I understand that the Atlas mistook the granting of a special licence for the solemnization of the nuptials.[1]

Then began for Caroline a blissful married life such as she had never known before. She longed to go at once with William to Keir, but she was not well enough and, anyway, he had his parliamentary duties to perform. They promised each other that they would go in the early summertime. She and William had so much in common. He came home in the evenings to tell her all that had taken place in the House, and she corresponded with both her family and his. Her health improved a little, so that she was able to move between Sir William's house at 10 Upper Grosvenor Street, and her own home in Chesterfield Street. She wrote to an old friend, Colonel Johnstone, to thank him

for his best wishes: 'You must come to my new address to be thanked.
I am not able for the journey to our home in Yorkshire, so I only flit
from one town house to another. My little stepsons are to arrive on
Wednesday from Scotland – but by the end of the week I hope to be
settled enough to have comfortable and leisurely chats with friends
who call to see me . . . next to a good man's faithful regard, – nothing
can brighten "The evening of a clouded day" more than kind words
from friends . . .'[2]
She even discovered a new zest for domestic detail and the energy
to supervise tradesmen; a note to one of them reads:

> Lady Stirling Maxwell (Honble Mrs Norton) begs Mr Smethurst
> to warn his lampist to be careful in her house 3 Chesterfield
> Street. Mrs Norton found some oil had dropped as he was
> attending to the lamps in the Drawing room this morg. The carpet
> is quite new & cost 45 Guineas. Some bath waterproof must be
> laid down carefully before working there. Lady SM is not well
> enough to superintend herself.[3]

Caroline and William agreed that, before Scotland, she needed the sun
again, to make her better. So a holiday was planned. In July they
would take ship for the south, and visit Brinsley, now the fourth Baron
Grantley, in Capri. She was worried by reports of his health. As soon
as they returned, they would go up to Stirling, to see Dunblane and
the Bridge of Allan, and finally to come home to Keir. She could think
of nothing else. But in early summer, she was suddenly taken ill. For
a few days she declined and then, on 15 June 1877, she died.
The Pictorial World informed its readers:

> The death of the lady known for many years as the Hon.
> Mrs Norton, is an event of some Scottish interest, since the
> deceased was married to a distinguished representative of a
> leading Scottish county. Mrs Norton was married to Sir William
> Stirling Maxwell on 2nd March last. There had long been a tender
> attachment between the erudite baronet of Keir and the once-
> beautiful grand-daughter of Richard Brinsley Sheridan. The
> marriage when it did take place, evoked many comments, but it
> was generally looked upon as a romantic supplement to the 40
> years of friendship according to Plato. The bridegroom was 64
> [sic] and the bride 69. People wondered why the marriage ever
> took place. If Sir William had a vision of a coronet, which he

desired his old friend to share with him, the vision has been disrupted by death.[4]

Caroline was married to George Norton for forty-five years. Her second marriage lasted three months.

PART THREE

AFTERWORDS

XXXVI

RETURN TO SCOTLAND

BRINSLEY NORTON WAS TOO UNWELL to leave Italy and attend his mother's funeral. He was obliged to remain with his wife Maria in Capri, while their children, Richard and Carlotta, both in their early twenties, followed Caroline to her grave. Then, while they were away from home, news reached them that their father had died of tuberculosis, on 24 July 1877, just five weeks after his own mother's death.

The third Lord Grantley had not succeeded in having Brinsley's name removed as heir to the Grantley lands and title, despite the fact that Norton himself had always made plain his suspicions that Brinsley was, in reality, the son of Lord Melbourne. Brinsley had succeeded to the title in 1875, when Grantley died, and Maria became the most improbable of Lady Grantleys. And so, John Richard Norton, son of Brinsley and Maria, became the fifth Baron Grantley.

These deaths, hard upon each other's heels, naturally distressed the young people, who had come to grieve in a strange land, only to face a deeper grief at home. So, when it was decided that Richard must remain in England in order to settle inheritance problems, Sir William, in his kindly way, insisted on accompanying Carlotta home to Capri, where he intended to offer any help he could to Maria.

On his journey back to Scotland, he put up for the night at the Lana Hotel, in Venice. The following morning, an English lady, a Mrs Wingfield, heard that a fellow-countryman of hers was lying alone and ill in an adjoining bedroom. He had contracted fever. She did what she could to help him, but it was no use. Sir William Stirling-Maxwell died of typhoid, in Venice, on 15 January 1878, exactly seven months after the death of his wife.

Over the next 112 years, the whereabouts of the bodies of Caroline and her husband were forgotten, though the Stirling-Maxwell family always understood that Sir William had been buried in Venice. During that time, the story of Caroline Norton was retold a number of times and the widest audience it achieved was probably in the broadcasting of *A Scandalous Woman*, by the present author, on BBC Radio 4, on Wednesday, 29 August 1990, at 11.02 in the morning.

By extraordinary coincidence, and unknown to the author, at that very moment, workmen were opening the family vault of the Stirling-Maxwells at Lecropt, near Keir, in Stirlingshire, in order to make good an outbreak of dry rot.[1] In the tomb they discovered three coffins. One was that of Lady Anna Stirling-Maxwell, Sir William's first wife, and close by was that of Sir William. The other coffin was that of his second wife, Lady Caroline Elizabeth Sarah Stirling-Maxwell, sometimes known as Caroline Norton.

XXXVII

ANOTHER STORY: DIANA OF THE CROSSWAYS

AFTER HER DEATH, Caroline became a character in other people's stories, and, as might be expected, she provoked another scandal. It was her old friend, Benjamin Disraeli, who first put her in a novel, when he drew upon recollections of her in the Thirties, to create the character of Berangaria Montfort, for his novel, *Endymion*, published in 1880.

Caroline's friends and relatives were not particularly disturbed by Disraeli's satirical portrait, but it was a different matter when George Meredith published *Diana of the Crossways*, in 1885, in which the eponymous heroine was, as Meredith told Robert Louis Stevenson, 'partly modelled upon Mrs Norton'.[1]

Meredith had not especially admired or liked Caroline when he had met her at the Duff Gordons, and had no great opinion of her intelligence. But he had perceived a sort of epic quality in her story, which fitted her to be the model for the new woman of the twentieth century. He had, he thought, only to endow her 'with brains' which she did not possess,[2] and to heighten the melodrama in her story, to have a plot for a best-seller. He was right. *Diana of the Crossways* was his first success, and went into many editions.

Diana's history closely follows that of Caroline. Her dead father was the famous Irishman, 'Dan Merion' (Richard Brinsley Sheridan); she is aristocratic but impoverished, and at a Society ball is recognized, by common consent, to be 'in the market' for a husband. Diana is a wit and a beauty whom men find fascinating. Her closest friend is Lady Dunstane (Lucy Duff Gordon). She has an elderly admirer, the Cabinet Minister, Lord Dannisburgh, who, like Lord Melbourne, is 'a man of ministerial tact, official ability, Pagan morality . . . but . . . careless of social opinion, unbuttoned, and a laugher' . . . Yet Diana assures Lady Dunstane that their friendship is Platonic: 'He is near what Dada's age would have been, and is, I think I can affirm, next to my dear father and my Emmy, my dearest friend. I love him. I could say it in the street without shame; and you do not imagine me shameless . . . I see him almost daily; it is not possible to think I can be deceived, and as long as he does me the honour to esteem my poor portion of brains by coming to me for what he is good enough to call my counsel, I shall let the world wag its tongue.'[3]

Like Caroline, Diana makes an unfortunate marriage, leaves her husband, and is eventually obliged to live alone in London, and to brave the disapproval of polite Society. Her beauty and charm ensure that she is not completely ostracized, but she now has to become a 'character', dining out on her wit: 'She discovered the social uses of cheap wit; she laid ambushes for anecdotes . . . Irish anecdotes are always popular in England, as promoting, besides the wholesome shake of the sides, a kindly sense of superiority.' She becomes a dinner-table charmer and professional talker. The friends of her own class stay loyal to her, but the new, moralistic middle-class women, such as Lady Wathin, detest her.

So much Caroline's surviving friends and family might have tolerated, but it was when Meredith touched upon her friendship with Herbert, here called Percy Dacier, that they took offence. For Diana (Caroline) is depicted as almost yielding to his suggestion that they should elope. What is worse, she later drives straight from a meeting with Dacier, in which he has told her of a sensational change in Cabinet policy, to sell the information to the editor of a national newspaper. In this way, Meredith resurrected the old calumny about Caroline's selling the Corn Law secrets to Delane of *The Times*, and the story became a subject for London gossip again.

Caroline's relatives were not without influence, indeed, her nephew, Lord Dufferin, had become Viceroy of India in 1884. He was especially annoyed that this young, Radical novelist should have revived the forty-year-old scandal about his aunt selling secrets to the newspapers. He wrote to the *St James's Gazette* for 12 December 1895:

Sir – As reference has been made in an article in the 'St James's Gazette' of the 6th inst. to the story of Mr Sidney Herbert having told Mrs Norton of the intention of Sir Robert Peel's government to repeal the Corn Laws, and of Mrs Norton having communicated the fact to Mr Delane, the editor of 'The Times', perhaps you will permit me to state that I am in a position to prove that neither Mrs Norton, nor Mr Herbert were in any way concerned in the transaction referred to . . .[4]

He then quoted Henry Reeve's review of *Diana of the Crossways* of 1885. Henry Reeve was a senior civil servant of the time, and should have known the truth. Reeve wrote: 'We observe with regret that Sir

William Gregory has revived a callumnious and unfounded anecdote, to which Mr Meredith had given circulation in this novel. We are enabled to state, and we do state from our personal knowledge, that the story is absolutely false in every particular, and the persons thus offensively referred to had nothing to do with the matter.' He added that the story was also denied by Sidney Herbert's biographer, Lord Stanmore, and by the late Mr Hayward of *The Times*.

Dufferin gave orders, and George Meredith was spoken to. Shortly afterwards, Dufferin could write confidently to Richard Norton, Caroline's grandson, now Lord Grantley:

My dear Grantley,
    With reference to my letter of a few days ago, you will be glad to hear that, in compliance with a suggestion which I made to him, Mr George Meredith, the author of 'Diana of the Crossways' has promised to introduce a note in the next edition of his novel, acknowledging that the incident which connected his heroine, with the sale of a Cabinet secret to a newspaper, has been proved to be quite baseless and unfounded.
                        Ever yours sincerely,
                        Dufferin & Ava[5]

Meredith was as weak as his word. All future editions of the novel contained a notice which read:

A lady of high distinction for wit and beauty, the daughter of an illustrious Irish House, came under the shadow of a calumny. It has been examined and exposed as baseless. The story of 'Diana of the Crossways' is to be read as fiction.

BIBLIOGRAPHY

WORKS BY CAROLINE NORTON

(The place of publication is London unless otherwise stated.)

POETRY

The English Bijou Almanack, Poetically illustrated. Undated.
The Sorrows of Rosalie, A Tale with Other Poems, John Ebors & Co., 1829.
The Undying One and Other Poems, H. Colburn & R. Bentley, 1830.
Poems and Sketches in *The Court Magazine* and *La Belle Assemblée* for
    1832–4, J. Bull.
Poems in *The English Annual* for 1834–5.
Poems in *The Keepsake* for 1836.
A Voice from the Factories, John Murray, 1836.
The Dream and Other Poems, Henry Colburn, 1840.
The Child of the Islands, Chapman & Hall, 1845.
Poems in *Fisher's Drawing-Room Scrap-book*, 1846–9.
Aunt Carry's Ballads for Children, 1847.
Bingen On The Rhine, John Walker & Co., undated.
The Centenary Festival (verses on Burns), 1859.
The Lady of La Garaye, Macmillan & Co., 1862.
Poems and Sketches in *Macmillan's Magazine*, 1861–75.
'Crippled Jane' in *Home Thoughts & Home Scenes*, Routledge, Warne &
    Routledge, 1865.

FICTION

The Wife, and Woman's Reward, two prose tales, Saunders & Otley, 1835.
Stuart of Dunleath, a novel, George Routledge & Sons, 1851.
Lost and Saved, a novel, Hurst & Blackett, 1863.
Old Sir Douglas, a novel, first serialized in *Macmillan's Magazine*, from
    January, 1866, and in a two-volume edition by Bernhard Tauchnitz
    (Leipzig) in 1867, and also elsewhere in three volumes.

Pamphlets

Observations on the Natural Claim of a Mother to the Custody of her Children as affected by the Common Law Right of the Father, John Murray, 1837, for private circulation.

The Separation of Mother & Child by the Law of Custody of Infants, Considered, Roake & Varty, 1838.

A Plain Letter to the Lord Chancellor on the Infant Custody Bill, by 'Pearce Stevenson Esq' (Caroline Norton), James Ridgeway, 1839.

'Letters to the Mob', first published in *The Morning Chronicle*, collected 1848.

English Laws for Women in the Nineteenth Century, privately published, 1854.

A Letter to the Queen on Lord Chancellor Cranworth's Marriage & Divorce Bill, Longman, Brown, Green and Longman, 1855.

A Review of the Divorce Bill of 1856, with propositions for an amendment of the laws affecting married persons, John W. Parker, 1857.

Letters

Letters &c Dated from June 1836, to July 1841, privately printed, in the British Library.

Some Unrecorded Letters of Caroline Norton, In the Altschul Collection of the Yale University Library, by Bertha Coolidge, privately printed, Boston, 1834.

The Letters of Caroline Norton to Lord Melbourne, ed. Hoge, James O., and Olney, Clarke, Ohio State University Press, 1974.

Miscellaneous

A History of the Fishes of Madeira by Richard T. Lowe, with original figures by the Hon. C. E. Norton, 1843.

A Residence in Sierra Leone, 'By A Lady' (Mrs Elizabeth Helen Melville), ed. Mrs Norton, John Murray, 1849, repr. Frank Cass & Co.

Prefatory Note in *The Pastor of Silverdale*, by Miss Stapleton, William Mackintosh, 1867.

The Rose of Jericho, ed. the Hon. Mrs Norton (translated from the French by her mother, Mrs Sheridan), Tinsley Bros, 1870.

Selected Writings of Caroline Norton, ed. Facsimile Reproductions with an Introduction and Notes by James O. Hoge & Jane Marcus, Scholars' Facsimile Reprints, Delmer, New York, 1978.

Biography

Fitzgerald, Percy, *The Lives of the Sheridans*, Richard Bentley & Son, two vols, 1886.

Perkins, Miss Jane Gray, *The Life of Mrs Norton*, John Murray, 1910.
Acland, Alice, *Caroline Norton*, Constable, 1948.
Moore, Katherine, *Victorian Wives*, Allison & Busby, 1975.
Forster, Margaret, *Significant Sisters*, Penguin, 1984.

There are also biographical portraits in:
Disraeli, Benjamin, *Endymion*, 1880, and
Meredith, George, *Diana of the Crossways*, 1885.

References in the Notes refer to these items by author, e.g. 'Hoge & Olney', 'Perkins', etc.

NOTES

2. AT SPRING GARDENS

1. Hoge & Olney, p. 87, Caroline Norton to Lord Melbourne, 21 June 1836.
2. *Op. cit.*, p. 89, CN to LM, 21 June 1836.

3. CRIMINAL CONVERSATION

1. Acland, p. 89.
2. Fitzgerald, p. 411.
3. See *The Courier*, 22 June 1836, p. 2.
4. *Ibid.*
5. This was the same Lord Lucan (1800–1888) who later commanded the Cavalry in the Crimea.
6. *The Times*, 23 June 1836. This is the source of information about the trial unless otherwise stated.
7. *The Courier*, 26 June 1836.
8. *The Satirist*, 26 June 1836, p. 205.
9. See Charles Dickens, *The Posthumous Papers of the Pickwick Club*, 1837, Chapter XXXIV.
10. The press coverage of the trial was thoroughly confused about the names of some of the witnesses. In *The Times* 'Fluke' is sometimes 'Flook', and elsewhere he is referred to as 'John Hook'. In *The Courier* for 22 June, he was 'John Monk', but in a later edition became 'John Fluke'. Mrs Cummins is at times referred to as 'Comyns', and sometimes as 'Mrs Owen', which was her true name.
11. *The Courier*, 23 June 1836, p. 1.
12. *The Satirist* for 26 June hints at the delight taken in Fluke by the scandal-loving middle class: 'We like the quiet philosophy in the following passage of his evidence: "Then you sometimes had a drop too much?" "Why Sir, I don't know who don't; the best of us takes it at times, masters and servants." (Laughter) The infirmity is universal and consequently Fluke consoles himself for his own participation. Everybody gets drunk now and then, in the opinion of the witness, and the sin is therefore divided or diluted among the world at large. If it be a vice, there are plenty of shoulders to bear the consequences.'

4. From a Dark Wood

1. Perkins, pp. 4–5.
2. *Ibid.*, p. 7.
3. *Ibid.*, p. 6.

5. A School for Scandal

1. Perkins, pp. 9–10.
2. *The Undying One*, pp. 231–2.
3. *Dictionary of National Biography (DNB).*

6. In the Market

1. *DNB.*
2. In later years Mr Gladstone was unpopular with some of his parliamentary colleagues, for helping to close down an 'introducing house' in St George's Road, near Lupus Street, that 'catered almost exclusively to Members of Parliament'. See Pearsall, Ronald, *The Worm in the Bud*, Penguin, 1971, p. 314.
3. Perkins, p. 12.
4. See Gibbs, Lewis, *Sheridan*, J. M. Dent, 1947, p. 264.
5. See the Epilogue to *Pizarro*, by Sheridan, 'Written by the Hon. William Lamb; Spoken by Mrs Jordan', in *The Plays of R. B. Sheridan*, ed. John Hampden, Nelson, p. 528.

7. Braving Mr Norton

1. *English Laws for Women in the Nineteenth Century (ELWNC)*, p. 32.
2. Perkins, p. 17.
3. *ELWNC*, p. 32.
4. *Perkins*, p. 17.
5. *ELWNC*, pp. 32–3.
6. *The Wife, & Woman's Reward* quoted in Perkins, pp. 73–4.
7. *ELWNC*, p. 33.

8. Temptations

1. Fitzgerald, vol. 2, pp. 353–4.
2. Hoge & Olney, p. 4.
3. The description of Trelawny is by Mary Shelley, quoted in *Shelley and his World*, by Tomalin, Clare, Thames & Hudson, 1980, p. 106.
4. See Ransome, Eleanor, *The Terrific Kemble*, Hamish Hamilton, 1978, p. 4.
5. Acland, p. 37.

9. POETIC AGONY

1. *The Sorrows of Rosalie, A Tale with Other Poems*, John Ebors & Co., London, 1829, published anonymously. The book carries a dedication to Lord Holland and an epigraph from Byron's *The Giaour*.
2. *Ibid.*, p. 97.
3. *Ibid.*, p. 94.
4. Sheridan, Richard Brinsley, *Clio's Protest*.
5. See Blake, Robert, *Disraeli*, Eyre & Spottiswoode, 1966, p. 81.
6. Perkins, p. 27.
7. Perkins, p. 19.
8. Hoge & Olney, p. 56.
9. Perkins, p. 24.
10. *The Undying One and Other Poems*, London, Henry Colburn and Richard Bentley, 1830.
11. *Ibid.*, Canto III, p. 97.
12. *Ibid.*, p. 202.
13. *Ibid.*
14. *Op. cit.*, pp. 269–72.
15. *Ibid.*

10. SHERIDAN'S FRIEND

1. See Cecil, David, *Melbourne*, Constable, 1955, p. 168.
2. *Ibid.*, p. 254.
3. Perkins, p. 37.
4. Fitzgerald, vol. 2, p. 334.
5. Hoge & Olney, p. 25.
6. *Ibid.*, p. 37.
7. *Ibid.*, p. 46.
8. *Ibid.*, p. 42.

11. THE WIFE, AND WOMAN'S REWARD

1. See Woodward, E. L., *The Age of Reform 1815–1870*, Oxford, 1946, pp. 82–7.
2. Atkins, p. 60.
3. See *ELWNC*.
4. Acland, p. 46.
5. See *La Belle Assemblée or Court & Fashionable Magazine*, January–June 1832. The story 'Leaves of a Life; or the Templar's Tale' is signed 'Cxxxy'. Caroline often signed her letters 'Cary'.
6. *ELWNC*, p. 33.
7. *Ibid.*, p. 34.
8. Cecil, *op. cit.*, pp. 222–4.
9. See *ELWNC*, pp. 36–8.

10. *Ibid.*
11. Perkins, pp. 60–2.
12. Perkins, p. 64.
13. *Ibid.*

12. PUBLIC AFFAIRS

1. *The Satirist*, 5 April 1835, 'Chit-Chat' column.
2. Blake, *op. cit.*, p. 127.
3. *The Satirist*, 24 May 1835.
4. *ELWNC*, p. 38.
5. *Ibid.*, p. 39.

13. AT FRAMPTON COURT

1. I am indebted to the Dorset County Museum for information concerning Frampton Court.
2. *ELWNC*, pp. 40–1.
3. Hoge & Olney, p. 68.
4. Perkins, pp. 83–4.
5. *Ibid.*, p. 85.
6. *Ibid.*, p. 86.
7. Hoge & Olney, p. 70.
8. The balustraded stone bridge is still to be found in the grounds at Frampton. The house was demolished in the late 1930s to avoid death duties, and only a stable-block remains.

14. SCANDAL

1. *The Satirist*, 3 May 1835.
2. *Ibid.*, 21 June 1835.
3. *Ibid.*, 5 July 1835.
4. *Ibid.*, 12 July.
5. *Ibid.*, 28 June.
6. Hoge & Olney, p. 72.
7. Stephen Lushington (1782–1873) was a famous barrister who advised Caroline and her lawyers for some years after the trial. It was Lushington who had advised Lady Byron in her separation proceedings in 1816, and who was, therefore, indirectly responsible for Byron's exile. He was also one of the counsels for Queen Caroline in 1820, in her divorce trial before the House of Lords. See Hoge & Olney, p. 74.
8. Hoge & Olney, p. 75.
9. Perkins, p. 99.
10. Perkins, p. 91.
11. Perkins, p. 93.

12. Ziegler, Philip, *Melbourne*, Collins, 1976, p. 232.
13. Cecil, *op. cit.*, p. 261.
14. Acland, p. 88.
15. See also Hoge & Olney, p. 75.

15. VERDICTS

1. Perkins, p. 95.
2. Hoge & Olney, p. 82.

16. A WOMAN WAITING

1. Hoge & Olney, p. 107, Caroline Norton to Lord Melbourne, late summer 1836.
2. *Ibid.*, p. 96, CN to LM, 8 July 1836.
3. Perkins, p. 114, CN to John Murray, 19 October 1836.
4. Acland, pp. 93–4.
5. Perkins, p. 184, CN to Mary Shelley, undated.

17. STRANGER AND FRIENDS

1. Hoge & Olney, p. 95, CN to LM, 1 July 1836.
2. *Ibid.*, pp. 96–8, CN to LM, 8 July 1836.
3. *Ibid.*
4. *Ibid.*, p. 102, CN to LM, late 1836.
5. Perkins, pp. 106–7, LM to CN, 24 July 1836.
6. Hoge & Olney, pp. 107–9, CN to LM, late summer, 1836.
7. *Ibid.*, p. 112, CN to LM, 6 March 1837.
8. *Ibid.*
9. *Ibid.*, p. 115, CN to LM, late March 1837.
10. *Ibid.*, p. 121, CN to LM, late March 1837.
11. Dedication to *The Dream & Other Poems*, by the Hon. Mrs Norton, London, Henry Colburn, 1840.
12. Perkins, p. 137, letter from Mary Shelley to E. Trelawny, 12 October 1835.
13. Perkins, p. 142, CN to Mary Shelley, 1838.

18. A DREAM OF CHILDREN

1. See *Letters &c. Dated from June 1836, to July 1841*, privately printed, First Correspondence, pp. 12–13. (FC)
2. *Ibid.*
3. Hoge & Olney, p. 102.
4. See *A Voice From the Factories in Serious Verse*, Dedicated to the Right Honourable Lord Ashley, London, John Murray, 1836, published anonymously.

5. *Ibid.*, Stanzas III, IV, and VI.
6. Perkins, pp. 115–16.
7. *FC*, p. 17.
8. *Ibid.*, p. 30.

19. CAMPAIGN AND QUARREL

1. See Holcombe, Lee, *Wives & Property*, Martin Robertson, Oxford, 1983, p. 18.
2. Perkins, pp. 149–50.
3. See *Letters &c Dated from June 1836, to July 1841*, British Library, pp. 26–31.
4. *Ibid.*, p. 36.
5. Acland, p. 109, CN to George Norton, 1 June 1837.
6. Fitzgerald, p. 433.
7. *Ibid.*, p. 434.
8. *DNB*.
9. Fitzgerald, p. 438.
10. Holcombe, *op. cit.*, p. 53.
11. Hoge & Olney, pp. 142–3.

20. THE RIVALS

1. Hoge & Olney, pp. 112–13, CN to LM, 16 March 1837.
2. *Ibid.*, p. 115, CN to LM, 17 March 1837.
3. *Ibid.*, pp. 120–1, CN to LM, late March 1837.
4. *Ibid.*, pp. 124–5, CN to LM, April (?) 1837.
5. *Ibid.*, pp. 130–1, CN to LM, late spring 1837.
6. See Longford, Elizabeth, *Victoria RI*, Pan Books, 1964, p. 77.
7. *Ibid.*, p. 83.
8. *Ibid.*, p. 98.
9. *Ibid.*, p. 99.
10. *Ibid.*, pp. 112–13.
11. Hoge & Olney, p. 148.
12. Longford, *op. cit.*, p. 165.
13. Perkins, pp. 178–9.
14. *Ibid.*

21. INFANT CUSTODY

1. This is Acland's speculation, see p. 111.
2. *Ibid.*, p. 112.
3. See *The Separation of Mother & Child by the Law of Custody of Infants Considered*, London, Roake & Varty, 31 Strand, 1838, anonymous, but it is by CN.
4. *Ibid.*, pp. 16–17.

5. *Ibid.*
6. *Ibid.*, pp. 26–7.
7. Hoge & Olney, p. 144.
8. Perkins, p. 124.
9. *Ibid.*, pp. 145–6.
10. Acland, p. 122.
11. See *A Plain Letter to the Lord Chancellor on the Infant Custody Bill*, by 'Pearce Stephenson, Esq.' (a nom-de-plume for Caroline Norton), London, James Ridgeway, Piccadilly, 1839.
12. Altschul, p. 5.
13. Perkins, p. 146.
14. *Ibid.*, pp. 154–5.

22. THE COMPANY OF WRITERS

1. See Strong, L. A. G., *The Minstrel Boy*, Hodder & Stoughton, 1937, p. 164.
2. See 'The Summer Fête', in *The Poetical Works of Thomas Moore*, Frederick Warne, 1892, pp. 661–3.
3. Strong, *op. cit.*, p. 162.
4. *Ibid.*, pp. 216–17.
5. See Ellis, Robert R., *Samuel Rogers & His Circle*, Methuen, 1910, pp. 273–5.
6. *Ibid.*, p. 61.
7. *Ibid.*, p. 209.
8. *Ibid.*
9. *Ibid.*, pp. 98–101.
10. Pearson, Hesketh, *The Smith of Smiths*, The Hogarth Press, 1984, p. 185.
11. Crabb Robinson, quoted in Martin, Robert, *Tennyson: The Unquiet Heart*, Faber & Faber, 1983, p. 284.
12. Pearson, Hesketh, *Dickens: His Character, Comedy and Career*, Methuen, 1949, p. 105.
13. Maurois, André, *Disraeli*, Penguin, 1939, pp. 60–1.
14. *The Dream & Other Poems*, Henry Colburn, 1840.
15. *Ibid.*, p. 180.
16. *Ibid.*, pp. 54–5.
17. See Baxter, Lucy ('Leader Scott'), *The Life of William Barnes*, Macmillan, 1887, pp. 74–9.

23. NOT QUITE NICE

1. Perkins, pp. 191–2.
2. Forster, Margaret, *Significant Sisters*, Penguin, 1986, p. 31.
3. Monsarrat, Ann, *An Uneasy Victorian*, Cassell, 1980, pp. 194–5.

4. *Ibid.*, pp. 185–6.
5. Forster, *op. cit.*, p. 43.

24. MELBOURNE AGAIN

1. Perkins, p. 160.
2. Hoge & Olney, p. 156.
3. *Ibid.*, p. 157.
4. See Raymond, John, *Queen Victoria's Early Letters*, Batsford, 1963, pp. 71–2.
5. Ziegler, Philip, *Melbourne*, Collins, 1976, pp. 344–9.
6. Raymond, *op. cit.*, p. 72.
7. Ziegler, *op. cit.*, p. 345.

25. LITTLE BOY LOST

1. Perkins, p. 101.
2. Acland, p. 131.
3. *Ibid.*, p. 132.
4. *Ibid.*, p. 161.
5. *Ibid.*, p. 164.
6. *Ibid.*, p. 167.
7. *Ibid.*, p. 169.
8. Altschul, p. 10, letter from CN to Dr Hawtrey, Headmaster of Eton.
9. Perkins, p. 206.

26. MY SECRETARY

1. Acland, p. 165.
2. Hoge & Olney, pp. 165–6.
3. Acland, p. 166.
4. *Lost and Saved*, Cap. XXIII, p. 110, Hurst & Blackett, London, 1863.
5. *DNB.*
6. Acland, p. 169.
7. Acland, p. 170.
8. *Lost and Saved*, Cap. XXXII, p. 174.
9. *DNB.*
10. See Woodham-Smith, Cecil, *Florence Nightingale*, Penguin 1951, p. 249.
11. *The Lady of La Garaye*, Macmillan, 1862, pp. 145–6.

27. CHANGING ROLES

1. See Forster, *op. cit.*, p. 44.
2. Hoge & Olney, pp. 163–71.
3. *Ibid.*, p. 165.
4. *Ibid.*
5. *Ibid.*, p. 168.

6. Ziegler, *op. cit.*, p. 361.
7. *The Child of the Islands*, Chapman & Hall, 1845. In this book she quotes approvingly a speech by Sidney Herbert at the Salisbury Diocesan Conference Church Meeting, 11 November 1842.
8. *Ibid.*, 'Spring', Stanza XXIX.
9. *Morning Chronicle*, 'Letters to the Mob', collected 1848, and reprinted by Thomas Bosworth. Caroline signed herself 'Libertas'.
10. *Aunt Carry's Ballads for Children*, with illustrations by John Absalom, Joseph Cordell, 1847.
11. *Stuart of Dunleath*, a novel, George Routledge & Sons, 1851.
12. *Ibid.*, Chapter XX.

28. NORTON VERSUS NORTON

1. *ELWNC*. Quoted in Perkins, pp. 228–9.
2. *Ibid.*, Perkins, pp. 230–1.

29. PROPERTY

1. Perkins, p. 235.
2. *ELWNC*.
3. Perkins, p. 240.
4. *Ibid.*, pp. 241–2.
5. *Stuart of Dunleath*.
6. Holcombe, *op. cit.*, pp. 9–13.

30. A RACE TO REFORM

1. Information concerning the Women's Committee is taken from Holcombe, *op. cit.*, pp. 47–70.
2. *Ibid.*, pp. 57–62.
3. *Ibid.*, p. 65.
4. *Ibid.*, p. 70.
5. Mrs Gaskell quoted in Holcombe, p. 73.
6. *Ibid.*, p. 237.
7. *Ibid.*
8. *A Letter to the Queen on Lord Chancellor Cranworth's Marriage & Divorce Bill*, Longman, Brown, Green, Longman, 1855.
9. *Ibid.*, p. 154.
10. *Ibid.*, p. 16.
11. *Ibid.*, p. 13.
12. *Ibid.*, p. 153.
13. *A Review of the Divorce Bill of 1856, with propositions for an amendment of the laws affecting married persons*, John W. Parker & Son, West Strand, 1857. Quoted in Perkins, pp. 221–3.

31. DANGEROUS, TERRIBLE, BEAUTIFUL

1. Perkins, p. 216.
2. Altschul, p. 20.
3. See the Diary of Richard Brinsley Sheridan (Jun). MP for Shaftesbury 1845–1852, Dorchester 1852–1868. Entry for 11 May 1857, Dorset County Record Office. (*DCR*)
4. Perkins, pp. 258–9.
5. *Ibid.*, pp. 260–1.
6. *Ibid.*, pp. 255–6.
7. *Ibid.*, p. 222.
8. *Ibid.*, p. 262.

32. SHAME AND GRIEF

1. Perkins, p. 254.
2. Fitzgerald.
3. Caroline's poem, 'The Centenary Festival', was printed in *The Daily Scotsman*.
4. Perkins, pp. 264–5.
5. *Ibid.*, pp. 267–8.
6. Acland, p. 212.

33. LOST AND SAVED

1. Perkins, p. 270.
2. *Macmillan's Magazine*, February 1862, p. 343.
3. *The Lady of La Garaye*, p. vii.
4. *Lost and Saved*, Chapter 3, pp. 14–15.
5. *The Times*, 18 January 1863.
6. Acland, p. 212.
7. *DCR*, Sheridan papers.
8. Altschul, p. 23.

34. A VISITOR TO CHESTERFIELD STREET

1. Acland, p. 214.
2. *Ibid.*
3. See Williams, David, *George Meredith*, Hamish Hamilton, 1977, p. 173.
4. Acland, p. 216.
5. Altschul, p. 24.
6. Acland, p. 221.
7. *Ibid.*, pp. 222–3.
8. Perkins, p. 295.

35. LADY STIRLING-MAXWELL

1. *Pictorial World*, 10 March 1877.
2. Acland, pp. 225–6.
3. Altschul, p. 25.
4. *Pictorial World*, 25 July 1877.

36. RETURN TO SCOTLAND

1. This information was supplied by Mr A. Stirling of Keir, in personal letters to the author, dated 17 September 1990, and 5 August 1991.

37. ANOTHER STORY: DIANA OF THE CROSSWAYS

1. Acland, p. 171.
2. See Sassoon, Siegfried, *Meredith*, Arrow Books, 1959.
3. See Meredith, George, *Diana of the Crossways*, 1885, reprinted Virago Books, 1980.
4. Acland, pp. 179–80.
5. Acland, p. 181.

INDEX